MW01224130

# Health Informatics

*(formerly Computers in Health Care)*

---

Kathryn J. Hannah  Marion J. Ball
Series Editors

**Springer**
*New York*
*Berlin*
*Heidelberg*
*Hong Kong*
*London*
*Milan*
*Paris*
*Tokyo*

## Health Informatics Series
*(formerly Computers in Health Care)*

---

*Series Editors*
Kathryn J. Hannah Marion J. Ball

Dental Informatics
*Integrating Technology into the Dental Environment*
L.M. Abbey and J. Zimmerman

Ethics and Information Technology
*A Case-Based Approach to a Health Care System in Transition*
J.G. Anderson and K.W. Goodman

Aspects of the Computer-Based Patient Record
M.J. Ball and M.F. Collen

Performance Improvement Through Information Management
*Health Care's Bridge to Success*
M.J. Ball and J.V. Douglas

Strategies and Technologies for Healthcare Information
*Theory into Practice*
M.J. Ball, J.V. Douglas, and D.E. Garets

Nursing Informatics
*Where Caring and Technology Meet*, Third Edition
M.J. Ball, K.J. Hannah, S.K. Newbold, and J.V. Douglas

Healthcare Information Management Systems
*A Practical Guide*, Second Edition
M.J. Ball, D.W. Simborg, J.W. Albright, and J.V. Douglas

Healthcare Information Management Systems
*Cases, Strategies, and Solutions*, Third Edition
M.J. Ball, C.A. Weaver, and J.M. Kiel

Clinical Decision Support Systems
*Theory and Practice*
E.S. Berner

Strategy and Architecture of Health Care Information Systems
M.K. Bourke

Information Networks for Community Health
P.F. Brennan, S.J. Schneider, and E. Tornquist

Informatics for the Clinical Laboratory
*A Practical Guide*
D.F. Cowan

*(continued after index)*

Reinhold Haux Alfred Winter
Elske Ammenwerth Birgit Brigl

# Strategic Information Management in Hospitals

## *An Introduction to Hospital Information Systems*

With a Foreword by Reed M. Gardner

With 110 Illustrations

Springer

Reinhold Haux, Ph.D
Professor for Medical Informatics
Institute for Health Information Systems
University for Health Informatics and Technology Tyrol (UMIT)
6020 Innsbruck, Austria
reinhold.haux@umit.at

Alfred Winter, Ph.D
Professor for Medical Informatics
Institute for Medical Informatics, Statistics and Epidemiology
University of Leipzig
04103 Leipzig, Germany
winter@imise.uni-leipzig.de

Elske Ammenwerth, Ph.D
Assistant Professor for Medical Informatics
Research Group Assessment of Health Information Systems
University for Health Informatics and Technology Tyrol (UMIT)
6020 Innsbruck, Austria
elske.ammenwerth@umit.at

Birgit Brigl, Ph.D
Institute for Medical Informatics, Statistics and Epidemiology
University of Leipzig
04103 Leipzig, Germany
birgit.brigl@t-online.de

*Series Editors:*
Kathryn J. Hannah, Ph.D., R.N.
Adjunct Professor, Department of Community Health Sciences
Faculty of Medicine
The University of Calgary
Calgary, Alberta, T3B 4Z8 Canada

Marion J. Ball, Ed.D.
Vice President, Clinical Solutions
Healthlink, Inc.
2 Hamill Road
*and*
Adjunct Professor
The Johns Hopkins University School of Nursing
Baltimore, MD 21210, USA

Library of Congress Cataloging-in-Publication Data
Strategic information management in hospitals : an introduction to hospital information systems / Reinhold Hauz ... [et al.].
p.; cm—(Health informatics series)
Includes bibliographical references and index.
ISBN 0-387-40356-6 (hardback : alk. paper)
1. Information storage and retrieval systems—Hospitals. 2. Medical informatics. I. Haux, R. (Reinhold) II. Health informatics.
[DNLM: 1. Hospital Information Systems. 2. Information Management. 2. Models, Theoretical. WX 26.5 S898 2003.]
R858.S77 2003
362.11'0285—dc22 2003059129

ISBN 0-387-40356-6 Printed on acid-free paper.



Printed in the United States of America. **(RW/MVY)**

9 8 7 6 5 4 3 2 1 SPIN 10936962

Springer-Verlag is a part of *Springer Science+Business Media*
*springeronline.com*

# Foreword

Healthcare management is a complex and ever-changing task. As medical knowledge increases, as clinical management strategies or administrative management strategies change, and as patients move from one city to another or from one country to another, the challenges of managing health care have changed and will continue to change. Central to all of these changes is a need to store and process administrative and clinical records for the patient. For the reasons listed above, computerization of record systems in hospitals and clinics has been and continues to be a slow and complex process. Developing a strategy to provide the best healthcare service at the lowest possible cost is a common goal of almost every healthcare system in the world. Care given in the hospital is typically the most advanced, the most complex, and the most expensive. As a consequence, understanding and managing health care in hospitals is crucial to every healthcare delivery system. This book provides a wonderful overview for students and medical informatics professionals. It also provides the background that every medical informatics specialist needs to understand and manage the complexities of hospital information systems.

This book deals primarily with the underlying administrative systems that are in place in hospitals throughout the world. These systems are fundamental to the development and implementation of the even more challenging systems that acquire, process, and manage the patient's clinical information. Hospital information systems provide a major part of the information needed by those paying for health care, be they hospital administrators, health insurance companies, public health authorities, or local or national political leaders. As a consequence, an important and complex set of strategies has been implemented to document medical problems and procedures that hospitals are dealing with. Problems are usually coded with International Classification of Diseases (ICD-9 or ICD-10) coding systems, while medical procedures are designated using Current Procedural Terminology (CPT) codes. Typically, these codes are used to generate bills to an insurance company or governmental unit. As a consequence, these data must be generated, transmitted, and processed accurately and promptly. Computer technology enhances the ability of hospital clinical and administrative staff to provide these data.

Because of the complexities and changing needs of medical information, the field of medical informatics is in need of a growing number of professionals who understand how to use computers and are familiar with the administrative requirements of the healthcare field and clinical medicine. Having a person who has knowledge in all of these fields is unusual. However, I am convinced that the rate at which medicine is able to better use computer technology is limited by the lack of a sufficient number of well-trained professionals who have an understanding of all of these fields. As a consequence, I congratulate each of you who is studying hospital information systems and encourage you to take what you will learn from this book and move the field forward.

After you have an understanding of what is presented in this text, I encourage you to take on the challenge of clinical informatics. Study and learn how computers can be used to advantage by those providing clinical care—physicians, nurses, pharmacists, therapists, and other caregivers. In the future we must all work toward developing computer and communications systems that will enhance the acquisition of clinical data so that the data can be used to provide better patient care and more efficient and better administrative documentation.

Enjoy this book. Its clearly written materials and exercises should give every reader a challenge and opportunity to learn. I found Appendix A, the thesaurus, a treasure of important information. The thesaurus will be very handy for everyone for years to come. I congratulate the authors for their knowledge, skillfulness, and dedication in writing and publishing this book.

*Reed M. Gardner*
Professor and Chair, Department of Medical Informatics
University of Utah & LDS Hospital, Salt Lake City, Utah, USA
Reed.Gardner@hsc.utah.edu

# Series Preface

This series is directed to healthcare professionals who are leading the transformation of health care by using information and knowledge. Launched in 1988 as Computers in Health Care, the series offers a broad range of titles: some addressed to specific professions such as nursing, medicine, and health administration; others to special areas of practice such as trauma and radiology. Still other books in the series focus on interdisciplinary issues, such as the computer-based patient record, electronic health records, and networked healthcare systems.

Renamed Health Informatics in 1998 to reflect the rapid evolution in the discipline now known as health informatics, the series will continue to add titles that contribute to the evolution of the field. In the series, eminent experts, serving as editors or authors, offer their accounts of innovations in health informatics. Increasingly, these accounts go beyond hardware and software to address the role of information in influencing the transformation of healthcare delivery systems around the world. The series also will increasingly focus on "peopleware" and organizational, behavioral, and societal changes that accompany the diffusion of information technology in health services environments.

These changes will shape health services in the next millennium. By making full and creative use of the technology to tame data and to transform information, health informatics will foster the development of the knowledge age in health care. As coeditors, we pledge to support our professional colleagues and the series readers as they share advances in the emerging and exciting field of health informatics.

*Kathryn J. Hannah*
*Marion J. Ball*

# Preface

What is a hospital information system? The literature defines hospital information systems in many different ways and presents various views. Some articles focus on information processing functions, while others focus on the technology used. To begin with, we understand a hospital information system as the information processing and information storing subsystem of a hospital.

This book discusses the significance of information processing in hospitals, the progress in information and communication technology, and the importance of systematic information management. Nearly all people working in a hospital have an enormous demand for information, which has to be fulfilled in order to achieve high-quality and efficient patient care. The management of a hospital needs up-to-date information about the hospital's costs and services. The quality of information processing is also important for the competitiveness of a hospital. Hospital information systems can be regarded as the memory and nervous system of a hospital.

The subject of information processing is quite complex. Nearly all groups and all areas in a hospital depend on the quality of information processing. The amount of information processing is tremendous. Additionally, the information needs of the different groups are often based on the same data. Therefore, integrated information processing is necessary. If hospital information systems are not systematically managed and operated, they tend to develop chaotically. This, in turn, leads to negative consequences, such as low data quality and increasing costs of patient care.

Well-educated health informatics specialists, with the knowledge and skills to systematically manage and operate hospital information systems, are therefore needed to appropriately and responsibly apply information and communication technology to the complex information processing environment of a hospital.

This book discusses hospital information systems and their systematic management. Information management comprises those activities in a hospital that deal with the management of information processing and therefore with the management of its hospital information system.

The goal of this book is to introduce healthcare and health informatics professionals, as well as students in medical informatics/health informatics and health information management, to the strategic management of hospital information systems. The book should be regarded as an introduction to this complex subject. For a deeper understanding, the reader will need additional knowledge and, foremost, practice in this field.

After reading this book, a reader should be able to answer the following questions:

- Why is systematic information processing in hospitals important?
- What do hospital information systems look like?
- What are good hospital information systems?
- How can we strategically manage hospital information systems?

We hope that the reader will find this book useful. Any comments on it or suggestions for improvements are warmly welcome.

*Reinhold Haux*
*Alfred Winter*
*Elske Ammenwerth*
*Birgit Brigl*

# Acknowledgments

We would like to express our thanks to all of our colleagues who contributed to this book, especially Reed Gardner, who commented on it and wrote the Foreword. Thanks also to many other people who helped to produce this book, especially Frieda Kaiser and Gudrun Hübner-Bloder.

We would also like to thank the following colleagues for helping to obtain figures and screen shots: Marc Batschkus, Thomas Bürkle, Andrew Grant, Torsten Happek, Marianne Kandert, Thomas Kauer, Georg Lechleitner, Otwin Linderkamp, André Michel, Gerhard Mönnich, Oliver Reinhard, Christof Seggewies, Pierre Tetrault, Raimund Vogl, and Immanuel Wilhelmy. In particular, we are grateful to Ursula and Markus Beutelspacher for allowing us to take a picture of their Heidelberg quintuplets for the cover (quintuplet picture by Bernd Krug).

Not least, we want to thank our students, who kept asking critical questions and drew our attention to incomplete and indistinct arguments.

*Reinhold Haux*
*Alfred Winter*
*Elske Ammenwerth*
*Birgit Brigl*

"Any technology sets a relationship between human beings and their environment, both physical and human. No technology can be seen as merely instrumental. This is especially relevant when dealing with large automatic information systems, developed to contribute to the management and integration of large organizations, such as hospitals."

Jean-Marie Fessler and Francois Grémy
Ethical Problems with Health Information Systems.
Methods of Information in Medicine 2001; 40: 359-61.

"Health and medical informatics education is of particular importance at the beginning of the $21^{st}$ century for the following reasons...:

1. progress in information processing and information and communication technology is changing our societies;
2. the amount of health and medical knowledge is increasing at such a phenomenal rate that we cannot hope to keep up with it, or store, organize, and retrieve existing and new knowledge in a timely fashion without using a new information processing methodology and information technologies;
3. there are significant economic benefits to be obtained from the use of information and communication technology to support medicine and health care;
4. similarly the quality of health care is enhanced by the systematic application of information processing and information and communication technology;
5. it is expected that these developments will continue, probably at least at the same pace as can be observed today;
6. healthcare professionals who are well-educated in health or medical informatics are needed to systematically process information in medicine and in health care, and for the appropriate and responsible application of information and communication technology."

Recommendations
of the International Medical Informatics Association (IMIA)
on Education in Health and Medical Informatics.
Methods of Information in Medicine 2000; 39: 267-77.
Available at http://www.imia.org.

# Contents

# List of Tables and Figures

## Tables



## Figures

## *Annotation to the Figures*

All persons shown in the photos have given their permission. With the exception of the Heidelberg quintuplets, no real patients are shown. The patients in the figures are mostly the authors, their families, or medical informatics VIPs.

We have partly used screen shots from commercial software products in this book. This use cannot be regarded as a recommendation for those products. We only want to illustrate typical functionality and typical user interfaces of software products that support specific hospital functions. Therefore, we did not mention the product names.

## *Figure Credits*

- Centre Hospitalier Universitaire de Sherbrooke, Quebec, Canada: 3.35, 3.48
- Cerner Immediate Support Services, Kansas City, Missouri: 5.7
- Diakonissehjemmets Sykehus Haraldsplass, Bergen, Norway: 4.5
- German Cancer Research Center, Heidelberg, Germany: 4.4
- LDS Hospital, Salt Lake City, Utah: 1.11, 3.5
- National Library of Medicine, Bethesda, Maryland: 3.4, 3.36
- One of the author's home office, Meckesheim, Germany: 3.41
- Selayang Hospital, Kuala Lumpur, Malaysia: 1.7, 3.10, 3.38, 3.53, 5.5
- Siemens Medical Solutions Health Services, Malvern, Pensylvania: 3.34, 3.46
- Specialist Practice Dr. Fröhlich, Bammental, Germany: 2.6, 3.7, 3.65
- University Medical Center Erlangen, Germany: 1.4, 2.1, 2.2, 2.3, 3.8, 3.11, 3.44
- University Medical Center Heidelberg, Germany: 1.1, 1.2, 1.3, 1.8, 1.10, 1.12, 1.13, 1.14, 1.15, 2.4, 2.5, 2.7, 2.8, 3.1, 3.2, 3.6, 3.12, 3.13, 3.15, 3.30, 3.33, 3.40, 3.45, 3.47, 3.49, 3.50, 3.64, 3.67, 4.1, 4.2, 4.3, 4.7, 5.6
- University Medical Center Innsbruck, Austria: 1.5, 1.9, 3.9. 3.14, 3.37, 3.39, 3.42, 3.43, 3.51, 3.52, 3.63, 3.66, 3.68, 4.6
- University Medical Center Munich-Grosshadern, Germany: 1.6
- University Medical Center Münster, Germany: 3.32
- Weinberg Cancer Center Johns Hopkins, Baltimore, Maryland: 3.3
- Zürcher Höhenkliniken Wald-Davos, Switzerland: 3.31

# 1 Introduction

## 1.1 Significance of Information Processing in Hospitals

### *Information Processing Is an Important Quality Factor*

Almost all healthcare professionals need a vast amount of information. It is essential for the quality of patient care and for the quality of hospital management to fulfill these information needs.

When a patient is admitted to a hospital, a physician or a nurse first needs information about the reason for admission and about the history of the patient. Later, she or he needs results from clinical, laboratory, and radiology examinations (Figure 1.1) which are some of the most frequent diagnostic procedures. In general, clinical patient-related information should be available on time, and it should be up-to-date and valid (e.g., the recent lab

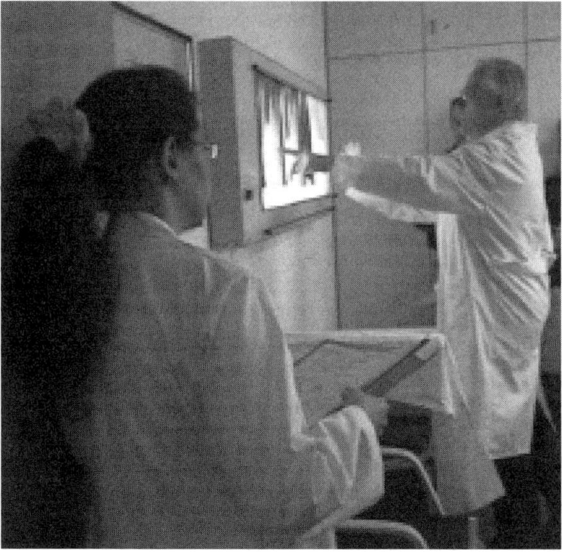

Figure 1.1: Radiological conference in a radiodiagnostic department.

report should be available on the ward within 2 hours). If this is not the case, if it comes too late, or is old or even wrong, the quality of patient care is at risk (e.g., an incorrect lab report may lead to erroneous and even harmful treatment decisions). If this causes repetition of examinations or expensive searches for information, the costs of health care may increase. Information should be documented adequately, enabling healthcare professionals to access the information needed and to make sound decisions.

People working in hospital administration also must be well informed in order to carry out their tasks. They should be informed in a timely fashion and receive current information. If the information flow is too slow, bills are written days or even weeks after the patient's discharge. If information is missing, payable services cannot be billed, and the hospital's income will be reduced.

Hospital management also has an enormous information need. Up-to-date information about costs and proceeds are necessary as a basis for controlling the enterprise. Information about the quality of patient care is equally important, for example, about the form and severity of patients' illnesses, about nosocomial infections, or about complication rates of therapeutic procedures. If this information is not accurate, not on time, or incomplete, the hospital's work cannot be controlled adequately, increasing the risks of management errors.

Thus, information processing is an important quality factor in health care and, in particular, in hospitals.

## Information Processing Is an Enormous Cost Factor

In 1996 in the European Union (EU), the costs for health care, including the costs for the approximately 14,000 hospitals, amounted to 814 billion €, which is 8.7% of the total gross domestic product (GDP) of all EU countries.[1] In 1998, the costs for the approximately 2,200 German hospitals with their 570,000 beds amounted to 107 billion €; 1.1 million people worked in these institutions in Germany, and 16 million inpatients were treated.[2]

A relevant percentage of those costs is spent on information processing. However, the total percentage of information processing can only be estimated. Already in the 1960s, studies observed that 25% of a hospital's costs are due to (paper-based and computer-based) information processing.[3] However, such an estimate depends on the definition of information processing. In general, the investment costs (including purchase, adaptation, intro-

1. Organization for Economic Co-operation and Development (OECD). OECD Health Data 2000. http://www.oecd.org/els/health/software.

2. Statistical Federal Office. Statistical Yearbook 2000 for the Federal Republic of Germany. Stuttgart: Metzler-Poeschel; 2000. pp. 428, 431, 438.

3. Jydstrup R, Gross M. Cost of information handling in hospitals. Health Services Research 1966; 1: 235-71.

duction, training) must be distinguished from the regular costs (including staff), and the costs for computer-based from the costs for paper-based information processing (which today are often much higher in hospitals).

Looking at computer-based information processing, the annual budget that healthcare institutions spend on information and communication technology (including computer systems, computer networks, and computer-based application components) is, according to different sources, between 2.8%[4] and 4.6%.[5] In regard to the technical progress, this rate may continue to increase.

When looking at paper-based information processing, the numbers become increasingly vague. However, we can expect that, for example, the annual operating costs (including personnel costs) for a paper-based archive, storing about 400,000 new patients records each year, may easily amount to more than 500,000 €. A typical, standardized, machine-readable form, including two carbon copies (for example, a radiology order) costs approximately 0.50 €. A typical inpatient record at a university hospital consists of about 40 documents.

Based on these figures, it becomes apparent that information processing in health care is an important cost factor and considerably significant for a national economy. It is clear that, on the one hand, efficient information processing offers vast potential for cost reductions. On the other hand, inefficient information processing leads to cost increases.

## *Information Becomes a Productivity Factor*

In the 19th century, many societies were characterized by rising industry and industrial production. By the second half of the 20th century, the idea of communicating and processing data by means of computers and computer networks was already emerging. Today we speak of the 21st century as the century of information technology, or of an "information society." It is expected to become a century in which informatics and information and communication technology (ICT) will play a key role. Information, bound to a medium of matter or energy, but largely independent of place and time, shall be made available to people at any time and in any place imaginable. Information shall find its way to people, not vice versa.

Today, information belongs to the most important productivity factors of a hospital. For high-quality patient care and economic management of a

---

4. Garets D, Duncan M. Enterprisewide Systems: Fact of Fiction? Healthcare Informatics Online, Febr. 1999. http://www.healthcare-informatics.com/issues/1999/02_99/garets.htm.

5. Healthcare Information and Management Systems Society (HIMSS). The 11th Annual HIMSS Leadership Survey Sponsored by IBM: Trends in Healthcare Information and Technology—Final Report. 2000. http://www.himss.org.

hospital, it is essential that the hospital information system can make correct information fully available on time. This is also increasingly important for the competitiveness of hospitals.

## *Information Processing Should Offer a Holistic View of the Patient and of the Hospital*

Information processing in a hospital should offer a comprehensive, holistic view of the patient and of the hospital. "Holistic" in this context means a complete picture of the care of a patient, independent of where in the hospital the patient has been or will be treated. This holistic view on the patient can reduce the undesired consequences of highly specialized medicine with various departments and healthcare professionals involved in patient care. Despite highly differentiated diagnostics and therapy, and the multitude of people and areas in a hospital, adequate information processing (and a good hospital information system) can help to make information about a patient completely available (Figure 1.2). As specialization in medicine and health care increases, so does the fragmentation of information, which makes combining information into such a holistic view more and more necessary. However, it must be clearly ensured that only authorized personnel can access patient data and data about the hospital as an enterprise.

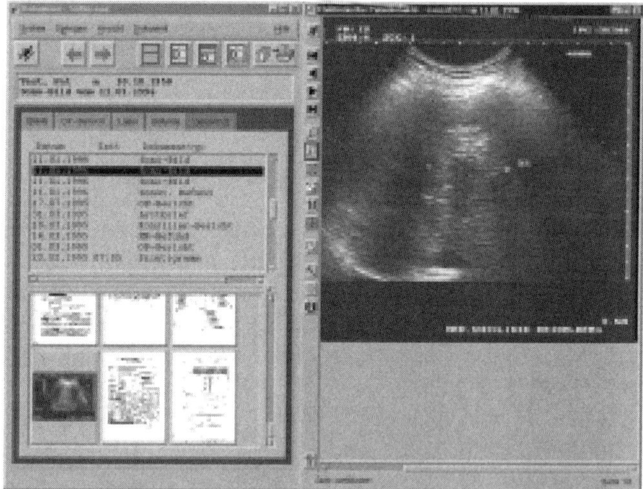

Figure 1.2: An example of an electronic patient record, comprising documents as well as images.

## *A Hospital Information System as the Memory and the Nervous System of a Hospital*

Figuratively speaking, a hospital information system might be regarded as the memory and the nervous system of a hospital. A hospital information system, comprising the information processing and storage in a hospital (Figures 1.3 and 1.4), to a certain extent can be compared to the information processing of a human being. The hospital information system also receives, transmits, processes, stores, and presents information. The quality of a hospital information system is essential for a hospital, again figuratively, in order to be able to adequately recognize and store facts, to remember them, and to act on them.

Figure 1.3: A paper-based patient record archive as one information storing part of the hospital's memory and nervous system.

Figure 1.4: A server room of a hospital as one information processing part of the hospital's memory and nervous system.

## 1.2 Progress in Information and Communication Technology

Progress in information and communication technology (ICT) changes societies and affects the costs and quality of information processing in health care. It is thus useful to take a look at the world of information and communication technology.

## *Information and Communication Technology Has Become Decisive for the Quality of Health Care*

Tremendous improvements in diagnostics have been made available by modern technology, for example in the area of medical signal and image processing. Magnetic resonance imaging and computed tomography, for example, would not have been possible without improvements in information processing and information methodology and without modern information and communication technology (Figure 1.5). Such improved diagnostics then lead to an improvement in therapy. Some therapies, for example in neurosurgery or radiotherapy, are possible mainly due to the progress in ICT.

Important progress due to improvements in modern ICT can also be observed in information systems of healthcare institutions. The role of computer-supported information systems, together with clinical documentation and knowledge-based decision support systems, can hardly be overestimated in respect to the quality of health care, as the volume of data available today is much greater than it was a few years ago.

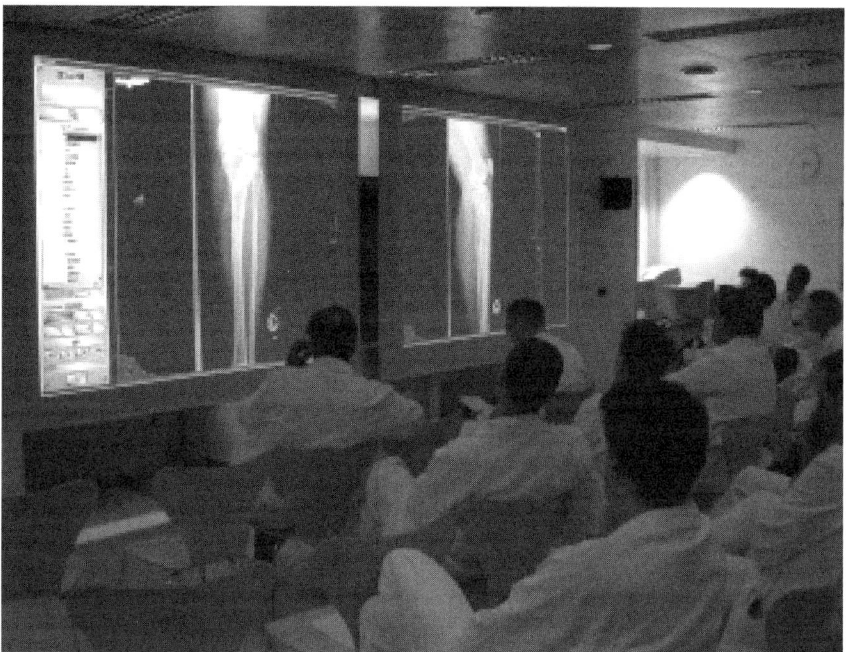

Figure 1.5: Radiological conference using a picture archiving and communication system for image presentation.

Thus, there is a significant relevance of modern ICT for the quality of health care. High-level information and communication technology forms a basis for high-level information processing in health care.

## *Information and Communication Technology Has Become Economically Important*

For many countries, the vision of an "information society" is becoming a reality. More personal computers are sold worldwide today than cars.[6] Nearly every part of a modern economic system is shaped by information processing and information and communication technology. The leading industrialized countries in 1999 spent between 5% and 7.7% of their gross domestic product (GDP) on information and communication technology.[7]

In 1999, the worldwide market for information and communication technology was 1,592 billion €, with an estimated growth rate of 9.3 percent per year.[7] The U.S. ICT market was about 564 billion €, and the European ICT market (including Eastern Europe) was about 493 billion €.[7] Germany's expected total annual turnover on information and communication technology was approximately 104 billion €.[7] Generally, half of this money is spent on information technology (data processing and data communication equipment, software, related services) and the other half on communication technology (telecommunication equipment and related services).[7]

The percentage of healthcare ICT on the worldwide ICT market is difficult to estimate. The following numbers may indicate the significance of ICT in health care: The estimated size of the overall healthcare IT market in the United States was about 16.5 billion € in 1998.[8] For hospital information systems alone, 3 billion € were spent in the United States, compared to 2.6 billion in the EU.[9] In 1999 the German Research Association funded hardware and software investments for 36 German university hospitals with 27 million €. The total amount of investments for hardware and software of

6. German Ministry of Economy. Info 2000: Germany's way to the information society (in German). Bonn: German Ministry of Economy; 1996. pp. 7.

7. European Information Technology Observatory (EITO). The new edition of the European Information Technology Observatory. Frankfurt: EITO; 2000. pp. 378, 384, 434. http://www.eito.com.

8. Solberg C. Prove It! IT Vendors need to show results to the healthcare industry. Healthcare Informatics Online, June 1999. http://www.healthcare-informatics.com/issues/1999/06_99/prove.htm.

9. Iakovidis I. Towards a Health Telematics Infrastructure in the European Union. In: Balas EA, Boren SA, Brow GD, editors. Information technology strategies from US and the European Union: Transferring research to practice for healthcare improvement. Amsterdam: IOS press. pp. 23-33.

these German hospitals was estimated to be in the range of 100 to 200 million €.

One might have doubts about the validity of these rather rough numbers. However, they all exemplify the following: There is a significant and increasing economic relevance for information and communication technology in general and in medicine and health care.

## *Information and Communication Technology Will Continue to Change Health Care*

Now once more, what changes in health care we expect through information and communication technology?

The developments mentioned will probably continue into the next decade at least at the same rate as given today. The development of information and communication technology will continue to have a considerable effect on our societies in general and on our healthcare systems in particular.[10]

The use of computer-based tools in health care will dramatically increase, and new technologies such as mobile devices and multifunctional bedside terminals will proliferate. Those mobile information processing tools will offer both communication and information processing functionality. Wireless networks will be standard in many hospitals. Computer-based training systems will strongly support efficient learning for healthcare professionals (Figure 1.6). Documentation efforts will increase and lead to more sophisticated computer-based documentation tools (see Figures 1.7 and 1.8). Decision support tools will be integrated and support high-quality care. Communication will be increasingly supported by electronic means. The globalization of providing health care and the cooperation of healthcare professionals will increase, and patients and healthcare professionals will seek health information on the Internet more and more. Large health databases will be available for everyone at his or her workplace.

Providing high-quality and efficient health care will continue to be strongly correlated with high-quality information and communication technology and a sound methodology for systematically processing information. However, the newest information and communication technologies do not guarantee high-quality information processing. Both information processing technologies and methodologies must adequately and responsibly be applied and, as will be pointed out later on, systematically managed.

---

10. President's Information Technology Advisory Committee (PITAC). Transforming Healthcare Through Information Technology—PITAC report to the president. Arlington: Nation Coordination Office for Computing; 2001. http://www.hpcc.gov/pubs/pitac/pitac-hc-9feb01.pdf.

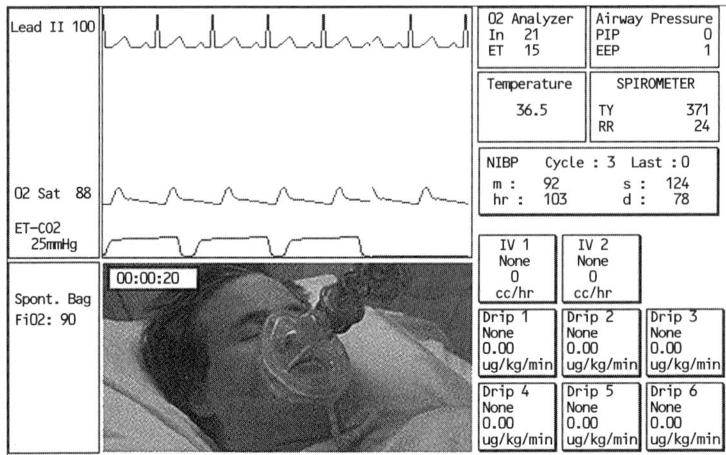


Figure 1.6: A computer-based training system for critical care, simulating a patient and various intensive care parameters.

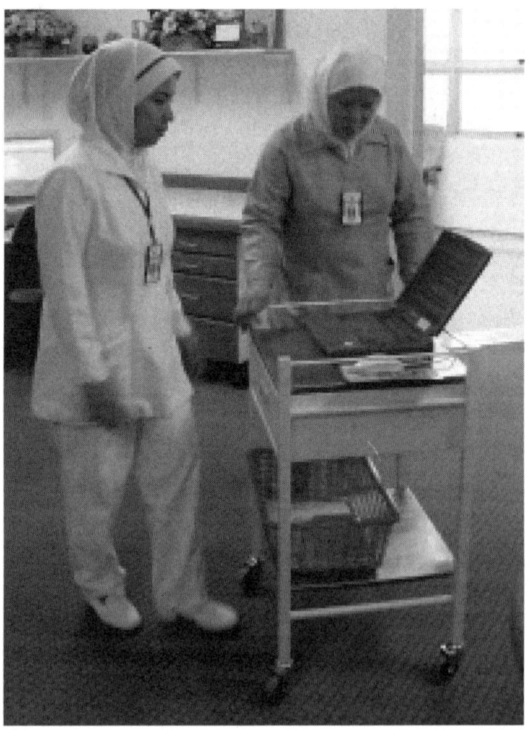

Figure 1.7: A mobile computer on a ward to support medical documentation and information access.

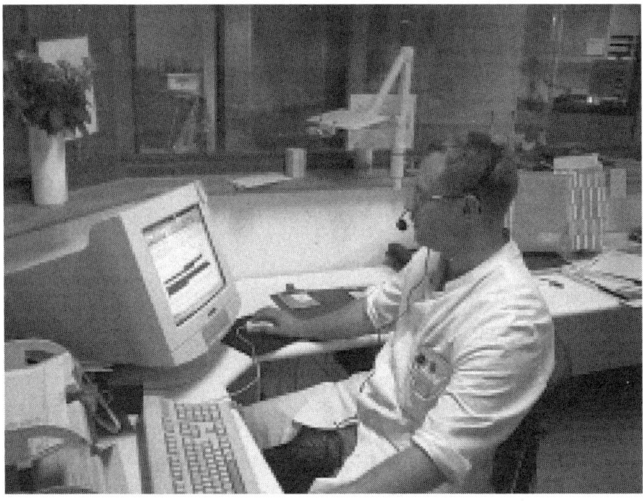

Figure 1.8: Writing a discharge summary using speech recognition.

# 1.3 Importance of Systematic Information Management

## *All People and All Areas of a Hospital Are Affected by the Quality of Its Information System*

Nearly all people and all areas of a hospital are affected by the quality of the information system, as most of them need various types of information (e.g., about the patient) in their daily work. The patient can certainly profit most from high-quality information processing since it contributes to the quality of patient care and to reducing costs.

The professional groups working in a hospital, especially physicians, nurses, and administrative personnel, but also others, are also directly affected by the quality of the information system. As they spend 25% or even more of their time on information handling, they directly profit from good and efficient information processing. But they will also feel the consequences if information processing is poor.

## *The Amount of Information Processing in Hospitals Is Considerable*

The amount of information processing in hospitals, especially in larger ones, should not be underestimated. Let us look at a typical German university medical center. It is an enterprise encompassing a staff of approximately

6,000 people, an annual budget of approximately 500 million € and, as a maximum care facility, numerous tasks in research, education, and patient care. It consists of up to 60 departments and up to 100 wards with approximately 1,500 beds and about 100 outpatient units. Annually, approximately 50,000 inpatients and 250,000 outpatients are treated, and 20,000 operation reports, 250,000 discharge letters, 20,000 pathology reports, 100,000 microbiology reports, 200,000 radiology reports, and 800,000 clinical chemistry reports are written (Figure 1.9).

Figure 1.9: Multitude of paper-based forms in an outpatient unit.

Each year, approximately 400,000 new patient records, summing up to approximately 8 million pieces of paper, are created. When stored in a paper-based form, an annual record volume of approximately 1,500 meters is generated (Figure 1.10). In Germany, for example, they should be archived over a period of 30 years. When stored digitally, the annual data volume needed is expected to be around 5 terabytes, including digital images and digital signals, and increasing.

The computer-based tools of a university medical center encompass hundreds of computer-based application components, thousands of workstations and other terminals, and up to a hundred servers (larger computer systems that offer services and functionality to other computer systems), which usually belong to a network.

The numbers in the majority of hospitals are much smaller. In larger ones we will find, for example, about 10 departments with 600 beds and about 20,000 inpatients every year. In industrialized countries 1,500 staff members would work there, and the annual budget of the hospital would be about 80 million €. Especially in rural areas we can also find hospitals with only one department and fewer than 50 beds.

Figure 1.10: Searching for patients records in a patient record archive.

## *Different Healthcare Professionals Often Need the Same Data*

There are different reasons for pursuing holistic—integrated—information processing. The most important reason is that various groups of healthcare professionals within and outside hospitals need the same data (Figure 1.11).

For example, a surgeon in a hospital documents the diagnoses and therapies of an operated patient in an operation report. This report serves as basis for the discharge letter. The discharge letter is also an important document to communicate with the admitting institution, normally a general practitioner. Diagnosis and therapy are also important for statistics about patient care and for quality management. Equally, they contain important information for the systematic nursing care of a patient. Diagnostic and therapeutic data are also relevant for billing.

Figure 1.11: Regular clinical round by different healthcare professionals on a ward.

In Germany, for example, some basic administrative data must be communicated to the respective health insurance company online within 3 days after patient admission and after discharge. In a coded form, they are the basis for accounting. Additionally, managing and controlling a hospital is possible only if the costs (such as consumption of materials or drugs) of the treatment can be compared to the form and the severity of the illness, characterized by diagnosis and therapy.

## *Integrated Information Processing Is Necessary to Efficiently Fulfill Information Needs*

Information processing has to integrate the partly overlapping information needs of the different groups and areas of a hospital (see Figures 1.12, 1.13, and 1.14)

It has been shown that systematic, integrated information processing in a hospital has advantages not only for the patient, but also for the healthcare professionals, the health insurance companies, and the hospital's owners. If information processing is not conducted globally across the institutions, but locally, for example in professional groups (physicians, nurses, administrative staff) or areas (clinical departments, institutes, administration), this corresponds to traditional separation politics and leads to isolated information processing groups, such as 'the administration' or 'the clinic'. In this case, the quality of the hospital information system clearly decreases while the costs for information processing increase due to the necessity for multiple data collection and analysis. Finally, this has disadvantages for the patient and, when seen from a national economical point of view, for the whole population.

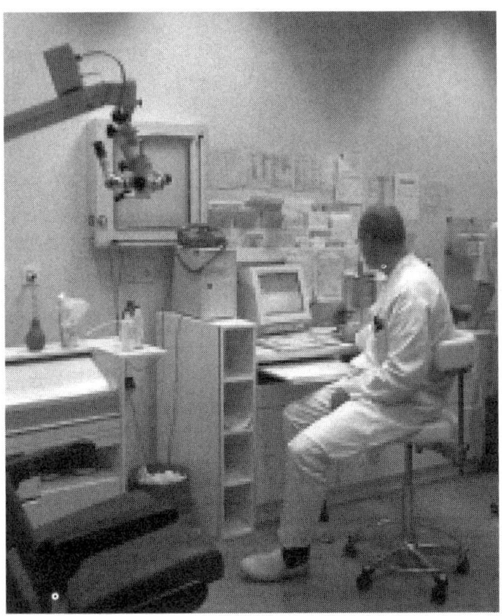

Figure 1.12: A physician in an examination room of an outpatient unit.

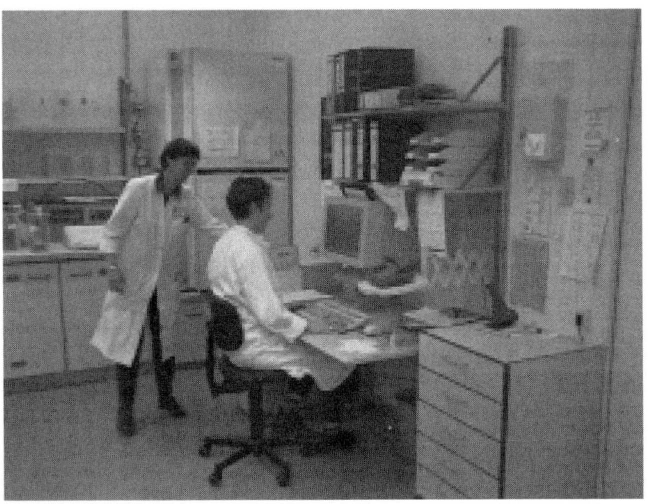

Figure 1.13: A medical-technical assistant and a microbiologist in a laboratory unit.

Figure 1.14: A nurse on an ophthalmology ward.

However, integration of information processing should consider not only information processing in one healthcare institution, but also information processing in and among different institutions or groups of institutions (such as integrated healthcare delivery systems). The achievements of modern medicine, particularly in the field of acute diseases, have led to the paradoxical result that chronic diseases and multimorbidity increasingly gain in importance. Among other reasons, this is due to people being able to live to old age. Moreover, in many countries an increasing willingness to switch doctors and a higher regional mobility exist among patients. The degree of highly specialized and distributed patient care creates a great demand for integrated information processing among healthcare professionals and among healthcare institutions such as hospitals, general practices, laboratories, etc. In turn, this raises the need for more comprehensive documentation and efficient, comprehensive information systems.

### *Systematic Information Processing Raises the Quality of Patient Care and Reduces Costs*

What does "systematic" mean in this context? "Unsystematic" can, in a positive sense, mean creative, spontaneous, or flexible. However, "unsystematic" can also mean chaotic, purposeless, and ineffective, and also entail high costs compared to the benefits gained.

"Systematic" in this context means purposeful and effective, and with great benefit regarding the costs. Bearing this in mind, it is obvious that information processing in a hospital should be managed systematically. Due to the importance of information processing as a quality and cost factor, a hospital has to invest systematically in its hospital information system. These investments concern both staff and tools for information processing. They aim at increasing quality of patient care and at reducing costs.

Unsystematic information processing normally leads to a low quality hospital information system, and the information needs of the staff and departments cannot be adequately satisfied. When hospital information systems are not systematically managed, they tend to develop in a chaotic way. This has severe consequences: decreased data quality, and higher costs, especially for tools and information processing staff, not to mention aspects such as data protection and data security violation.

To adequately process information and apply information and communication technology, knowledge and skills for these tasks are required.

### *Systematic Management of the Hospital Information System Is Essential for Systematic Information Processing*

If the hospital management decides to invest in systematic information processing (and not in fighting the effects of chaotic information processing, which normally means much higher investments), it decides to manage the hospital information system in a systematic way. The management of a hospital information system forms and controls the information system, and it ensures its efficient operation.

## 1.4 Examples

### Example 1.4.1: Improving Patient Care Through the Use of Medical Knowledge Servers

Imagine the following situation: Ursula B. was pregnant with quintuplets. She had already spent more than 5 months in the Heidelberg University Medical Center. She had to spend most of this time lying in bed. During the course of her pregnancy, her physical problems increased. From the 28th week on, she suffered severe respiratory distress.

The pediatrician, who was also involved in her treatment, had the following question: What are the chances of the infants being born healthy at this gestational age?

He went to a computer, a "healthcare professional workstation" available on his ward and in his office. Such a workstation can be used for a variety of tasks. It is connected to the computer network of the Heidelberg University Medical Center. The physician called up a "medical knowledge server" and one of its components, a bibliographic database (MEDLINE[11]) (Figure 1.15). This database contains the current state of the art of medical knowledge worldwide. The medical knowledge server can be accessed at any time and from any of the more than 3,000 healthcare professional workstations of the Heidelberg University Medical Center.

Figure1.15: Prof. Otwin Linderkamp, head of the Department of Pediatrics in Heidelberg, working with the medical knowledge server.

The following information resulted from this consultation of the medical knowledge server: Several publications stated that only slim chances exist for all infants to survive in good health. If they are born during the 28th week of pregnancy, the chance for survival is about 15%. In case of birth during the 30th week, their chances would improve to about 75%. Also, according to the literature, further delay of the delivery does not improve the prognosis of the quintuplets. The physician discussed the results with the expectant mother. Despite her respiratory problems, she had the strength to endure two more weeks. On January 21st, 1999, the quintuplets were born well and healthy at the Heidelberg University Medical Center (Figure 1.16). A team of 25 physicians, nurses, and midwives assisted during the delivery.

11. Offered for free by the National Library of Medicine (NLM), Bethesda, USA, http://www.ncbi.nlm.nih.gov/entrez/query.fcgi.

The costs for such a medical knowledge server for a complete medical center are generally lower than the costs for one ultrasound scanner, provided that the information system of the medical center offers a minimum infrastructure. Every hospital in the developed world can afford such a tool.

Figure 1.16: The Heidelberg quintuplets.

A medical knowledge server, as an integrated part of a hospital information system, can be used at any time at the healthcare professional's workplace. Such a medical knowledge server was introduced by the Department of Medical Informatics of the University of Heidelberg in 1992. At that time, it was one of the first installations of its kind in the world. Today, the medical knowledge server is maintained and under further development in cooperation with the Heidelberg University Library. In April 2001, for example, the medical knowledge server was called upon about 600 times a day by healthcare professionals of the Heidelberg University Medical Center.

**Example 1.4.2: Evaluation of a Decision-Support Program for the Management of Antibiotics**[12]

A decision-support program linked to computer-based patient records was developed to assist physicians in the use of antiinfective agents. The pro-

12. This example is taken from: Evans R, Pestotnik S, Classen D, et al. A Computer-Assisted Management Program for Antibiotics and Other Antiinfective Agents. New England Journal of Medicine 1996; 338(4): 232-60.

gram can recommend antiinfective regimens and courses of therapy for particular patients and provide immediate feedback. The program alerts physicians to the latest pertinent information on the individual patient at the time therapeutic decisions are made. It suggests an appropriate antiinfective regimen for the patient, using decision-support logic, based on admission diagnoses, laboratory parameters, surgical data, chest radiographs, and information from pathology, serology, and microbiology reports. The precondition for this antibiotic assistant is a structured data entry into a clinical database.

To analyze the effects of using this program, its usage in a 12-bed intensive care unit for 1 year was prospectively studied. During the intervention period, all 545 patients admitted to the unit were cared for with the aid of the antiinfective-management program. Measures of processes and outcomes were compared with those for the 1,136 patients admitted to the same unit during the 2 years before the intervention period.

The use of the program led to significant reductions in orders for drugs to which the patients had reported allergies (35 vs. 146 during the preintervention period), excess drug dosages (87 vs. 405), and antibiotic-susceptibility mismatches (12 vs. 206). There were also marked reductions in the mean number of days of excessive drug dosage (2.7 vs. 5.9), and in adverse events caused by antiinfective agents (4 vs. 28). Those who always received the regimens recommended by the program had significant reductions in cost of antiinfective agents (114 vs. 374 € of the preintervention period), in total hospital costs (28,946 vs. 38,811 €), and in the length of the hospital stay (10.0 vs. 12.9 days).

The results show that this computerized antiinfective-management program can improve the quality of patient care and reduce costs.

### Example 1.4.3: Nonsystematic Information Processing in Clinical Registers

The following example shows what can happen when information processing is done in a nonsystematic (or, better, chaotic?) manner from yet another point of view.[13] Let us analyze a (fictitious) clinical register from the (fictitious) Plötzberg Medical Center and Medical School (PMC). PMC will be used in examples and exercises in this book.

Table 1.1 shows statistics with patients having diagnosis Δ, e.g., rheumatism, and treated during the years δ, e.g., 1991-2001, at PMC. The patients have either received standard therapy, Verum, or a new therapy, Novum.

Comparing the success rates of Novum and Verum, one might conclude that the new therapy is better than the standard therapy. Applying an appro-

---

13. The example is based on a similar one in: Green SB, Byar DP. Using Observational Data from Registries to Compare Treatments: The Fallacy of Omnimetrics. Statistics in Medicine 1984; 3: 361-70.

priate statistical test would lead to a low $p$-value and a significant result. The success rate was also analyzed by sex. This resulted in Verum leading in female patients as well as in male patients.

Is one of our conclusions erroneous? Or maybe both? What would a systematic design and analysis of such a register be? After looking at the data, one can identify a fairly simple reason for this so-called Simpson's paradox. The methodology for processing information systematically ought to prevent such errors; however, it is far more complex.

Table 1.1: Example of Simpson's paradox. Success rates of Novum and Verum treatments for patients with diagnosis Δ, treated during the years δ at the Plötzberg Medical Center and Medical School (PMC).

| *all patients* | | | | |
|---|---|---|---|---|
| | | success | | success |
| | yes | no | Σ | rate |
| Novum | 333 | 1143 | 1476 | (23%) |
| Verum | 243 | 1113 | 1356 | (18%) |
| Σ | 576 | 2256 | 2832 | |

| *male patients* | | | | |
|---|---|---|---|---|
| | | success | | success |
| | yes | no | Σ | rate |
| Novum | 24 | 264 | 288 | (8%) |
| Verum | 147 | 906 | 1053 | (14%) |
| Σ | 171 | 1170 | 1341 | |

| *female patients* | | | | |
|---|---|---|---|---|
| | | success | | success |
| | yes | no | Σ | rate |
| Novum | 309 | 879 | 1188 | (26%) |
| Verum | 96 | 207 | 303 | (32%) |
| Σ | 405 | 1086 | 1491 | |

### Example 1.4.4: Relevance of Information Processing, as Seen from a Healthcare Professional's Point of View

In our field, the relevance of medical informatics both for patient care and for scientific research cannot be overestimated. In many medical fields, basic technologies have developed so far that their wise application and exhaustive use have led to better results and to their improvement.

The revolution of radiology diagnostics by computed tomography exemplifies this. Here, a 100-year-old principle was tremendously improved by the means of data processing. For my field, this means very burdening invasive patient treatments can be avoided by using the high quality, non-invasive picture generation.

Due to computer-based registration of medical reports and patient data, similar revolutionary developments can be found in other medical tasks. Quality assurance and resource controlling are only two examples. Effective controlling is needed to avoid low-informative diagnostics and low-efficient therapy. Effective controlling would not be possible without modern information systems. This is true for both the individual hospital departments and for healthcare services as a whole. Those who have worked with patients in a responsible clinical position know that experiences based on individual cases are rather deceptive and that a rational and quantifiable evaluation of their own tasks and the resulting effects is necessary. The new, widely basic data set documentation, which is just being introduced nationwide in my field, offers possibilities for such a rational and sober assessment of success treatment and for resource controlling which has not been possible in the past.[14]

# 1.5 Exercises

### Exercise 1.5.1: Amount of Information Processing in Typical Hospitals

Estimate the following figures for a typical university medical center and for a typical rural hospital. To solve this exercise, look at the strategic information management plan for information processing of a hospital, or proceed with your own local investigations.

- Number of (inpatient) clinical departments and institutes.
- Number of wards and outpatient units.
- Number of employees.
- Annual budget.
- Number of beds, inpatients, and outpatients per year.
- Number of new patient records per year.
- Number of discharge letters per year.
- Number of computer servers, workstations, and terminals.
- Number of operation reports, clinical chemistry reports, and radiology reports per year.

---

14. Speech of the Vice Dean of the Medical Faculty of the University of Heidelberg, Professor Christoph Mundt, to the graduates of the Heidelberg/Heilbronn Medical Informatics Program, during the commencement celebration of the University of Applied Sciences Heilbronn, October 4th 1996.

### Exercise 1.5.2: Information Processing in Different Areas

Find three examples of information processing for each of the following areas in a hospital, taking into account the different healthcare professional groups working there. Which information is processed during which activities, and which tools are used? Take paper-based and computer-based information processing into consideration in your examples.

- Information processing on a ward.
- Information processing in an outpatient unit.
- Information processing in an operating room.
- Information processing in a radiology department.
- Information processing in the hospital administration.

### Exercise 1.5.3: Good Information Processing Practice

Have a look at the following typical functions of hospitals. Try to find two examples of "good" information processing practices in these functions, and two examples of "poor" information processing practices. Which positive or negative consequences for the patients could they have?

- Administrative patient admission.
- Clinical documentation.
- Laboratory diagnostics.
- Patient records archiving.

## 1.6 Summary

Information processing is an important quality factor, but also an enormous cost factor. It is also becoming a productivity factor. Information processing should offer a holistic view of the patient and of the hospital. A hospital information system can be regarded as the memory and nervous system of a hospital.

Information and communication technology has become economically important and decisive for the quality of health care. It will continue to change health care.

The integrated processing of information is important, because

- all groups of people and all areas of a hospital depend on its quality,
- the amount of information processing in hospitals is considerable, and
- healthcare professionals frequently work with the same data.

The systematic processing of information

- contributes to high-quality patient care, and
- it reduces costs.

Information processing in hospitals is complex. Therefore,

- the systematic management and operation of hospital information systems, and
- health informatics specialists responsible for the management and operation of hospital information systems are needed.

# 2
# Basic Concepts

## 2.1 Introduction

Every domain usually has its own terminology, which often differs from the ordinary understanding of concepts and terms. This chapter presents the terminology for hospital information systems and its information management, as used in this book. It is therefore essential to read this chapter carefully. All relevant concepts can also be found in the thesaurus in Appendix A.

After reading this chapter, you should be able to answer the following questions:

- What is the difference between data, information, and knowledge?
- What are information systems, and what are their components?
- What are hospital information systems?
- What are health information systems?
- What does information management mean?

## 2.2 Data, Information, and Knowledge

*Data* constitute reinterpretable representations of information, or knowledge, in a formalized manner suitable for communication, interpretation, or processing by humans or machines. Formalization may take the form of discrete characters or of continuous signals (e.g., sound signals). To be reinterpretable, there has to be agreement on how data represent information. For example, "Peter Smith" or "001001110" are data. A set of data that is put together for the purpose of transmission and that is considered to be one entity for this purpose is called a *message*.

There is no unique definition of *information*. Depending on the point of view, the definition may deal with a syntactic aspect (the structure), a semantic aspect (the meaning), or a pragmatic aspect (the intention or goal of information). We will simply define information as specific knowledge about entities such as facts, events, things, persons, processes, ideas, or concepts.

For example, when a physician knows the diagnosis (facts) of a patient (person), then he or she has information.

*Knowledge* is general information about concepts in a certain (scientific or professional) domain (e.g., about diseases, therapeutic methods). Knowledge contrasts with specific information about particular individuals of the domain (e.g., patients). The knowledge of a nurse, for example, comprises how to typically deal with patients suffering from decubitus.

For the sake of simplicity, we will often use the term *information processing* when we mean processing of data, information, and knowledge.

## 2.3 Information Systems and Their Components

### *Systems and Subsystems*

Before talking about information systems, let us first define the concept "system." As defined here, a *system* is a set of persons, things, and/or events that forms an entity, together with their relationships. We distinguish between natural systems and artificial (man-made) systems. For example, the nervous system is a typical natural system, consisting of neurons and their relationships. A man-made system is, for example, a hospital, consisting of staff, patients, and relatives, and their interactions. If a (man-made) system consists of both human and technical components, it can be called a *sociotechnical system.*

A system can, in principle, be divided into *subsystems* that comprise a subset of the components and the relationships between them. For example, a possible subsystem of the nervous system is the sympathetic nervous system. A subsystem of a hospital is, for example, a ward with its staff and patients. Subsystems themselves are again systems.

### *Models of Systems*

When dealing with systems, we usually work with *models* of systems. A model is a description of what the modeler thinks to be relevant of a system.

In the sciences, models commonly represent simplified depictions of reality or excerpts of it. Models are adapted to answer certain questions or to solve certain tasks. Models should be appropriate for the respective questions or tasks. This means that a model is only "good" when it is able to answer such a question or solve such a task. For example, a model that only comprises the patients (and not the nurses) of a ward cannot be used for nurse staffing and shift planning.

## Information Systems

An *information system* is that part of an enterprise that processes and stores data, information, and knowledge. It can be defined as the socio-technical subsystem of an enterprise, which comprises all information processing as well as the associated human or technical actors in their respective information processing roles.

"Socio-" refers to the people involved in information processing (e.g., healthcare professionals, administrative staff, computer scientists), whereas "technical" refers to information processing tools (e.g., computers, telephones, patient records). The people and machines in an enterprise are considered only in their role as information processors, carrying out specific actions following established rules.

An information system that comprises computer-based information processing and communication tools is called a *computer-supported information system*. An information system can be divided (like any system) into subsystems, which are called *sub-information systems*. The sub-information system where computer-based tools are used is called the computer-supported part; the rest is called the conventional or paper-based part of an information system.

## Components of Information Systems

When describing an information system, it can help to look at the following typical *components* of information systems: enterprise functions, business processes, application components, and physical data processing components.

An *enterprise function* describes what acting human or machines have to do in a certain enterprise to contribute to its mission and goals. For example, "patient admission," "clinical documentation," or "financial controlling" describe typical enterprise functions. Enterprise functions are ongoing and continuous. They describe what is to be done, not how it is done. Enterprise functions can be structured into a hierarchy of functions, where a function can be described in more detail by refined functions. Enterprise functions are usually denoted by nouns or gerunds (i.e., words ending with -ing).

An *activity* is an instantiation of an enterprise function working on an individual entity. For example, "Dr. Doe admits patient Jane Smith" is an activity of the enterprise function "patient admission." Just as enterprise functions, they can be put together in a hierarchy of activities. In contrast to enterprise functions, activities have a definite beginning and end.

To describe the chronological and logical sequence of a set of activities, *business processes* are useful. They describe the sequence of activities together with the conditions under which they are invoked, to achieve a certain enterprise goal. Business processes are usually denoted by verbs (for example, “dismiss a patient,” “document a diagnosis,” or “write a discharge letter”). As they are composed of individual activities, they also have a definite beginning and end. While enterprise functions concentrate on the “what,” business processes focus on the “how” of activities.

We will refer only to enterprise functions and business processes with respect to information processing.

Whereas enterprise functions and business processes describe what is done, we now want to consider tools for processing data, in particular so-called application components and physical data processing components. Both are usually referred to as *information processing tools*. They describe the means used for information processing.

*Application components* support enterprise functions. We distinguish computer-based from paper-based application components. Computer-based application components are controlled by *application programs*, which are adapted *software products*. A software product is an acquired or self-developed piece of software that is complete in itself and that can be installed on a computer system. For example, the application component “patient management system” stands for the installation of a software product to support the enterprise functions of patient admission, transfer, and discharge.

Paper-based application components are controlled by working plans that describe how people use paper-based physical data processing components. For example, the application component “nursing documentation organization” contains rules regarding how and in which context to use the given forms for nursing documentation. Paper-based in this sense comprises not only paper as the main documentation carrier, but also other nonelectronic documents such as radiology films or teeth impressions.

Communication and cooperation among application components must be organized in such a way that the enterprise functions are adequately supported.

*Physical data processing components,* finally, describe the information processing tools that are used to realize the computer-based and the paper-based application components (Figure 2.1). Physical data processing components can be human actors (such as the person delivering mail), paper-based physical tools (such as printed forms, telephones, books, patient record), or computer systems (such as terminals, servers, personal computers). Computer systems can be physically connected via data wires, leading to physical networks.

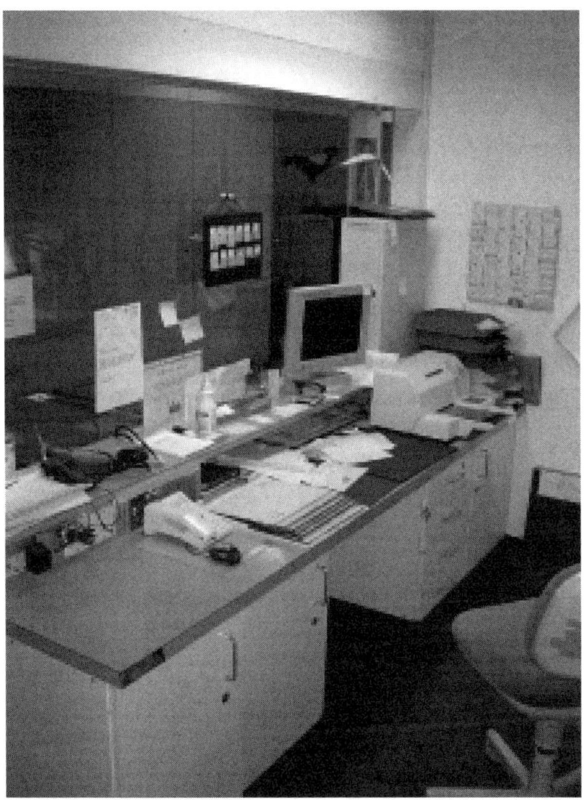

Figure 2.1: Typical physical data processing components (e.g., computer, printer telephone, paper-based patient record, blackboards) on a ward.

## *Architecture and Infrastructure of Information Systems*

The *architecture* of an information system describes its fundamental organization, represented by its components, their relationships to each other and to the environment, and by the principles guiding its design and evolution.[15] The architecture of an information systems can be described by the enterprise functions, the business processes, and the information processing tools, together with their relationships.

There may be several architectural views of an information system, e.g., a functional view looking primarily at the enterprise functions, a process view looking primarily at the business processes. Architectures that are

15. Institute of Electrical and Electronics Engineers (IEEE). Std 1471-2000: Recommended Practice for Architectural Description of Software-Intensive Systems. September 2000. http://standards.ieee.org.

equivalent with regard to certain characteristics can be summarized in a certain *architectural style*.

When the focus is put onto the types, number, and availability of information processing tools used in a given enterprise, this is also called the *infrastructure* of its information system.

## 2.4 Hospital Information Systems

With the definition of information systems in mind, a hospital information system can be easily defined. A *hospital information system* is the socio-technical subsystem of a hospital, which comprises all information processing as well as the associated human or technical actors in their respective information processing roles. Typical components of hospital information systems are enterprise functions, business processes, application components, and physical data processing components (see section 2.3). For the sake of simplicity, we will denote the enterprise functions of a hospital as *hospital functions*.

As a consequence of this definition, a hospital has a hospital information system from the beginning of its existence. Therefore, the question is not whether a hospital should be equipped with a hospital information system, but rather how its performance can be enhanced, for example, by using state-of-the- art information processing tools, or by systematically managing it.

All groups of people and all areas of a hospital must be considered when looking at information processing. The sensible integration of the different information processing tools in a hospital information system is important.

Hospital staff can be seen as part of the hospital information system. For example, when working in the department of patient records, or as an operator in an ICT department, staff members directly contribute to information processing. In their role as user of the hospital information system, they use information processing tools (e.g., a nurse may use a telephone or a computer). Each employee may continuously switch between these two roles.

The *goal* of a hospital information system is to sufficiently enable the adequate execution of hospital functions for patient care, including patient administration, taking into account economic hospital management as well as legal and other requirements. Legal requirements concern data protection or reimbursement aspects, for example. Other requirements can be the decision of a hospital executive board on how to store patient records, for example.

To support patient care and the associated administration, the *tasks* of hospital information systems are:

- to make information, primarily about patients, available: current information should be provided on time, at the right location, to authorized staff, in an appropriate and usable form. For this purpose, data must be correctly collected, stored, processed, and systematically documented to ensure that correct, pertinent, and up-to-date patient information can be supplied, for instance, to the physician or a nurse (Figure 2.2);

- to make knowledge, for example, about diseases, about side effects, and interactions of medications, available to support diagnostics and therapy;
- to make information about the quality of patient care and the performance and cost situation within the hospital available.

Figure 2.2: A healthcare professional accessing patient information.

In addition to patient care, university medical centers undertake research and education to gain medical knowledge and to teach students.

When hospital information systems make available

- the right information and knowledge

- at the right time
- at the right place
- to the right people
- in the right form,

so that these people can make the right decisions, this is also described as *information and knowledge logistics*.

Hospital information systems have to consider various *areas* of a hospital, such as

- wards,
- outpatient units,
- service units: diagnostic (e.g., clinical laboratory, radiological department), therapeutic (e.g., operation room) and others (e.g., pharmacy, patient records archive, library, blood bank),
- hospital administration areas (e.g., general administration, patient administration and accounting, technology, economy and supply, human resources),
- offices and writing services for (clinical) report writing.

In addition, there are the management areas, such as hospital management, management of clinical departments and institutes, administration management, and nursing management.

These areas are related to patient care. They could be broken down further. For university medical centers, additional areas, needed for research and education, must be added to the above list.

Obviously, the most important *people* in a hospital are the patients and, in certain respect, their visitors. The most important groups of people working in a hospital (Figure 2.3) are

- physicians,
- nurses,
- administrative staff,
- technical staff, and
- health informaticians, health information management staff.

Within each group of people, different needs and demands on the hospital information system may exist, depending on the tasks and responsibilities. Ward physicians, for example, require different information than physicians working in service units or than senior physicians.

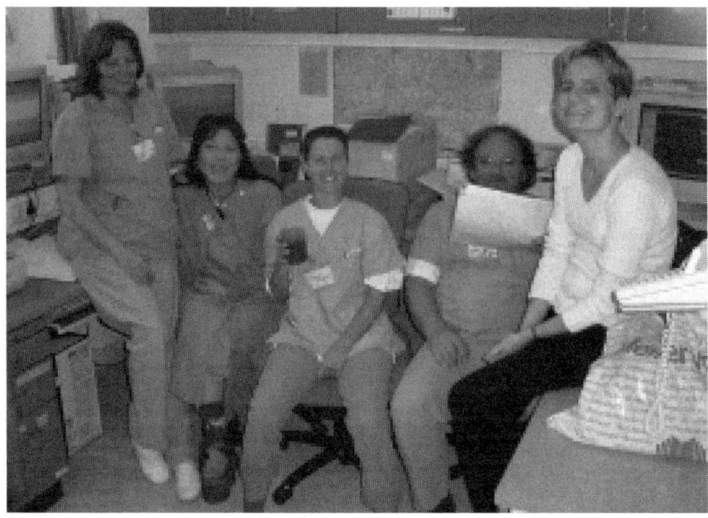

Figure 2.3: Different people working in a hospital (here, nurses and physicians in an emergency department).

## 2.5 Health Information Systems

### *From Hospital Information Systems to Health Information Systems*

In many countries, the driving force for health care and for ICT in health care has recently been the trend toward a better coordination of care, combined with rising cost pressure. One consequence is the shift toward better integrated and shared care. This means that the focus changes from isolated procedures in one healthcare institution (e.g., one hospital or one general practice) to the patient-oriented care process, encompassing diagnosis and therapy, spreading over institutional boundaries (Figure 2.4).

In the United States, for example, healthcare organizations are merging into large *integrated healthcare delivery systems*. These are healthcare institutions that join together to consolidate their roles, resources, and operations to deliver a coordinated range of services and to enhance effectiveness and efficiency of patient care. The situation in Europe is also changing from hospitals as centers of care delivery to decentralized networks of healthcare delivery institutions that are called regional networks or healthcare networks. Enterprise boundaries are blurring. Hospital information systems will increasingly be linked with information systems of other healthcare organizations.

The future architecture of hospital information systems must take these developments into account. They must be able to provide access or to exchange patient-related and general data (e.g., about the services offered in the hospital) across its institutional boundaries.

Figure 2.4: A general practitioner contacting a hospital by phone.

A lot of technical and legal issues have to be solved before trans-institutional computer-supported *health information systems*, or information systems spreading over institutional boundaries in health care, will adequately support trans-institutional patient care. For example, a general willingness to cooperate with other healthcare providers must exist; optimal care processes must be defined, and recent business processes be redesigned; accounting and financing issues must be regulated; questions of data security and data confidentiality must be answered, together with questions on data ownership (patient or institution) and on responsibilities for distributed patient care; issues on long-term patient records (centralized or decentralized) must be discussed; and technical means for integrated, trans-institutional information processing must be offered (telemedicine, e-health), including general communication standards.

When dealing with hospital information systems, we will consider these aspects of health information systems.

## *Patient Care and the Web*

The Internet plays an increasingly important role within health care. First, many healthcare organizations offer information on their services on the Internet. Healthcare professionals and patients therefore can easily inform themselves on the available healthcare services in a city or area, and they can find specialized institutions for their needs. Second, more and more clinical knowledge is available on the Internet. For example, the National Library of Medicine grants free access to over 12 million MEDLINE citations back to the mid-1960s.[16] This clinical knowledge is available both for the healthcare practitioners as well as for patients and their relatives. Digital libraries will have a rising influence on the distribution of human knowledge.[17] Third, there are already several initiatives offering patients the possibility to manage their personal health record on the Internet. This means that the patient-related history is available anywhere at any time. Fourth, the rising connectivity of healthcare institutions and the rising bandwidth of the Internet allows telemedical applications. Telemedicine means to provide diagnostics and therapy even when the patient and the healthcare professional are at remote places. Applications can be found, for example, in the areas of teleradiology, teledermatology, and telesurgery.

The potential of Internet technologies to support health care thus seems tremendous. However, it is important to guarantee that the information offered on the Internet is valid, up-to-date, correct, and complete. Here, initiatives such as HON[18] offer ways to ensure the quality of health-related information on the Internet.

## 2.6 Information Management in Hospitals

In general, management comprises all leadership activities that determine the enterprises' goals, structures, and behaviors. Accordingly, *information management* in hospitals are those management activities in a hospital that deal with the management of information processing in a hospital and therefore of its hospital information system. The goal of information management is systematic information processing that contributes to the hospital's strategic goals (such as efficient patient care and high satisfaction of patients and staff). Information management therefore directly contributes to the hospital's success and ability to compete.

The general tasks of information management are planning, directing, and monitoring. In other words, this means

- planning the hospital information system and its architecture,
- directing its establishment and its operation, and

16. NLM. National Library of Medicine. PubMed. http://www.ncbi.nlm.nih.gov/entrez/query.fcgi.

17. President's information technology advisory committee (PITAC). Digital Libraries: Universal Access to Human Knowledge—PITAC report to the president. Arlington: Nation Coordination Office for Computing; 2001. http://www.ccic.gov/pubs/pitac/pitac-dl-9feb01.pdf.

18. HON. Health on the Net Foundation. http://www.hon.ch.

- monitoring its development and operation with respect to the planned objectives.

Information management encompasses the management of all components of a hospital information system—the management of information, of application components, and of physical data processing components.

Information management can be differentiated into strategic, tactical, and operational management. Strategic information management deals with information processing as a whole. Tactical information management deals with particular enterprise functions or with application components that are introduced, removed, or changed. Operational information management, finally, is responsible for operating the components of the information system. It cares for its smooth operation, for example, by planning necessary personal resources, by failure management, or by network monitoring. Information management in hospitals is discussed in detail in Chapter 5.

## 2.7 Examples

### Example 2.7.1: Architecture of a Hospital Information System

Here is an extract of the description of the architecture of the hospital information system of the Plötzberg Medical Center and Medical School (PMC). As mentioned, PMC is a fictitious institution, which will be used in examples and exercises in this book.

> The hospital information system of PMC supports the hospital functions of patient treatment with patient admission and discharge, decision support, order entry, clinical documentation and service documentation; handling of patient records; work organization and resource planning; and hospital administration.
>
> Those hospital functions are supported by some bigger and over a hundred smaller application components (partly computer-based, partly paper-based). The biggest application component is the patient management system (PMS), the computer-based application component that supports patient admission, transfer, and discharge. In addition, several computer-based departmental application components are used for work organization and resource planning (e.g., in the radiological department, in the laboratory department, and in outpatient units). Nearly all computer-based application components are interconnected, using a communication server. Some computer-based application components are isolated systems without interfaces.
>
> Paper-based application components are used for special documentation purposes (e.g., documentation in operation rooms), and for order entry and communication of findings.
>
> The application components are realized by physical data processing components. As computer-based physical data processing component, ap-

proximately 40 application and database servers are operated, and over 4,000 personal computers are used. Over 1,000 printers of different types are installed. Most computer-based physical data processing components are interconnected to a high-speed communication network.

As paper-based physical data processing components, over 2,000 telephones and 800 pagers are used. Over 2,000 different paper-based forms are used to support different tasks. More than 400,000 patients records are created and used each year, and a dozen local archives are responsible for patient record archiving. A paper-based mailing system allows for paper-based communication between departments.

## Example 2.7.2: Comments on the Future of Health Information Systems

For the physicians of the 1990s and beyond, computer workstations will be their windows on the world. Much of the necessary technology already exists. Desktop or bedside, in the office or at the hospital, computers can respond to a simple click of a mouse pointing device....In the future, the physician will be able to access the patient record largely by using the mouse and doing very little typing. Moreover, the record will include graphics and images as well as extensive text. Outpatient records will be integrated with inpatient data by using the capabilities of communications networks that link hospitals with the clinics and private offices of their medical staff members...."[19]

Through the further development of information systems at the university hospitals, the following goals are of special importance:

- Patient based (facility-wide) recording of and access to clinical data for team-based care.
- Workflow integrated decision support made available for all care takers through up-to-date, valid medical knowledge.
- Comprehensive use of patient data for clinical and epidemiological research, as well as for health reports....

The following tasks shall have priority and will be worked on in the next years:

- The introduction of a patient based, structured, electronic health record.
- The step-wise introduction of information system architectures that support cooperative, patient centered and facility-wide care.
- The establishment of a suitable network and computer infrastructure in order to be able to, via the Internet, inform about the care offered at a particular hospital.

---

19. Ball M, Douglas J, O'Desky R, Albrigh J. Healthcare Information Management Systems—A Practical Guide. New York: Springer; 1991. p. 3.

- The introduction of efficient, usable mobile information and communication tools for patient care....[20]

From the experience gained so far..., a number of direct benefits from health telematics can be identified:...

- More people can be diagnosed and treated at their local clinics or hospitals, though without the facilities of urban referral hospitals. For the first time, it is technically feasible to contemplate the provision of universal health care....
- Health telematics allows the global sharing of skills and knowledge. Access to international centers of excellence for various specialties becomes possible from many locations. Medical expertise can be available to anyone on request....
- Cost savings can be achieved by reducing the transport of patients and travel of healthcare professionals, as well as by allowing home care of patients who would otherwise require hospitalization....[21]

The future tasks of health care include: greater cooperation, more quality and economics and greater adjustment to the needs of patients. The information age offers great possibilities to solve these tasks, maybe even possibilities that we can't begin to imagine today.

The neuralgic point though in the discussion of telematics in health care is the uniting of data. Especially with regard to personal patient data, we are forthright dealing with the most personal of all data, and special caution is to be exercised when dealing with these data. After all, questions of power are raised through the uniting of data: greater transparency also means greater control.[22]

---

20. Deutsche Forschungsgemeinschaft (DFG): Informationsverarbeitung und Rechner an Hochschulen—Netze, Rechner und Organisation. Empfehlungen der Kommission für Rechenanlagen für 2001-2005 (information processing and computer systems for universities; in German), Kommission für Rechenanlagen der Deutschen Forschungsgemeinschaft. Bonn: DFG; 2001. http://www.dfg.de.

21. World Health Organization (WHO). A Health Telematics Policy, Report of the WHO Group Consultation on Health Telematics 11-16 December 1997. Geneva: World Health Organization; 1998.

22. Speech of German Minister for Health, Andrea Fischer, at the occasion of the first meeting of the symposium "telematics in healthcare," August 19, 1999, Bonn.

## 2.8 Exercises

### Exercise 2.8.1: HIS as a System

As introduced, a system can be defined as a set of people, things, and/or events that form an entity, together with their relationships. Which people, things, or events can you find when looking at a hospital information system? In what relationship do they stand to one another? To solve this exercise, take into account the components of hospital information systems as defined in section 2.3.

### Exercise 2.8.2: Goals of Models

Find two models that represent a city. What are the goals of these models? What are their components?

### Exercise 2.8.3 Information Processing Tools in a Hospital

Look at Figures 2.5, 2.6, 2.7, and 2.8. Which information and communication tools are used? Which hospital functions may be supported by those tools?

Figure 2.5: The office of a senior physician.

Figure 2.6: The office of a general practitioner.

Figure 2.7: An intensive care unit.

Figure 2.8: A laboratory unit.

### Exercise 2.8.4: Information Processing of Different Healthcare Professional Groups

Consider the different professional groups in a hospital (e.g., physician, nurse, administrative staff, hospital manager, patient, visitor), and describe some of their typical information processing needs.

### Exercise 2.8.5: Information and Knowledge Logistics

Select one typical business process in a hospital (such as admitting a patient, requesting an examination, planning of therapeutical procedures, documenting diagnoses, etc.) and find three examples how information and knowledge logistics can fail. Which consequences may arise for the quality and for the costs of patient care from this failure?

### Exercise 2.8.6: Buying an HIS

Look at the definition of hospital information systems in section 0. Based on this definition, is it possible to buy a hospital information system? Explain your answer. What do vendors of hospital information systems thus really sell?

### Exercise 2.8.7: Health Information Systems

Look at the comments on the future of health information systems in example 2.7.2. Which possible benefits are discussed, and which problems?

## 2.9 Summary

When working on hospital information systems, we must distinguish among data, information, and knowledge:

- Data can be defined as a representation of information, or knowledge, in a formalized manner, suitable for communicating, interpreting, or processing.
- Information can be defined as specific knowledge about entities such as facts, events, things, persons, processes, ideas, or concepts.
- Knowledge can be defined as general information about concepts in a certain domain.

A system is a set of people, things, and/or events that forms an entity, together with their relationships. Systems can be divided into subsystems and can be represented by using models. Models are a description of what the modeler thinks to be relevant to a system. Remember that models

- usually form a simplified representation of reality,
- should be adapted to a specific question or task, and
- should be appropriate to provide answers for these question or tasks.

A hospital information system can be defined as the socio-technical subsystem of a hospital that comprises all information processing functions and the human or technical actors in their information processing role. Typical components of hospital information systems are

- the hospital functions supported,
- the business processes that take place,
- the application components that support the hospital functions,
- the physical data processing components that realize the application components.

The subsystem of the HIS where computer-based tools are used is called the computer-supported part of the hospital information system. The architecture of an information system describes its fundamental organization, represented by its components, their relationships to each other and to the environment, and by the principles guiding its design and evolution.

The goal of an HIS is to

- adequately enable the execution of hospital functions for patient care,
- taking economic, legal, and other requirements into account.

When the HIS makes available

- the right information (about patients, ...) and the right knowledge (about diseases, ...)
- at the right time
- in the right place

- for the right people
- in the right form

so that these people can make the right decisions, this is called information and knowledge logistics.

When working on a hospital information system, you should consider all areas of a hospital, such as wards, outpatient units, service units, administration departments, reporting services, management units, as well as all groups of people in a hospital, such as patients, visitors, physicians, nurses, administrative staff, technical staff, and health informaticians.

Health information systems stand for trans-institutional information systems spreading over institutional boundaries in health care.

Information management in hospitals is those management activities in a hospital that deal with the management of information processing and therefore with the management of the hospital information system.

# 3
# What Do Hospital Information Systems Look Like?

## 3.1 Introduction

A hospital information system (HIS) was previously defined as the socio-technical subsystem of a hospital, which comprises all information processing as well as the associated human or technical actors in their respective information processing roles.

We now take a closer look at what hospital information systems look like. We present typical enterprise functions and processes of hospitals. We also discuss how to describe hospital information systems using appropriate modeling methods. We describe in detail the three-layer graph-based metamodel to describe HIS and discuss typical information processing tools and typical architectural styles of hospital information systems. Finally, integrity and integration within heterogeneous hospital information systems are discussed.

After reading this chapter, you should be able to answer the following questions:

- What are the main hospital functions?
- What are the typical metamodels for modeling various aspects of HIS?
- What is the three-layer graph-based metamodel (3LGM)?
- What are the typical information processing tools in hospitals?
- What are the architectural styles of HIS?
- How can integrity and component integration be achieved within HIS?

## 3.2 Hospital Functions

In this section, typical hospital functions are presented in greater detail, but we do not focus on how they are typically supported by various computer-based or paper-based information processing tools.

After this section, you should be able to answer the following question:

- What are the main hospital functions that have to be supported by an HIS?

## Patient Admission

Patient admission (Figure 3.1) aims at recording and distributing the patient demographics and insurance data. In addition, each patient must be correctly identified, and a unique patient and case identifier must be assigned.

Figure 3.1: A patient being admitted in a patient admission department.

Subfunctions are:

- Appointment scheduling: The hospital must be able to schedule an appointment for a patient's visit. In addition, unplanned admissions must be possible (e.g., in case of emergencies).
- Patient identification: A unique patient identification number (PIN) must be assigned to each patient. This PIN should be valid and unchangeable lifelong (i.e., the PIN should not be based on changeable patient's attributes such as the name). The PIN is the main precondition for a patient-oriented combination of all information arising during a patient's stay. Before a PIN can be assigned, the patient must be correctly identified, usually based on available administrative patient data. If the patient has already been in the hospital, she or he must be identified as recurrent, and previously documented information must be made available (such as previous diagnoses and thera-

pies). If the patient is in the hospital for the first time, a new PIN must be assigned. In addition, the hospital must be able to distinguish between different cases or hospital stays of a patient. Therefore, in addition to the PIN, a case identification is usually assigned.

- Administrative admission: Administrative admission starts following patient identification. Important administrative data such as insurance data, type of admission, details about special services, patient's relatives, admitting physician, and referral diagnoses must be recorded. In addition, a new visit number (case identifier) that identifies the recent stay is usually assigned. The patient is assigned to a ward and a bed. Some of the administrative data must be available to other hospital functions through the help of certain organization media (such as labels and magnetic cards; Figure 3.2). Administrative data form the backbone of information processing. In case of changes, patient data must be maintained and communicated. If the admitting physician has communicated relevant information (e.g., previous laboratory findings), this information must be communicated to the responsible physician in the hospital. Administrative admission is usually done either in a central patient admission or directly on the ward (e.g., during emergencies or on the weekend).

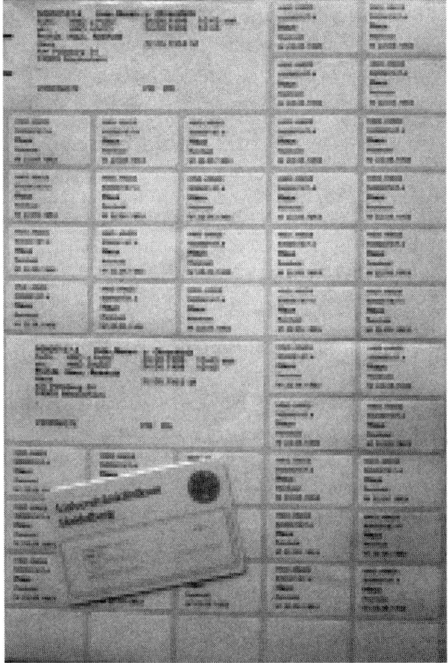

Figure 3.2: Typical organizational media: a magnetic card and stickers with patient identification data.

- Clinical admission: The responsible physician and nurse will proceed with the medical and nursing admission. This typically comprises the patient history, and the introduction of the patient to the ward. The basic patient history data have to be made available for other hospital functions.
- Information: The hospital management must always have an overview of the recent bed occupation, i.e., about the patients staying at the hospital. This is, for example, important for the clerks, who must be able to inform relatives and visitors correctly (Figure 3.3), and also for some general hospital management statistics.

Figure 3.3: Informing patient's relatives on a ward.

## *Planning and Organization of Patient Treatment*

All clinical procedures of healthcare professionals must be discussed, agreed upon, efficiently planned, and initiated. This process is initiated each time new information is available. Subfunctions are:

- Presentation of information and knowledge: Staff members must be able to access all relevant patient data specific to a situation, in addition to general clinical knowledge (e.g., guidelines and standards) supporting patient care (Figure 3.4).
- Decision making and patient information: Responsible team members must decide upon the next steps such as certain diagnostic or therapeutic procedures (Figure 3.5). Depending on the complexity of a diagnostic or therapeutic decision, they should be able to consult internal or external experts (e.g., in specialized hospitals) to get a second opinion. In this context, (tele-) conferences may help. Decisions

about clinical procedures must be documented. The patient should be involved in the decision-making process, and his or her informed consent must be documented as well.

- Care planning: The next steps now have to be planned in detail. For each procedure (such as an operation or a chemotherapeutic treatment), the type, extent, duration, and responsible person have to be determined. In nursing, care planning is documented in nursing care plans, containing nursing problems, nursing goals, and planned nursing procedures. If necessary, other healthcare professionals are ordered to execute the planned clinical procedures (e.g., medical bandaging orders, which have to be executed by a nurse).

Figure 3.4: Infrastructure to access medical knowledge in a clinical library.

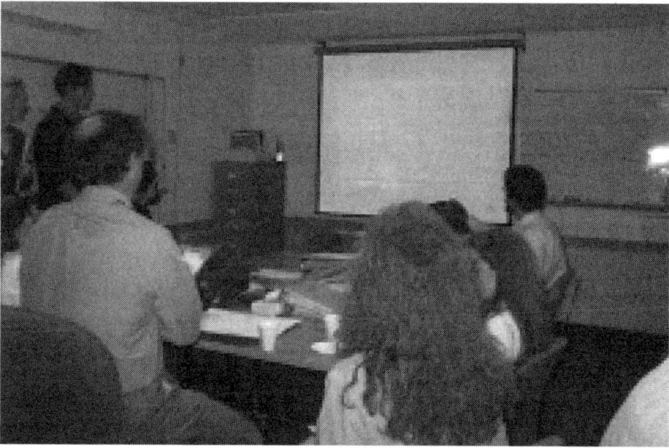

Figure 3.5: Regular meeting of healthcare professionals to discuss the next diagnostic and therapeutic steps for a patient.

## *Order Entry and Communication of Findings*

Diagnostic and therapeutic procedures must often be ordered at specialized service units (e.g., laboratory, radiology, or pathology). These units execute the ordered procedures and communicate the findings or results back to the ordering department. Subfunctions are:

- Preparation of an order: Depending on the available service spectrum offered by a service unit, which may be presented in the form of catalogs, the physician or nurse selects the appropriate service on an order entry form (Figure 3.6). Patient and case identification, together with relevant information such as recent diagnoses, the relevant questions, the service ordered (e.g., laboratory, radiology), and other comments (e.g., on special risks) are documented. An order should be initiated only by authorized persons. When computer-based tools for order entry are used, computerized decision support systems could alert the physician in case of medication errors, e.g. when a medication is ordered to which the patient is allergic.
- Taking samples or scheduling appointments and procedures: Depending on the type of order, specimens that must be unambiguously assigned to a patient are submitted (e.g., blood samples), or the patient's appointments must be scheduled (e.g., in radiological units). During scheduling, the demands of all parties (e.g., ordering physician, service unit, patient, transport unit) must be fairly balanced.
- Transmission of the order: The order must quickly and correctly be transmitted to the service unit. If a specimen is transferred, it must be guaranteed that the order and specimen can be linked to each other at the service unit. If necessary, modification to already transferred orders by the ordering physician or nurse should be possible.
- Reporting of findings (results review): Findings and reports must be transmitted (as quickly as necessary) back to the ordering unit and presented to the responsible healthcare professional. They must be unambiguously assigned to the correct patient. The responsible physician should be informed about new results, and critical findings should be highlighted.

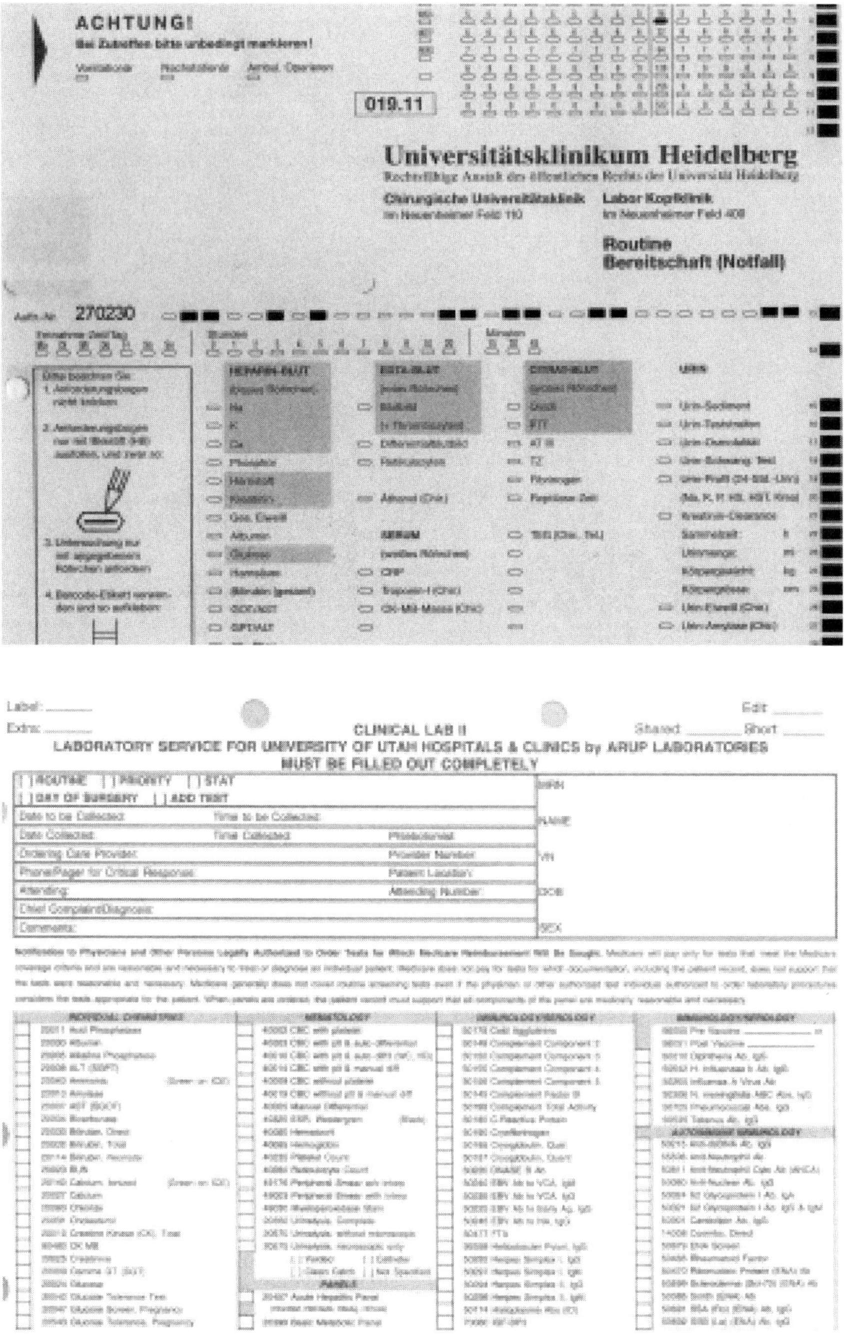

Figure 3.6: Extracts from paper-based order entry forms for laboratory testing.

## *Execution of Diagnostic or Therapeutic Procedures*

The planned diagnostic, therapeutic, or nursing procedures (such as operations, radiotherapy, radiological examinations, medication) must be executed (Figure 3.7). The hospital must offer adequate tools and resources (e.g., staff, room, equipment) for the execution of the necessary procedures.

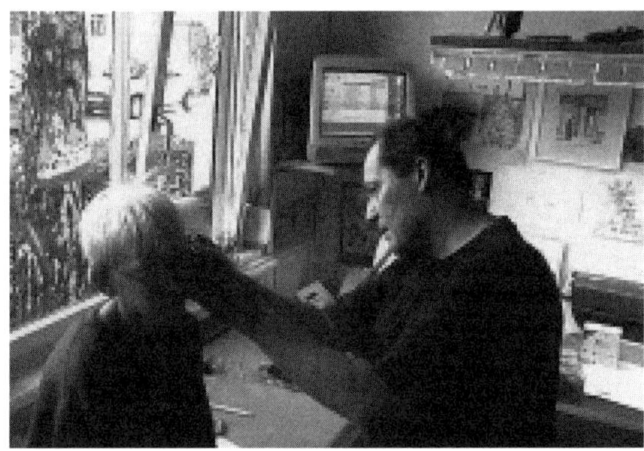

Figure 3.7: Clinical examination conducted by a pediatrician.

It is important that changes in care planning that may be due to new findings are directly communicated to all involved units and persons, enabling them to adapt to the new situation.

## *Clinical Documentation*

The goal of clinical documentation is to record all clinically relevant patient data (such as vital signs, orders, results, decisions) as completely, correctly, and quickly as possible. This supports the coordination of patient treatment among all involved persons, and also the legal justification for the actions taken. Data should be recorded in as structured a way as possible, so as to allow for data aggregation and statistics, computerized decision support, or retrieval of data. It is important that data can be linked by patient and case identification, even when data originate from different areas (such as ward, service unit, outpatient unit).

Usually, the hospital has to fulfill a lot of different legal reporting (such as epidemiological registers) and documentation requirements. Often, data must be adequately coded (for example, using the International Classification of Diseases, ICD-10[23] for diagnoses codes).

The content of clinical documentation depends partly on the documenting unit and the documenting healthcare professional group (such as documentation by nurses or physicians, documentation in outpatient units or in operation rooms). Clinical information should also be available for other purposes such as accounting, controlling, quality management, or research and education.

Subfunctions are:

- Nursing documentation (Figure 3.8) comprises the documentation of the nursing care process (nursing patient history, care planning, procedure documentation, evaluation, and reports writing), together with documentation of vital signs, medication, and other details of patient care.
- Medical documentation comprises the documentation of medical patient history, diagnoses, therapies, and findings (Figure 3.9), and also documentation for special areas (such as documentation in intensive care units) or special purposes (such as clinical trials). It also comprises order entry for service units as well as documenting orders for other healthcare professional groups (such as medication orders by physicians for nurses).

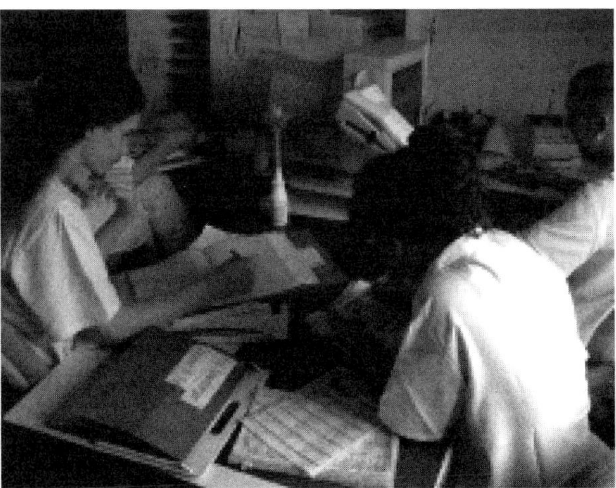

Figure 3.8: Paper-based nursing documentation on a ward.

---

23. World Health Organization (WHO): Tenth Revision of the International Statistical Classification of Diseases and Related Health Problems (ICD-10). Geneva: World Health Organization. http://www.who.int/whosis/icd10.

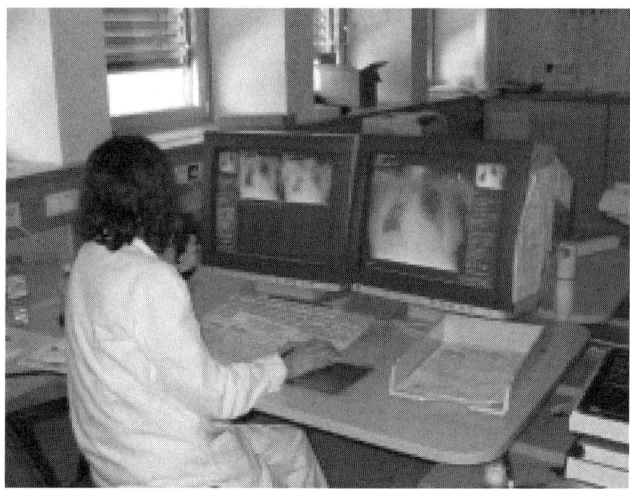

Figure 3.9: Dictation of findings in a radiological unit.

## *Administrative Documentation and Billing*

The hospital must be able to document all procedures carried out in a correct, complete, quick, and patient-oriented way. These data are the basis for the hospital's billing. The administrative documentation can also be used for controlling, cost center accounting and internal budgeting, cost responsibility accounting, and for other financial analyses. In addition, some of the data must be documented and communicated due to legal requirements.

During administrative documentation, diagnoses and procedures are recorded in a standardized way, and then processed. Administrative documentation should be at least partly derivable from clinical documentation. To support administrative documentation, adequate catalogs must be offered and maintained, containing lists of typical diagnoses and procedures relevant for a unit or a hospital.

## *Patient Discharge and Referral to Other Institutions*

When patient treatment is terminated, the patient is discharged and then sometimes referred to other institutions (e.g., a general practitioner, or a rehabilitation center) (Figure 3.10). The process of administrative patient discharge initiates final billing and the fulfillment of legal reporting requirements (e.g., statistics on diagnoses and procedures). Medical and nursing discharge entail the completing of documentation and the writing of a discharge report. The hospital must be able to transmit this and other information (e.g., radiological images) to other institutions as quickly as possible.

To speed up this process, a short report (i.e., physician's discharge letter) is often immediately communicated to the next institution containing, for example, the diagnoses and therapeutic treatments. It is then later followed by a more detailed report.

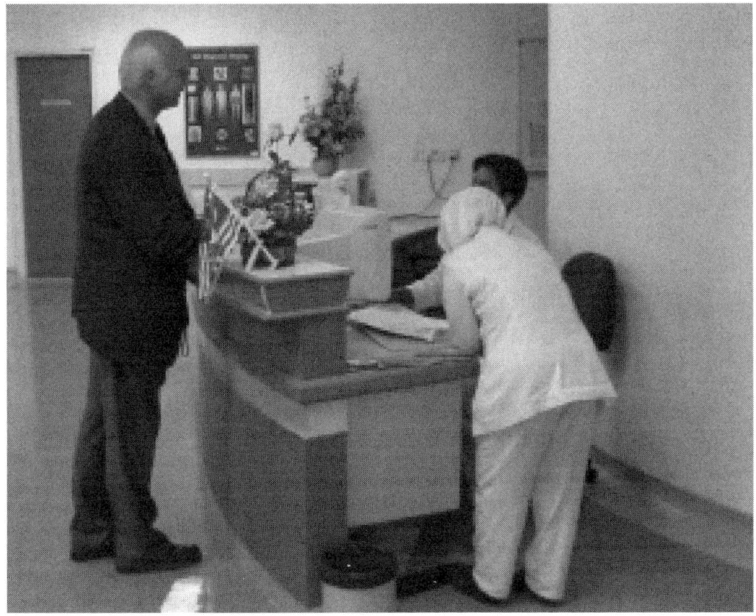

Figure 3.10: Preparing for the discharge of a patient from a ward.

## *Handling of Patient Records*

Relevant data and documents must be created, gathered, presented, and stored such that they are efficiently retrievable during the whole process of patient treatment. The storage of these data and documents is primarily done in patient records. Today, usually a mixture of paper-based and computer-based patient records is used. Certain legal requirements usually must be considered. Subfunctions are:

- Creation and dispatch of documents: Clinical documents, such as physician letters and surgical reports, should be easy to create, be available on time, and be patient-oriented. Already-documented information should be reusable as much as possible (e.g., laboratory results and coded diagnoses should be reusable for the discharge report). All documents should be signed by the author and the date of generation should be noted.

- Management of documentation for special areas or special purposes and of clinical registers: This documentation should by easy to create and maintain, for example, to support quality management, research, or individual departments. Already-documented data should be reusable as much as possible. Queries for a given subset of patients should be possible.
- Coding of diagnoses and procedures: Basic medical data such as diagnoses and procedures should be easy to document in a structured way. Basic dataset documentation serves for the internal hospital reporting structure as well as for the fulfillment of legal requirements. For coding of diagnoses, the International Classification of Diseases, ICD-10, is often used.
- Analysis of patient records (Figure 3.11): All data from patient records (whether computer-based or not) should be available during the whole process of patient care, on time, and in a user-friendly, comprehensive, and structured way. Therefore, a uniform structure for the patient record is useful. Health-related data are very sensitive; thus, the hospital must guarantee data protection and data security.
- Archiving of patient records: After discharge of the patient, patient records must be archived for a long time (e.g., for 10 or 30 years, depending on the legal regulations). The archive must offer enough space to allow the long-term storage of patient records. Their authenticity and correctness can be proven more easily, for example, in case of legal action, when they are archived in accordance with legal regulations.
- Administration of patient records: The hospital archive must be able to manage patient records and make them available upon request within a defined time frame. The exact location of each record should be known (e.g., in which archive, on which shelf). Lending and return of records (e.g., for patients coming for multiple visits) has to be organized (Figure 3.12), while respecting different access rights that depend on the role of the healthcare professionals in the process of patient care.

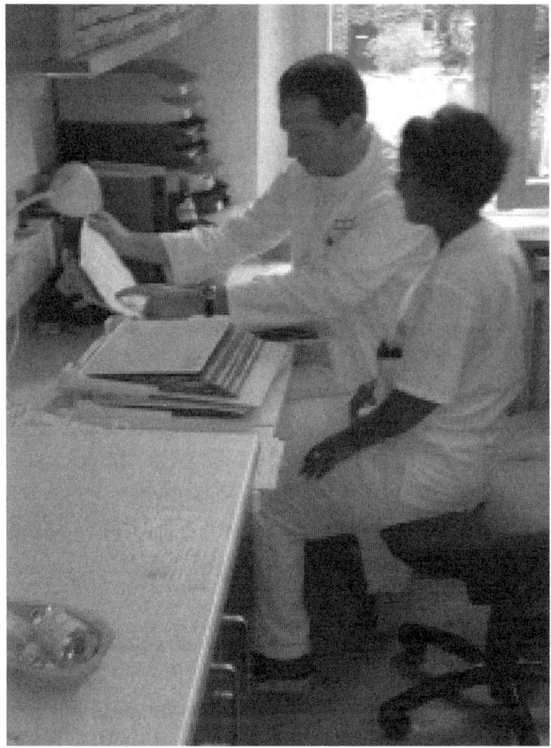

Figure 3.11: Analysis of a paper-based patient record.

Figure 3.12: Documenting the lending of patient records that have been ordered by clinical departments in a patient records archive.

## *Work Organization and Resource Planning*

The hospital must offer sufficient and well-organized resources for patient care. This is true for wards (ward management), outpatient units (outpatient management), and service units (department management). Subfunctions are:

- Scheduling and resource allocation: Various resources are needed for patient care, and resource management comprises staff planning, bed planning, room planning, and device planning. All resource planning activities must be coordinated. When procedures are scheduled, the demands of both the service unit and the ordering unit with regard to scheduling the appointment must be considered. Request, reservation, confirmation, notification, postponement, and cancellation must be supported. All involved staff members and patients should be informed about the appointments. Postponements and cancellations should be communicated in time to all involved persons.
- Materials and pharmaceuticals management (Figures 3.13 and 3.14): Supply and disposal of materials, food, drugs, and so on must be guaranteed. All departments of the hospitals should be able to order from up-to-date catalogs. The corresponding service units (stock, pharmacy, kitchen) must be able to deliver correctly and on time.
- Management and maintenance of equipment: Medical devices must be registered and maintained according to legislation.
- General organization of work: Efficient process organization is extremely important for hospitals, for example, in outpatient units or service units, and it can be supported by providing working lists for individual staff members, by issuing reminders about appointments, or by visualizing actual process flow.
- Office communication support (Figure 3.15): The hospital information system must be able to support communication between all persons involved in patient care. This comprises synchronous (e.g., telephone) and asynchronous (e.g., blackboards, brochures, e-mail) communication. Staff members must be able to be contacted within a prescribed period of time.
- Basic information processing support: The hospital information system must support basic information processing tasks such as writing reports or calculating statistics.

Figure 3.13: The stock of drugs on a hospital ward.

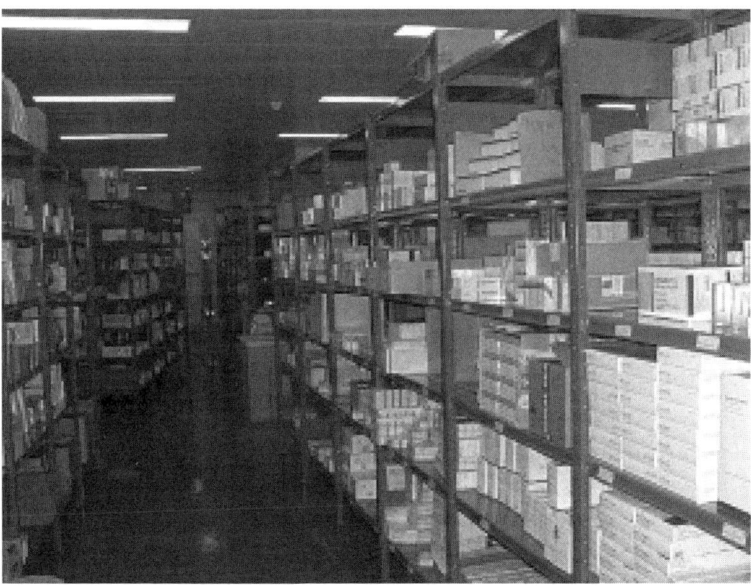

Figure 3.14: The central pharmacy of a hospital.

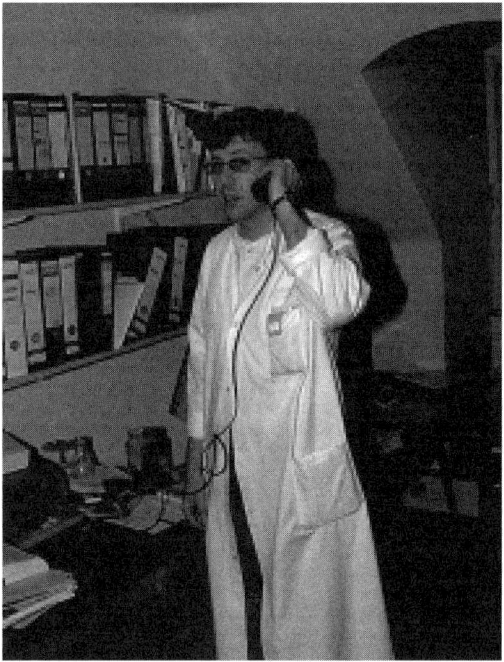

Figure 3.15: A physician communicating with a general practitioner by phone.

## *Hospital Administration*

Hospital administration supports the organization of patient care and guarantees the financial survival of the hospital. Subfunctions of hospital administration are:

- Quality management: Comprises all activities of a healthcare institution's management to assure and continuously improve the quality of patient care. This includes setting goals, defining responsibilities, and establishing and monitoring the processes to realize these goals. This covers, for example, internal reporting containing quality indices. Quality management requires information about patients and treatments as well as knowledge about diagnostic and therapeutic standards.
- Controlling and budgeting: The hospital must be able to gather and aggregate data about the hospital's operation in order to control and optimize it. This covers, for example, staff controlling, process controlling, material controlling, and financial controlling.
- Cost-performance accounting: For controlling purposes, it is necessary to keep track of services, their costs, and who has received them.

This covers, for example, accounting of cost centers, cost units, and process costs.

- Financial accounting: All the hospital's financial operations have to be systematically recorded to meet legal requirements. Financial accounting comprises, for example, debtor accounting, credit accounting, and facility accounting.
- Human resources management: This contains all tasks for the development and improvement of the productivity of staff. It comprises, for example, staff and position planning, the staff register, staff scheduling, and staff payroll.
- General statistical analysis: The hospital must support general statistical analysis, for example calculation and analysis of economic data.

## *Exercises*

### Exercise 3.2.1: Differences in Hospital Functions

Look at the hospital functions presented in this section. Now imagine a small hospital (e.g., 350 beds) and a big university medical center (e.g., 1,500 beds). What are the differences between these hospitals with regard to their functions? Explain your answer.

### Exercise 3.2.2: Different Healthcare Professional Groups and Hospital Functions

Look at the hospital functions listed in this section. Analyze the relationships between the hospital functions and the different healthcare professional groups (physicians, nurses, administrative staff, others) working in a hospital. Which hospital functions are performed by which healthcare professional group?

Create a table with healthcare professional groups as columns, hospital functions as rows, and the following symbols as content in the boxes:

'++': Function is primarily performed by this profession.
'+': Function is also performed by this profession.
'–': Function is not performed by this profession.
'.': Neither '++,' '+,' nor '–'.

### Exercise 3.2.3: Realization of Hospital Functions

As discussed at the beginning of this section, we have presented the main hospital functions that should be supported by a hospital information system. Look at a hospital you know and try to find out for each hospital function whether more computer-based or more paper-based information processing tools are used to support it.

### *Summary*

Typical main hospital functions are

- patient admission with appointment scheduling, patient identification, administrative admission, clinical admission, and information;
- planning and organization of patient treatment with presentation of information and knowledge, decision making and patient information, and care planning;
- order entry and communication of findings with preparation of an order, taking samples or scheduling appointments and procedures, transmission of the order, and reporting of findings;
- execution of diagnostic or therapeutic procedures;
- clinical documentation performed by physicians and nurses;
- administrative documentation and billing;
- patient discharge and referral to other institutions.

These hospital functions are typically supported by functions such as

- handling of patient records with creation and dispatch of documents, management of documentation for special areas or special purposes and of clinical registers, coding of diagnoses and procedures, and analysis, archiving, and management of patient records;
- work organization and resource planning with scheduling and resource allocation, materials and pharmaceuticals management, management and maintenance of equipment, support in the general organization of work, office communication support, and basic information processing support;
- hospital administration with quality management, controlling and budgeting, cost-performance accounting, financial accounting, human resources management, and general statistical analysis.

Those hospital functions describe what a hospital information system should support. It is not important at this point how they are supported—by paper-based or by computer-based information processing tools.

## 3.3 Modeling Hospital Information Systems

Modeling HISs is an important precondition for their management: What we cannot describe, we usually cannot manage adequately. We will present some types of information system metamodels, describing different aspects of HIS, and some smaller examples of HIS models.

After reading this section, you should be able to answer the following questions:

- What is a metamodel?

- What are the typical metamodels for modeling various aspects of HIS?
- What is a reference model of HIS?

## *HIS Models and Metamodels*

A model was defined in section 2.3 as a description of what the modeler thinks to be relevant to a system. The significance of models is based on their ability to present a subset of the (usually complex) reality and to aggregate the given information in order to answer certain questions or to support certain tasks. This means that models should present a simplified but appropriate view of an HIS in order to support its management and operation.

Models should be appropriate for respective questions or tasks. Examples of questions or tasks that are important with regard to hospital information systems could be:

- Which hospital functions are supported by an HIS?
- Which information processing tools are used?
- What are the steps of the business process of patient admission?
- What will happen if a specific server breaks down?
- How can the quality of information processing be judged?

A good model is able to answer given questions or to support a given task (such as detection of weaknesses, or planning the future state of the HIS). The better you can see an HIS, and the better a model assists you in managing it (e.g., in identifying good or critical parts of the HIS), the better the model is. Thus, the model you select depends on the problems or questions you have.

A large number of different classes of models exists. We can distinguish some typical *metamodels* that can be understood as a language for describing models of a certain class. A metamodel usually describes the modeling framework, which consists of

- modeling syntax and semantics (the available modeling objects together with their meaning),
- the representation of the objects (how the objects are represented in a concrete model, e.g., in a graphical way),
- and (sometimes) the modeling rules (e.g., the modeling steps).

Just as different views on HIS exist, there also exist various metamodels. Typical types of metamodels for HIS are

- functional metamodels, focusing on hospital functions that are supported by the information system, that is, on the functionality of an HIS;

- technical metamodels, which are used to build models describing the information processing tools used;
- organizational metamodels, which are used to create models of the organizational structure of an HIS;
- data metamodels, which are used for building models of the structure of data processed and stored inside an HIS;
- business process metamodels, which focus on the description of what is done in which chronological and logical order;
- enterprise metamodels, which combine different submodels into an integrated, enterprise-wide information system model.

Business process metamodels are also referred to as dynamic metamodels in contrast to the other previously described more static metamodels.

The art of HIS modeling is based on the right selection of a metamodel. Thus, for HIS modeling, you should consider the following steps:

1. Define the questions or tasks to be supported by the HIS model.
2. Select an adequate metamodel.
3. Gather the information needed for modeling.
4. Create the model.
5. Analyze and interpret the model (answer your questions).
6. Evaluate if the right metamodel was chosen, that is, if the model was adequate to answer the questions. If not, return to step 2.

In the next paragraphs, we will focus on some typical metamodels. We will answer the following questions for each metamodel:

- What elements does the metamodel offer?
- Which relationships between the elements can be modeled?
- Which questions can be answered by using this metamodel?
- What would a typical model look like when derived from this metamodel?

## Functional Modeling

Functional metamodels are used to build models that represent the functions of a hospital (what is to be done). The elements they offer are the hospital functions that are supported by the application components of the hospital information system. The relationships of the hospital functions can, for example, represent the information exchanged between them. In addition, functions are often described in a hierarchical way, comprising more global functions (such as patient management) and more specific (refined) functions (such as patient billing).

Typical questions to be answered with models derived from functional metamodels are:

- Which hospital functions are supported by which HIS components?

- Which specific hospital functions are part of which global hospital functions?
- Which hospital functions share the same data?
- Does the functional model correspond to a reference model?

Typical representations of functional models are (hierarchical) lists of functions, as well as graphical presentations of the hospital functions. Table 3.1 presents an extract from a three-level hierarchy of hospital functions for information processing in nursing:

Table 3.1: An extract from the functional HIS model, describing hospital functions relevant for nursing at the Plötzberg Medical Center and Medical School (PMC).[24]

| Management of the patient record | Nursing documentation | Documentation of patient's resources |
|---|---|---|
| | | Documentation of nursing goals |
| | | Planning and documentation of nursing tasks |
| | | Writing of nursing reports |
| | | |
| | Medical documentation relevant for nursing | Documentation of orders |
| | | Documentation of findings |
| | | |
| Patient-related ward organization | Patient management | Admission of a patient |
| | | Discharge of a patient |
| | | |
| | Generation of organizational tools | |

## Technical Modeling

Technical metamodels are used to build models that describe the information processing tools used. As elements, they typically describe physical data processing components (e.g., computer systems, telephones, forms, pagers, records) and application components. As relationships, they describe the data transmission between physical data processing components (e.g., network diagrams), or the communication between application components.

24. This example is an extract from Ammenwerth E, Haux R. A compendium of information processing functions in nursing—development and pilot study. Computers in Nursing 2000; 18(4): 189-96.

Typical questions that can be answered with models derived from technical metamodels are:

- Which information processing tools are used?
- Which application components communicate with each other?
- What are the data transmission connections between the physical data processing components?
- What does the network technology look like?
- What technical solutions are used to guarantee the security and reliability of information processing tools?

Technical models are typically presented as lists (e.g., lists of information processing tools used) or as graphs (e.g., graph of the network architecture of computer systems). Examples of graphical models are presented in Figures 3.16 and 3.17.

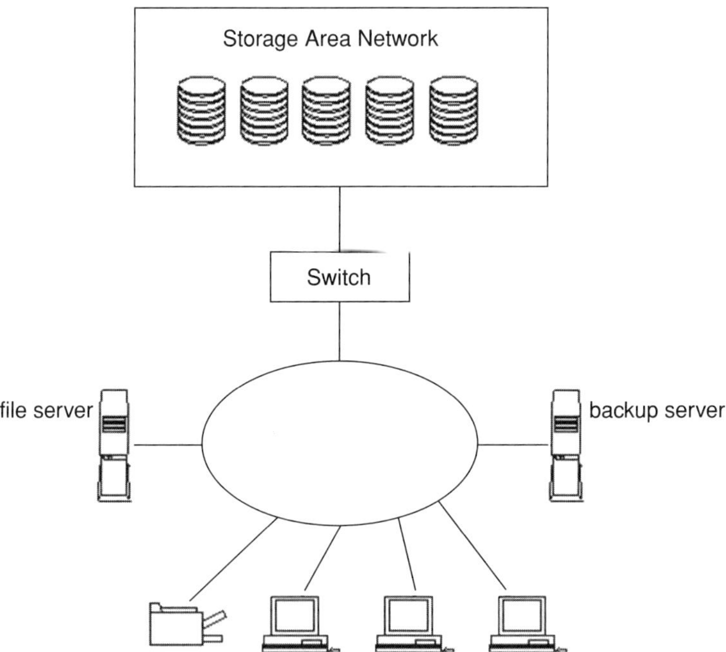


Figure 3.16: An extract of a technical HIS model with some physical data processing components and their data transmission links of the hospital information system of the Plötzberg Medical Center and Medical School (PMC). The oval in the middle symbolizes the network.

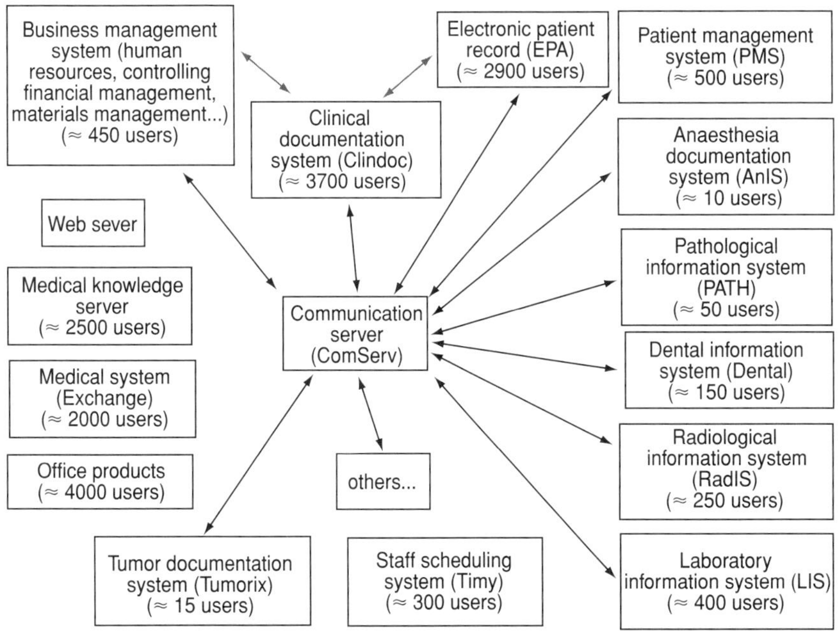


Figure 3.17: An extract of a technical HIS model with some application components and their communication links of the hospital information system of the Plötzberg Medical Center and Medical School (PMC).

## Organizational Modeling

Organizational metamodels are used to build models that describe the organization of a unit or area. For example, they may be used to describe the organizational structure of a hospital (e.g., consisting of departments with in- and outpatient units). In the context of HIS, they are often used to describe the organization of information management, that is, how it is organized in order to support the goals of the hospital.

The elements of those models are usually units or roles that stand in a certain organizational relationship to each other. Typical questions to be answered with models derived from organizational metamodels are:

- Which organizational units exist in a hospital?
- Which institutions are responsible for information management?
- Who is responsible for information management of a given area or unit?

Organizational models are typically represented as a list of organizational units (e.g., list of the departments and sections in a hospital), or as a graph (e.g., graphical description of the organizational relationships). An example is presented in Figure 3.18.

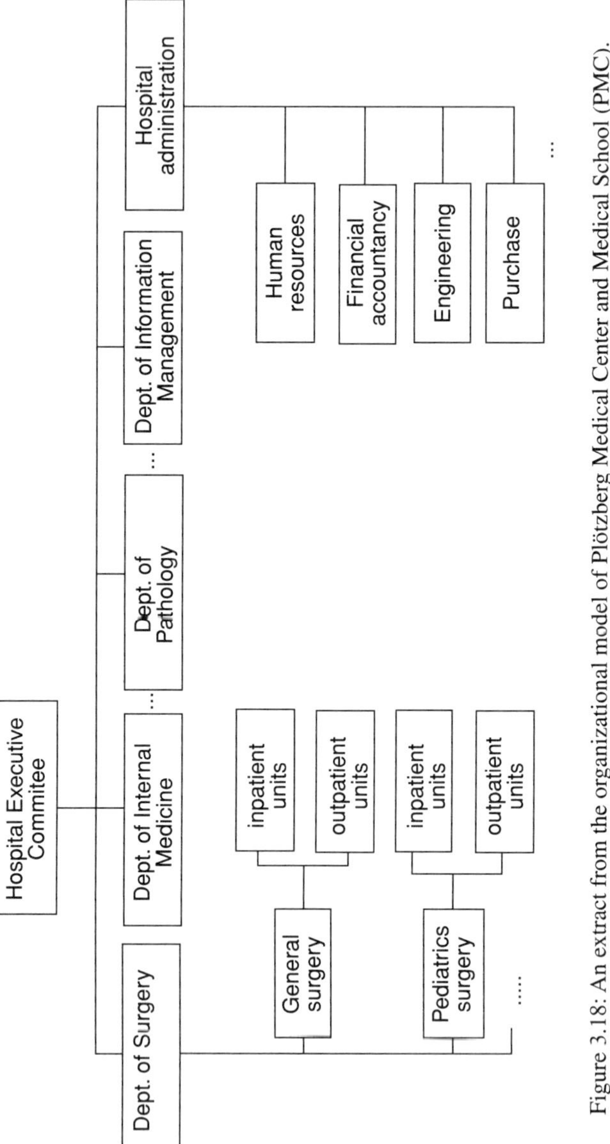


Figure 3.18: An extract from the organizational model of Plötzberg Medical Center and Medical School (PMC).

## Data Modeling

Data metamodels are used to create models that describe the data processed and stored in a hospital information system. The elements they offer are typically entity types and their relationships. Typical questions to be answered with models derived from data metamodels are:

- What data are processed and stored in the information system?
- How are data elements related?

A typical metamodel for data modeling is offered by the class diagrams in the Unified Modeling Language (UML).[25] An example is presented in Figure 3.19.

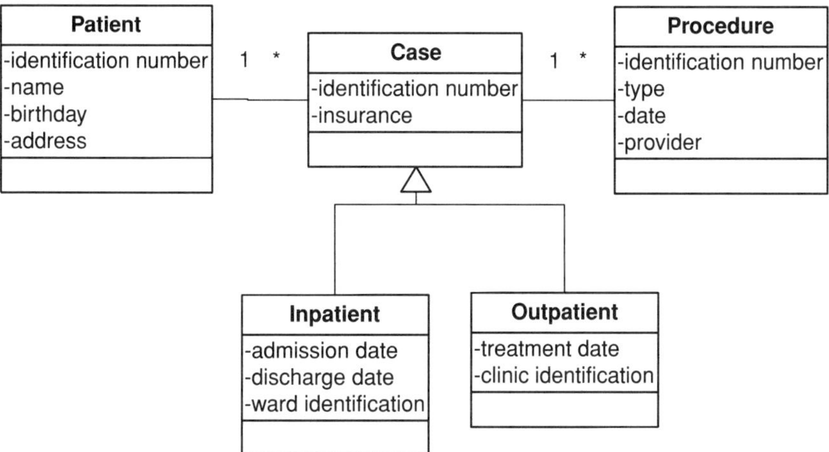


Figure 3.19: A simplified data model (UML class diagram), describing the relationships between the entity types patient, case, and procedure, as extract from the data model of the HIS of the Plötzberg Medical Center and Medical School (PMC).

## Business Process Modeling

Business process metamodels are used to create models that focus on a dynamic view of information processing. The elements used are activities and their chronological and logical order. Often, other elements are added, such as the role or unit that performs an activity, or the information processing tools that are used. The following perspectives usually can be distinguished:

- Functional perspective: What activities are being performed, and which data flows are needed to link these activities?

25. Object Management Group (OMG): Unified Modeling Language—UML. http://www.uml.org.

- Behavioral perspective: When are activities being performed, and how are they performed? Do they use mechanisms such as loops and triggers?
- Organizational perspective: Where and by whom are activities being performed?
- Informational perspective: Which entity types or entities (documents, data, products) are being produced or manipulated?

Typical questions to be answered with models derived from business process metamodels are:

- Which activities are executed with regard to a given hospital function?
- Who is responsible and which tools are used in a given process?
- Which activity is the pre- or postcondition for a given activity?
- What are the weak points of the given process and how can they be improved?

Due to the number of different perspectives, various business process metamodels exist. Examples are simple process chains, event-driven process chains, activity diagrams, and petri nets.

*Simple process chains* describe the (linear) sequence of process steps. They simply describe the specific activities that form a process, in addition to the responsible role (e.g., a physician).

*Event-driven process chains* add dynamic properties of process steps: events and logical operators (and, or, xor) are added to the functions, allowing the more complex modeling of branching and alternatives. In addition, some instances of event-driven process chains allow the addition of entities (e.g., a chart).[26]

*Activity diagrams* (as part of the modeling technique of the Unified Modeling Language, UML) also describe the sequence of process steps, using activities, branching, conditions, and entities (Figure 3.20). In addition, the method allows the splitting and synchronization of parallel subprocesses.[27]

Finally, *petri nets* also describe the dynamic properties of processes, but in a more formal way than the other methods.[28]

---

26. Scheer AW. ARIS—Business Process Frameworks. Berlin: Springer; 1999.

27. Object Management Group (OMG): Unified Modeling Language—UML. http://www.uml.org.

28. Mortensen KH, Christensen S, editors. Petri Nets World. http://www.daimi.au.dk/PetriNets.

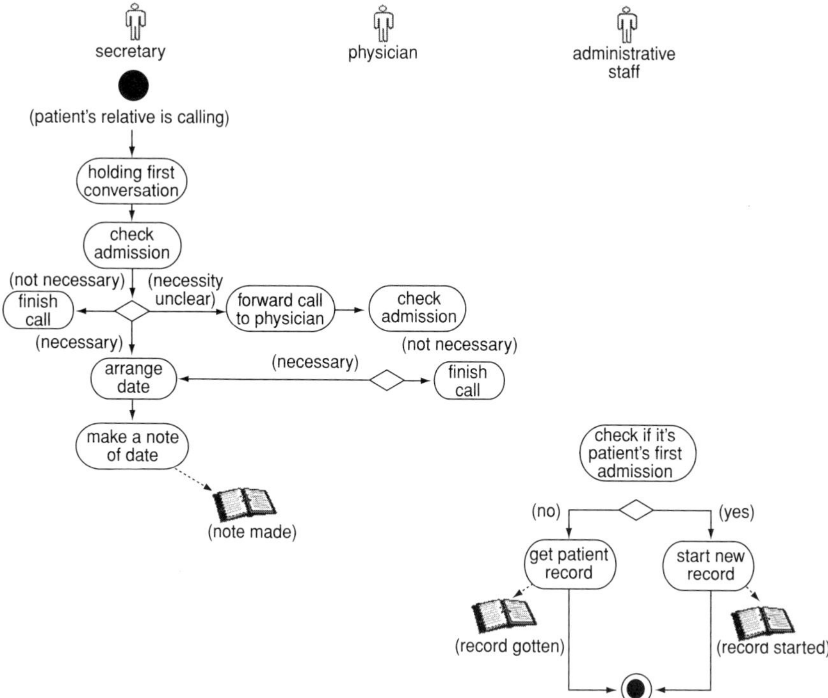


Figure 3.20: Example of a business process model, based on a UML activity diagram, describing a part of the admission process in the Department of Child and Juvenile Psychiatry at Plötzberg Medical Center and Medical School (PMC).

## Enterprise Modeling

Enterprise modeling comprises all modeling aspects discussed so far, that is, functional modeling, technical modeling, organizational modeling, data modeling, and process modeling. But beyond this, enterprise modeling considers the dependencies of these models and, therefore, offers a more holistic view.

Typical questions to be answered with enterprise modeling are:

- Which hospital functions are supported by which information processing tools?
- Are the information processing tools sufficient to support the hospital functions?
- Is the communication among the application components sufficient to fulfill the information needs?
- Which aims of the enterprise will be affected by a certain application component?

- In which area of the hospital are specific data on specific objects used?

Enterprise modeling frameworks help classify and organize these models and facilitate understanding their dependencies and the difficulties that may arise if certain aspects of enterprise modeling are not considered. Those frameworks are often presented as matrices where the rows reflect distinctive views on the enterprise and the columns describe different concepts related to the enterprise. Depending on the modeling goals, a model may be created for each cell of the matrix (which, of course, is normally based on a more specific metamodel).

A well-known enterprise modeling framework is the Zachman framework[29] for information systems architectures (Table 3.2).

Table 3.2: The Zachman enterprise architecture framework.

| | **Data (What)** | **Function (How)** | **Network (Where)** | **People (Who)** | **Time (When)** | **Motivation (Why)** |
|---|---|---|---|---|---|---|
| Scope (Contextual) | | | | | | |
| Enterprise Model (Conceptual) | | | | | | |
| System Model (Logical) | | | | | | |
| Technology Model (Physical) | | | | | | |
| Detailed Representations | | | | | | |

Individual modeling aspects as mentioned above can be found within this framework. Data models are placed in the data/enterprise model cell, if the more conceptual aspect is stressed, or in the data/system model cell, if the database aspect is stressed. Technological models may be found at the system model or the technology model level especially in the function and network rows. Organizational models are placed in the people row, and functional models in the function row. The difficulty in using such a comprehensive framework is in presenting the dependencies between the separated cells.

29. Zachman JA. A framework for information systems architecture. *IBM Systems Journal* 1999; 38(2&3): 454-70 (Reprint).

## *Reference Models for Hospital Information Systems*

Until now we talked about HIS metamodels, that is, about models to describe hospital information systems from various views. To support HIS modeling, it may also be helpful to use reference models. *Reference models* present a kind of model pattern for a certain class of aspects. On the one hand, these model patterns can help to derive more specific models through modifications, limitations, or add-ons (generic reference models). On the other hand, these model patterns can be used to directly compare models concerning their completeness (nongeneric reference models). As well as specific models, reference models are instances of metamodels. A specific model may be considered a variant of a reference model developed through specialization. This variant is an instance of that metamodel that also underlies the corresponding reference model.

A reference model is always directed toward a certain aspect. For example, we can define reference models for hospital information systems, for communication systems, or for the gastrointestinal system. A (general) model can be defined as a reference model for a certain class of aspects.

A reference model should be followed by a description of its usage, for example, how specific models can be derived from the reference model, or how it can be used for the purpose of comparison.

Specific models can be compared with a reference model, and consequently models can also be compared with each other, judging their similarity or difference when describing certain aspects.

Reference models can be normative in the sense that they are broadly accepted and have practical relevance. Reference models are more likely to be accepted if they are not only reliable and well-tested, but also recommended by a respected institution.

Different types of reference models can be described. For example, *business reference models* describe models of processes, data, and organization of a certain class of organizations (e.g., of a certain industrial branch). A subtype of these reference models are information system reference models. They focus on information processing of a class of organizations. These reference models will be based on the metamodels we have presented in this section. For example, data reference models can describe typical data structures for a hospital information system. Organizational reference models can describe typical organizational structures for information management. Enterprise reference models can describe typical functions and architectures of hospital information systems.

A second type of reference models is *software reference models*. They serve to derive models for different variants of a software product. Such a derived model can describe in which form a software product can be parameterized for a specific usage. These models normally integrate different views on the software product, such as a data, functional, or process view.

A third class of reference models is *procedure reference models*. They focus on how to do certain things, for example, how to introduce an information system component. Procedure reference models are also important in other areas; clinical guidelines present such reference models. Using such a reference model together with additional information, a project plan for a specific project to introduce a component can be established, or a specific treatment plan for a cancer patient can be derived.

Various reference models for hospital information systems exist.

The Common Basic Specification of the British National Health Service (NHS) from the early 1990s[30] is a functional reference model. It describes the functions of different institutions that have to be supported by a computer-based information system. All functions are described as activities, combining the tasks enable, plan, do, and execute. This also represents a part of a process reference model. In addition, a data reference model is described, which contains entity types that are usually processed in hospitals. The NHS reference models are partly compulsory for the NHS institutions.

In the framework of the European RICHE (Réseau d'Information et de Communication Hospitalier Européen) project, a process reference model for the description of activities in hospitals was established. This is the so-called order-and-act model.[31] Activities are seen as part of a process, where a client (for example, a physician) orders an activity (order). This order is communicated to the executing person (for example, a nurse), which carries out the order (act) and reports the results to the client.

A more recent example of a reference model for hospital functions is the Heidelberg reference model from 2000, developed with the support of the German Research Association.[32] It is presented in Figure 3.21. This reference model focuses on the process of patient care. It distinguishes between functions central to the patient care process and functions supporting the patient care process. The main hospital functions central to the process of patient care are presented as a sequence on the left side. The hospital functions that support patient care are presented on the right side.

---

30. Herbert I. The Common Basic Specification (version 4.4). Information Management Group (IMG), United Kingdom National Health Service (NHS); 1993.

31. Frandji B. Open architecture for healthcare systems: the European RICHE experience. In: Dudeck J, Blobel B, Lordieck W, Bürkle T, editors. New technologies in hospital information systems Amsterdam: IOS Press; 1997. pp. 11-23.

32. Ammenwerth E, Buchauer A, Haux R. A Requirements Index for Information Processing in Hospitals. Methods of Information in Medicine 2002; 41 (4): 282-8. The requirements index is available at: ttp://www.umit.at/reqhis.

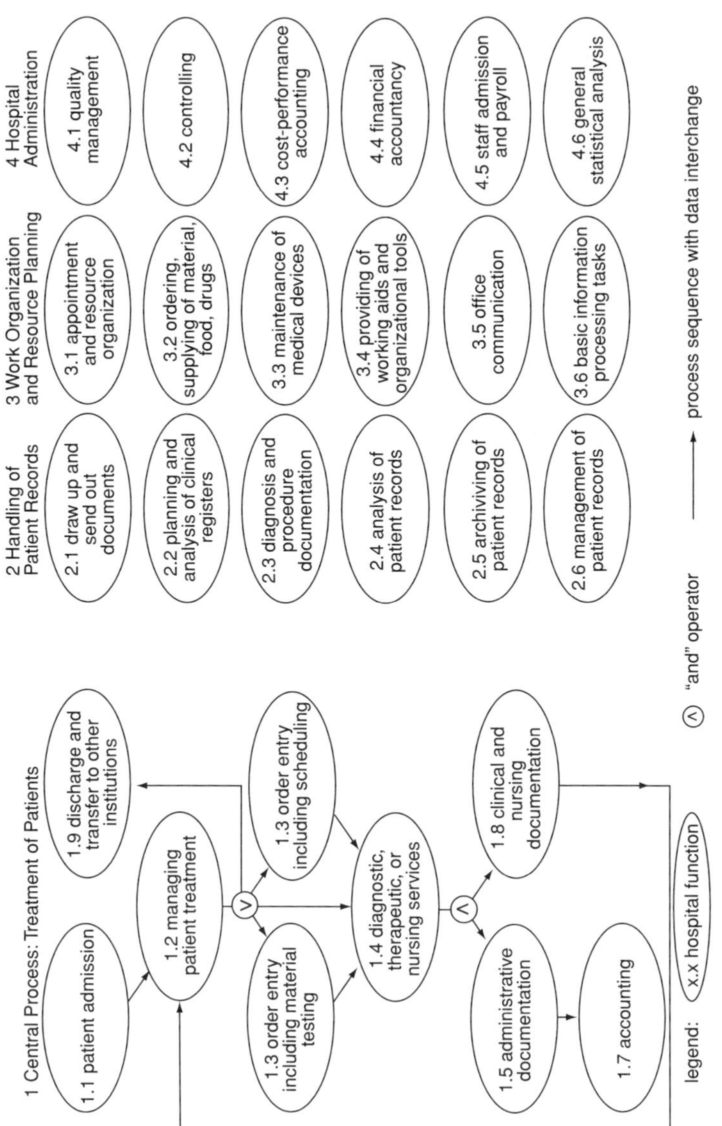


Figure 3.21: The Heidelberg reference model for hospital functions.

As of now, only a few reference models for typical functions, processes, or data of hospital information systems are available. Consultants sometimes create specific reference models for their clients. For example, a healthcare provider wants to standardize the business process of his hospitals. In this case, a system analysis will usually be performed in each hospital, and a general model of the planned state will be derived as the basis for detailed change planning. This is a (provider-specific) reference model and can be used to derive specific models to compare the current state with the planned state.

## *Example*

### Example 3.3.1: A Reference Model for Hospital Functions

Table 3.3 of hospital functions was established in 1997 by the German Research Association.[33] The following list presents that part of the reference model relevant for patient care.

Table 3.3: An example of a reference model for hospital functions.

| *Part I: Patient care* | |
|---|---|
| **1. General patient care functions** | **4. Diagnostic unit functions** |
| 1.1 Patient administration | 4.1 Clinical laboratory |
| 1.2 Management of the patient record | 4.2 Radiology (organization) |
| 1.3 Electronic archiving of patient records (for example digital-optical) | 4.3 Radiology (PACs—picture archiving and communication) |
| 1.4 Basic clinical documentation | 4.4 Immunology, microbiology, virology |
| 1.x Other functions | 4.5 Pathology |
| **2. Ward functions** | 4.x Other functions |
| 2.1 Ward management for physicians (including clinical documentation, writing documents, order entry, accounting) | **5. Therapeutic unit functions** |
| 2.2 Ward management for nurses (including nursing documentation, order entry, accounting) | 5.1 Anesthesia documentation |
| 2.3 Intensive care unit documentation | 5.2 Management of operating rooms (incl. documentation, reports, planning) |
| 2.x Other functions | 5.3 Radiotherapy |
| **3. Outpatient unit functions** | 5.x Other functions |
| 3.1 Management of outpatient units (including scheduling, process management, clinical documentation, document writing, order entry, accounting) | **6. Functions for other units** |
| 3.x Other functions | 6.1 Pharmacy |
| | 6.2 Blood bank |
| | 6.x Other functions |
| | **7. Other patient care functions** |
| | 7.1 Staff scheduling |
| | 7.2 Documentation, organization and billing for dentistry departments |
| | 7.3 Telemedicine (especially telediagnostics) |
| | 7.x Other functions |

33. Haux R, Michaelis J. Investitionsschema zur Informationsverarbeitung in Krankenhäusern (investment scheme for information processing in hospitals). Das Krankenhaus 1997; 7: 425-26.

Table 3.3 (*continued*): An example of a reference model for hospital functions.

| *Part II: Support of patient care* | |
|---|---|
| **1. Administrative functions**<br>1.1 Accounting (in- and outpatients)<br>1.2 Financial accounting<br>1.3 Maintenance of buildings<br>1.4 Calculation of costs and output, controlling<br>1.5 Stock management<br>1.6 Staff management<br>1.x Other functions | **2. Communication functions**<br>2.1 Office communication<br>2.2 Communication management (communication server)<br>2.3 Network management<br>2.x Other functions<br>**3 Other functions for the support of research, education, patient care**<br>3.1 Access to medical knowledge (for example Medline, diagnostic or therapeutic guidelines)<br>3.x Other functions |

## *Exercises*

### Exercise 3.3.1: Typical Realization of Hospital Functions

Look at the hospital functions presented in Figure 0.21 and describe how they are realized in your hospital. Try to classify each function according to how it is typically supported as

- primarily paper-based,
- mostly paper-based,
- mixed,
- mostly computer-supported, or
- primarily computer-supported.

For example, patient admission is typically primarily supported by computer-supported information processing tools, whereas nursing documentation is mostly supported by paper-based tools.

### Exercise 3.3.2: Comparison of Reference Models for Hospital Functions

Different reference models exist for hospital functions. Compare the reference model presented in Table 3.3 with the Heidelberg reference model of hospital functions (Figure 3.21).

- Which functions can be matched and which cannot?
- What could reasons for the differences be?

### Exercise 3.3.3: Modeling Business Processes with Activity Diagrams

*(a) Modeling a Given Process*

Design a graphical process model of nursing documentation. Use activity diagrams (compare Figure 3.20) with the typical symbols for activities, transitions, branching, conditions and synchronization, responsible roles, and entities to model the following process:

> Every time a patient is admitted to the ward, a new nursing plan is created: the nursing patient history is written down, together with the problems of the patients, the corresponding goals of the nursing treatment, and the tasks to be executed. The patient history is written on paper-based forms and then inserted in the paper-based patient record. The other parts are created with the aid of a computer-based application component known as NDS and then printed out and inserted in the paper-based patient record.
>
> At the beginning of each shift, the nurse reads the printed nursing plan to see which measures are to be executed. She copies the tasks to be executed during her shift onto a note that she carries with her. On this note, she marks the tasks which have been taken care of. At the end of each shift, the nurse documents which tasks that have been executed in the printed nursing plan (by signing each task). She writes a short report on a special form about special occurrences during her shift. Finally, she validates the nursing plan and adapts it to the new state of the patients problems and the nursing goals. During the patient's stay in the hospital, the nursing plan can be changed several times. The new plan is then again printed out and inserted into the paper-based record.

*(b) Weak Point Analysis of a Given Process*

Analyze the process modeled in (a) and try to find weaknesses in the process. Weak points can be, for example, double documentation, changes in tools used, or possible transcription errors. If you find weak points, discuss possible solutions and redesign the process based on your improvements.

## *Summary*

HIS models are used to support the description, management, and operation of HIS. A good model adequately supports information managers in these tasks.

According to their different purposes, different metamodels (models of models) exist for HIS. We can, for example, find functional metamodels, technical metamodels, organizational metamodels, data metamodels, business process metamodels, and enterprise metamodels.

Functional models describe the functions of a hospital. Technical models focus on the information processing tools used to support this functionality.

Organizational models describe the organization of areas or units. Data models describe the data processed and stored in an information system. Process models stress the dynamic aspects of HIS. Enterprise modeling comprises various modeling aspects and offers a more holistic view on an enterprise by considering the dependencies among various models.

Reference models are specific models that serve as model patterns. They can be used to derive concrete models or to compare models. A typical reference model for hospital functions is the Heidelberg reference model for hospital functions, which distinguishes functions central to the patient care process from functions supporting the patient care process.

## 3.4 A Metamodel for Modeling HIS: 3LGM

Let us now introduce a specific metamodel for modeling hospital information systems. This metamodel is called the three-layer graph-based metamodel (3LGM). It aims to support the systematic management of HIS as well as the quality assessment of information processing in hospitals. We will use this metamodel further on in this book.

3LGM combines a functional metamodel with technical metamodels. It is represented in UML notation. The 3LGM distinguishes three layers of information systems:

- domain layer,
- logical tool layer, and
- physical tool layer.

After reading this section, you should be able to answer the following questions:

- What is the aim of the three-layer graph-based metamodel (3LGM)?
- Which layers does the 3LGM distinguish?
- What do the interlayer relationships describe?

### *Domain Layer*

The *domain layer* (UML metamodel, Figure 3.22) describes a hospital independent of its implementation as a set of enterprise functions (compare section 2.3). Functions need information of a certain type about physical or virtual entities of the hospital. These types of information are represented as *entity types*. The access of a function to an entity type can be by using or updating information that is expressed by the attribute `access type` of the association class `access`. Functions and entity types can be hierarchically structured using is part of' relations.

An example of a domain layer is shown in Figure 3.23, where functions are represented as rectangles and entity types are represented as ovals. An arrow from an entity type to a function marks a using access, from a function to an entity type an updating access. Typical functions for the treatment of a patient are PATIENT ADMISSION, ORDER ENTRY, or CLINICAL DOCUMENTATION, and typical entity types are PATIENT, CASE, or RESULT. In the example, the association between the function PATIENT ADMISSION and the entity type PATIENT denotes that PATIENT ADMISSION uses information about patients, but also updates information (expressed by the bi-directional arrow).

Which entity types and which functions are modeled depends on the hospital. Reference models may offer recommendations about important entity types and functions for certain kinds of hospitals (compare section 3.3).

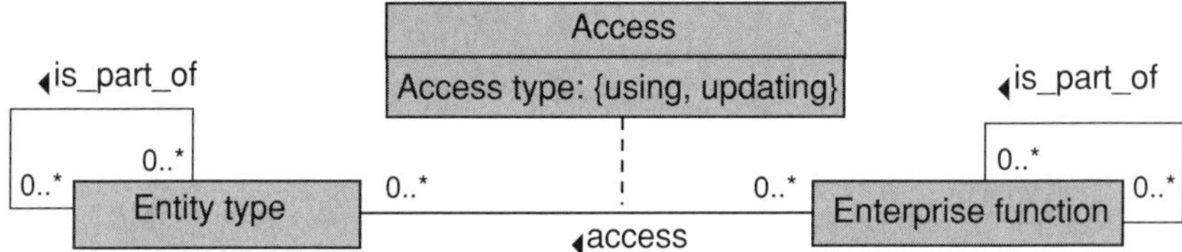


Figure 3.22: 3LGM domain layer.

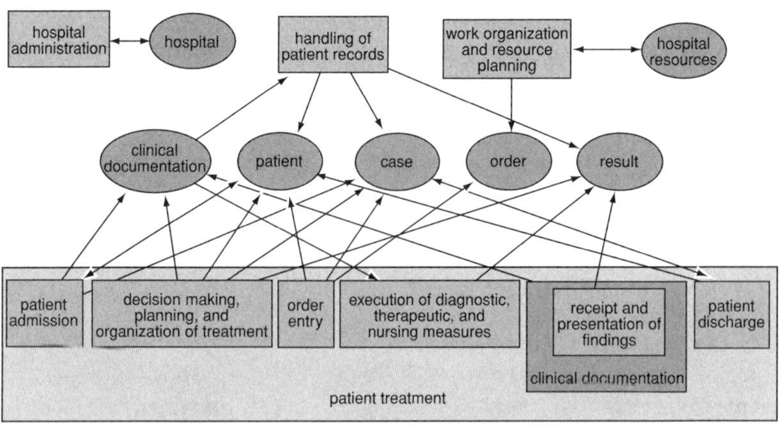


Figure 3.23: Example of a 3LGM domain layer.

Note that the metamodel of the domain layer just considers the static view of a hospital. Thus, there are no associations between functions that represent processes. This would be part of a dynamic view. The domain layer is restricted to entity types representing information, and to functions to be performed.

## *Logical Tool Layer*

At the *logical tool layer* (UML metamodel, Figure 3.24), *application components* are the center of interest. Application components support enterprise functions. Computer-based application components are controlled by *application programs*, which are adapted *software products* (this is what we can buy); paper-based application components are controlled by conventional working plans that describe how people use paper-based data processing components (compare section 2.3). Application components are responsible for the storage and for the communication of data about entities of a certain type. Therefore, we also have to describe how entity types are logically stored, and how application components have to communicate to ensure the access of the enterprise functions to entity types as described at the domain

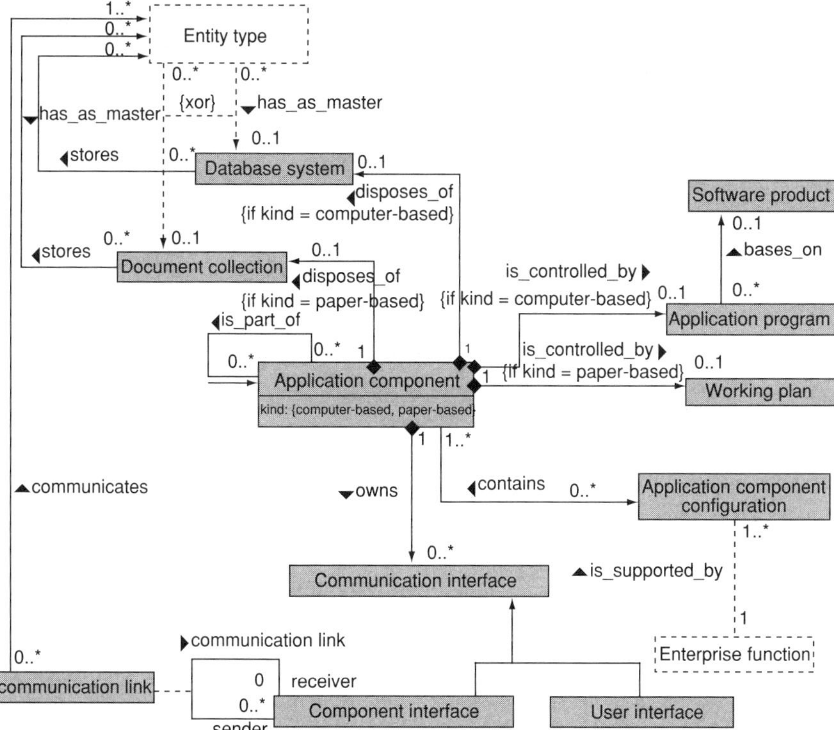


Figure 3.24: 3LGM logical tool layer. Dotted lines and symbols denote interlayer relationships between logical tool layer and domain layer.

layer. Computer-based application components may have a local database system to store data, and paper-based application components may file their documents in a document collection. Communication interfaces ensure the communication among application components (*component interfaces*), but also between an application component and a user (*user interfaces*). For communication among application components, *communication links* can be defined. Application components may be refined. The concept of application component configuration will be explained in detail later on.

Figure 3.25 shows an example of a logical tool layer. In this example the application components are depicted as large rounded rectangles, and the relationships between them via communication interfaces (small ovals) are depicted as arrows. The direction of the arrows represents the direction of the communication.

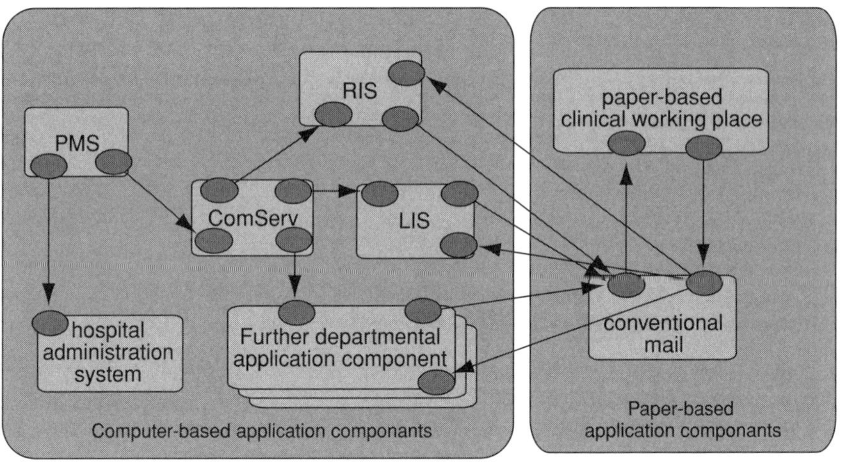


Figure 3.25: Example of a 3LGM logical tool layer.

The left part of the example shows computer-based application components: a patient management system (PMS), a radiological information system (RIS), a laboratory information system (LIS), a communication server (ComServ), a hospital administration system, and some further departmental application components (not otherwise specified). The right part shows paper-based application components: a conventional mailing system and a paper-based clinical working place.

This example is simplified and fictitious, but reflects a typical situation. Whereas hospital administration and all service units are supported by computer-based application components, typical clinical functions are supported by a paper-based application component. For the communication within the computer-supported part there is a communication server (introduced in section 3.7) available, but not all application components are able to use this communication service. As a consequence, a lot of proprietary interfaces are needed. The fact that typical hospital functions are not at all supported by computer-based application components makes a lot of communication links between the computer-based and the paper-based part of the HIS necessary, which might cause some problems due to media cracks (explained in more detail in section 4.3). Those digital-analog interfaces are, for example, realized through printers and document readers and the corresponding software.

## *Physical Tool Layer*

The *physical tool layer* (UML metamodel, Figure 3.26) is a set of physical data processing components. They can be human actors (such as the person delivering mail), paper-based physical tools (such as printed forms, telephones, books, paper-based patient record, administrative stickers), or computer systems (such as terminals, servers, personal computers, switches, routers). They are physically connected via so-called data transmission connections (e.g., data wires). The constellation of these connections leads to physical networks, which are based on network protocols. Arbitrary subnets can be defined as projections of the entire network. Note that physical as well as logical networks can be represented on the physical tool layer.

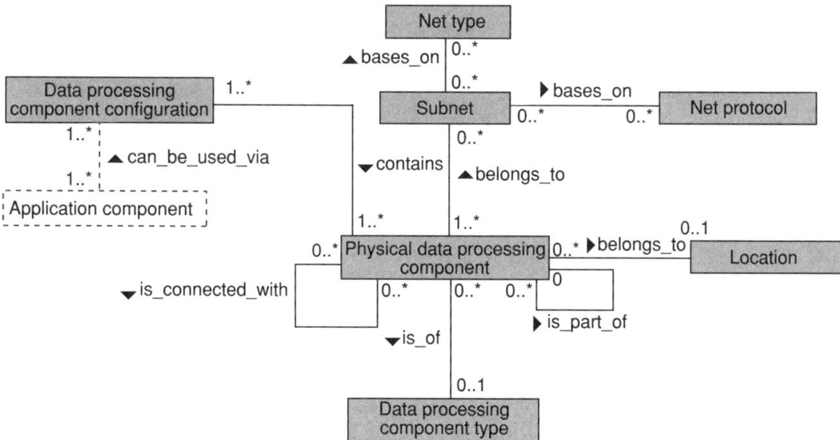


Figure 3.26: 3LGM physical tool layer. Dotted lines denote interlayer relationships between logical tool layer and physical tool layer.

Figure 3.27 shows an example of a physical tool layer. In this example we see a server for each departmental application component (a LIS server, a RIS server, a server for further departmental application components) and a central server where the PMS and the hospital administration system are installed. Each server is connected to a set of personal computers. The black dots represent network components. The data transmission from and to the paper-based part of the hospital information system is denoted only for the LIS data processing components. An order may come from the outbox of the clinical working place (CWP outbox) to the LIS inbox and be read by a form reader. A result is printed by the LIS printer and transferred via the LIS outbox to the CWP inbox. Data transmission connections are depicted as lines. In this example, there are no subnets specified. Information about network type or network protocol is not represented.

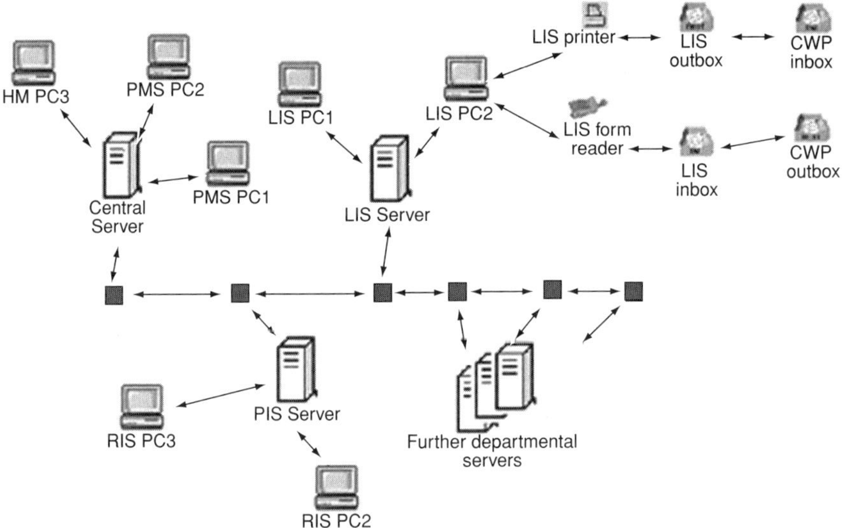


Figure 3.27: Example of a 3LGM physical tool layer.

## *Relationships Between Layers*

A variety of dependencies, called *interlayer relationships*, exist among components of different layers. Relationships exist between classes of the domain layer and the logical tool layer and between classes of the logical tool layer and the physical tool layer. Considering the domain layer and the logical tool layer, the most important relationship is between functions and application components, which is represented by a so-called *application component configuration*. It states that a hospital function in a specific organizational unit may be supported by several application components together, by a single application component, or by combinations of the two.

Two questions lead to the application component configurations for a specific function:

*Which application components are jointly necessary to support a function completely?*

An application component configuration contains all application components that together are directly necessary to support a function. If we remove an application component from this configuration, the function can no longer be supported.

*Which possible alternatives are there to support a function?*

An enterprise function may be supported by more than one application component configuration. If we remove such a configuration, the function is still supported by one of the remaining configurations, but may suffer from loss of quality.

Application component configurations can give hints not only about redundancies within hospital information systems, but also about weaknesses in the domain layer model. Figure 3.28 shows an example of application component configurations. The function PATIENT ADMISSION is supported by two application component configurations. In the light-gray one, the PMS has no own database system, but stores admission data in an application component MED DB, which contains the central database system. Thus, the function PATIENT ADMISSION can only be performed if both application components, PMS and MED DB, are available. The dark-gray box consists of just one application component WARD, which is sufficient to support the function PATIENT ADMISSION.

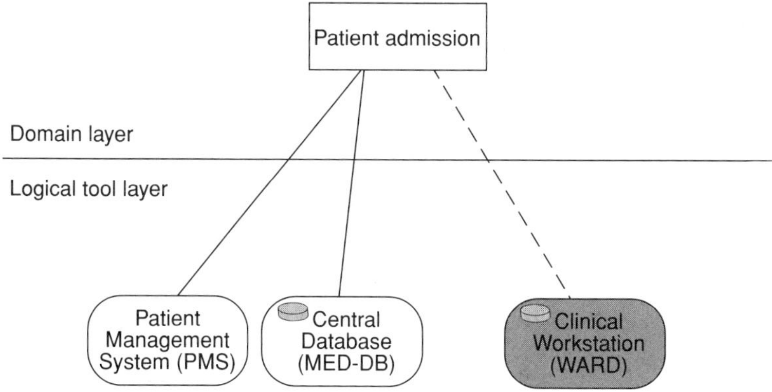


Figure 3.28: Example of two application component configurations of a hospital function.

Other relationships between classes of the domain layer and the logical tool layer are (compare Figure 3.24):

At the logical tool layer, entity types can be stored in a database system or in a document collection, and entity types can be communicated over communication links.

The 'has_as_master' relationship between entity type and the database system respectively document collection describes which database system respectively document collection is responsible for the storage of certain entity types, and, therefore, in case of redundant data storage, contains the current data.

Between the logical tool layer and the physical tool layer, there exists a relationship between application components and physical data processing components that is represented by a so-called *data processing component configuration*. It states that an application component may be installed on several data processing components together (e.g., typical client-sever installations), on a single data processing component (typical stand-alone application components), or through combinations of these two. Two questions lead to the data processing component configurations for a specific application component:

*Which physical data processing components are jointly necessary to support a application component completely?*

A data processing component configuration contains all physical data processing components that are together directly necessary to support an application component completely. If we remove a physical data processing component from this configuration, the application component will no longer work.

*Which possible alternatives are there to support an application component?*

An application component may be needed by more than one data processing component configuration. If we remove such a configuration, the application component still works through one of the remaining configurations, but may suffer from loss of quality. Application component configurations can give hints about physical redundancies within the hospital information systems.

Figure 3.29 shows a simple example of data processing configurations. The application component clinical workstation can be used via two data processing configurations, which are different with regard the used PCs, whereas the application server and the database server belong to both configurations.

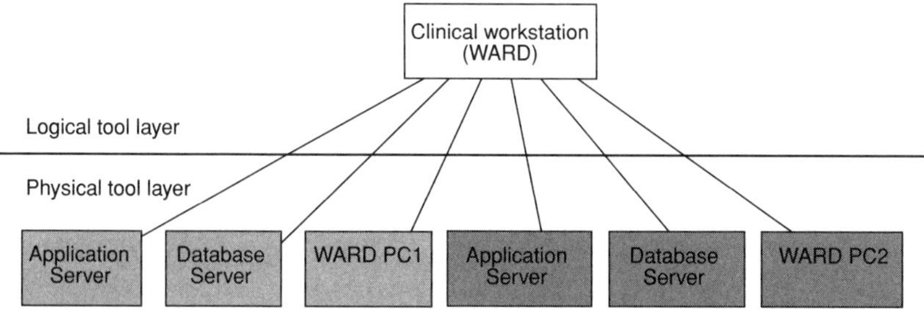


Figure 3.29: Example of two data processing component configurations of an application component.

## *Exercises*

### Exercise 3.4.1: 3LGM as a Metamodel

The 3LGM is a metamodel for hospital information systems. Look at the description of metamodels in section 0 and find the different elements of a metamodel in the 3LGM (e.g., for modeling syntax and semantics, representation, and modeling rules).

### Exercise 3.4.2: Modeling with 3LGM

The following description of a sub-information system of a hospital is given:

> The patient admission is supported by an application component called PATADMIN, which is installed at the hospital's central server. The administration personnel work with two personal computers. The patient data are stored in the Oracle-based medical database system (MEDDB). After the patient admission is completed, patient data are transmitted to the computer-based application components at the laboratory department (LABSYS) and at the radiology department (RADSYS), using an HL7-based message broker. For communication with paper-based application components, i.e., for ordering or clinical documentation, labels containing the identifying patient data as text and as barcodes are printed.

*(a) HIS components*

Identify the 3LGM-relevant components of the described HIS and assign them to one of the three layers. Which necessary information to get a complete model of this sub-information system is missing?

*(b) Create the model*

Design a 3LGM model with the three layers that includes the components and their relationships.

*(c) Interlayer relationships*
Describe which interlayer relationships are given and add them to the model.

*d) New function*
Add the function "nursing documentation" to the 3LGM of our example. In this example, nursing documentation is supported by paper-based information processing tools—nurses use paper-based forms to document their activities. The paper-based nursing documentation system (NursDocSys) describes how the nursing documentation has to be done and which forms have to be used. This function mainly requires general patient data, which are printed on labels and stuck to the forms.

Add the necessary elements in all three layers of the graphical model.

## *Summary*

A typical metamodel for modeling hospital information systems is the three-layer graph-based metamodel (3LGM). It is used to describe the static view of an HIS over three layers: the domain layer, the logical tool layer, and the physical tool layer.

The domain layer describes a hospital independent of its implementation as accumulation of its functions and the needed entity types. At the logical tool layer, application components that support the hospital functions are described. The physical tool layer comprises a set of physical data processing components that support the application components.

There are several relationships between classes of the different layers. The most important ones are application component configurations, which represent the relationships between hospital functions and application components, and data processing component configurations, which represent the relationships between application components and data processing components.

# 3.5 Information Processing Tools in Hospitals

After having looked at relevant functions of hospitals in section 3.2, we now describe typical information processing tools used in hospitals.

After reading this section, you should be able to answer the following questions:

- What are the typical application components in hospitals?
- What are the typical physical data processing components in hospitals?
- What are healthcare professional workstations?
- What are electronic patient record systems?

### *Typical Application Components*

As defined in section 2.4, a hospital information system is a subsystem of a hospital. Therefore, the application components that are used depend on the organizational structure of the hospital. However, typical application components that support different hospital functions as presented in section 0 can be defined. In this section, we take a closer look at typical computer-based application components used in computer-supported parts of hospital information systems.

## Application Components for Patient Administration

Application components for patient administration offer functionality for patient admission, discharge, and transfer (ADT), basic dataset documentation, and billing. During patient admission, these components must support the documentation of relevant patient data and must be able to check if a patient had previously stayed in the hospital. In this case, they should be able to provide administrative information from those earlier stays, together with the patient identification number (patient ID). In any other case, they must create a new unique patient ID. In addition, a new case ID has to be assigned. Both IDs must then be made available to all other patient-related application components in those areas where the patient will be treated. If the patient already has a paper-based patient record, the application component should automatically trigger the transfer of this record from the patient record archive to the admitting unit.

Closely connected to patient admission is the patient-related (not only case-related!) patient administration, which can be regarded as the center of the memory of the hospital information system. The application component for patient administration must be able to provide up-to-date administrative patient data for all other application components. In addition, all other application components must be able to transmit relevant administrative patient data (e.g., ADT data) to the patient administration component.

The application component for patient administration is usually called the *patient management system (PMS)* (Figure 3.30). The patient management system can be seen as a link between the clinical application components and the general administrative application components. Sometimes the PMS is closely connected to the general administrative application components (e.g., they present different modules of the same software product), which allows for good integration of patient administration and general administration. Often, the PMS is closely connected to the clinical application components, which allows for better integration of those two parts.

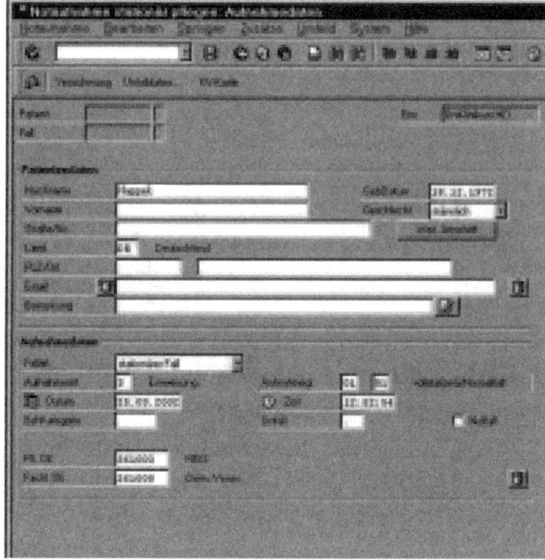

Figure 3.30: Screen shot of an application component for patient admission. Some basic data such as name and date of birth have just been entered.

## Application Components on Wards

Typically, the tasks of physicians, nurses, and other healthcare professionals on a ward are supported by application components for medical documentation, nursing documentation, order entry and result reporting, ward management, and knowledge access.

Application components for medical documentation (often called *medical documentation systems*) should support specific documentation tasks (e.g., patient history, care planning, progress notes, report writing) in different medical fields (e.g., ophthalmology, psychiatry). These components normally offer predefined forms for unstructured, semistructured or structured data entry, as well as reporting and analysis functionality (see Figures 3.31 and 3.32). The more data is structured, the easier are patient-related computer-based decision support and statistical data analysis. It is important that users are able to adapt the components to their needs (e.g., by defining which items have to be documented, and which constraints the entered data must meet).

The coding of diagnoses and procedures receives more and more attention, often due to increased legal requirements. Coding components must support the easy search for suitable classes and codes in catalogs for a given medical field (Figure 3.33). Typically, catalogs of already-coded terms that are created based on the terms of a clinical area (thesaurus or data dictionary; compare section 3.7) or of an institution (house catalogs) are used.

Alternatively, free text can be analyzed using natural language recognition methods. If these coding components are separate from the documentation components, it must be guaranteed that the codes can be transferred to medical documentation components. When reports are generated, the application components should support the reuse of already-documented data (e.g., coded admission diagnosis, laboratory results).

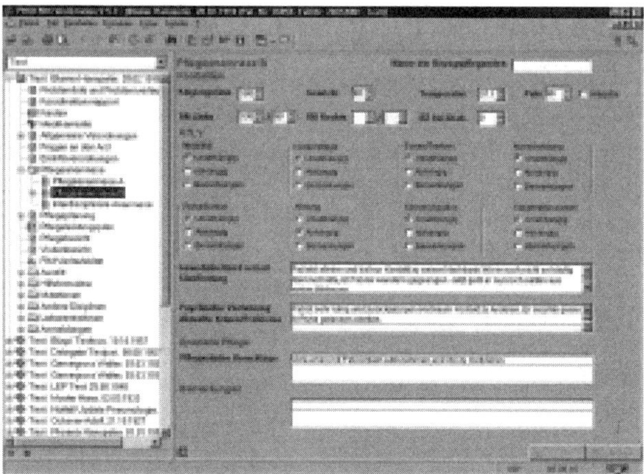

Figure 3.31: Screen shot of an application component for documenting the patient's history, supporting structured data entry with check boxes, as well as offering free-text fields.

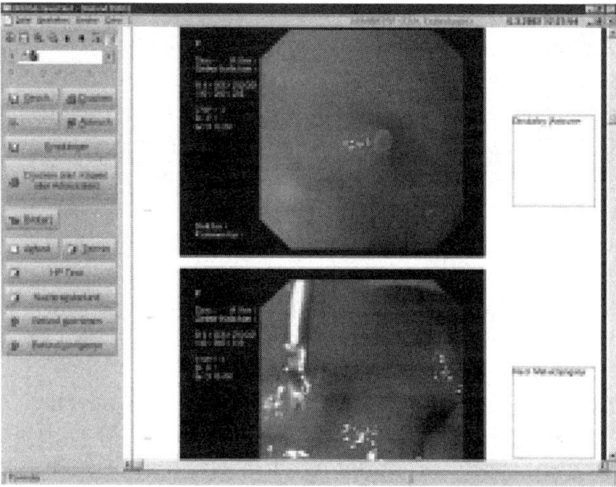

Figure 3.32: Screen shot of an application component for writing endoscopy reports, including both images and fields for free-text data entry.

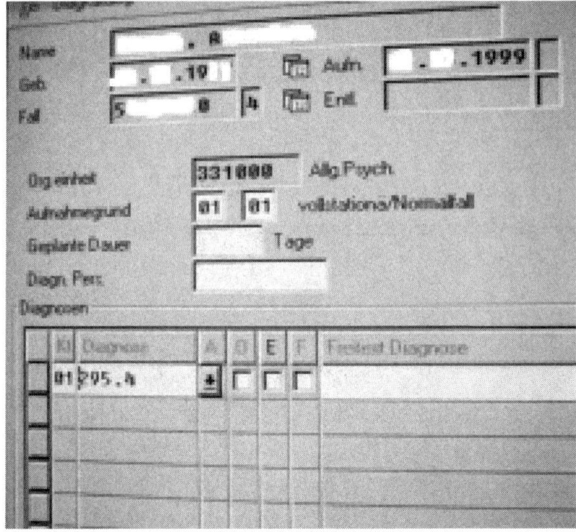


Figure 3.33: Screen shot of an application component for coding of diagnoses using the International Classification of Diseases (ICD-10).

The medical documentation system should also allow an adequate layout of diverse reports. When several persons are involved in the creation of a report (e.g., discharge letters may be dictated by a junior physician, written by a secretary, and approved by a senior physician), the application components should support the management and distribution of different versions of a document.

Application components for nursing documentation (often called *nursing documentation systems*) offer similar functionality as those for medical documentation. Nursing is usually oriented toward the so-called nursing process, which mainly comprises nursing patient history, nursing care planning, execution of nursing tasks, and evaluation of results. An application component should support the documentation of all of those steps. To support nursing care planning, the definition and use of predefined nursing care plans (comprising recent problems of the patient, nursing goals, and planned nursing tasks) is helpful. Application components for medical and nursing documentation should be closely connected, as both deal with clinical data of the same patient.

Application components for order entry and result reporting (also called *order entry systems*) comprise order entry of diagnostic or therapeutic procedures, appointment scheduling, printing of labels, as well as the communication and presentation of findings or reports. Supporting application components usually offer so-called service catalogs, which present the available service types of the different service units (e.g., laboratory, radiology, surgery). After selecting a service type and adding additional information (e.g., patient data, recent diagnoses, specific questions), the order is then transmitted to the service unit. After execution of the ordered procedure, the resulting report is communicated back to the ordering ward or healthcare professional (Figure 3.34). Such application components may also offer organizational support by listing open orders (Figure 3.35).

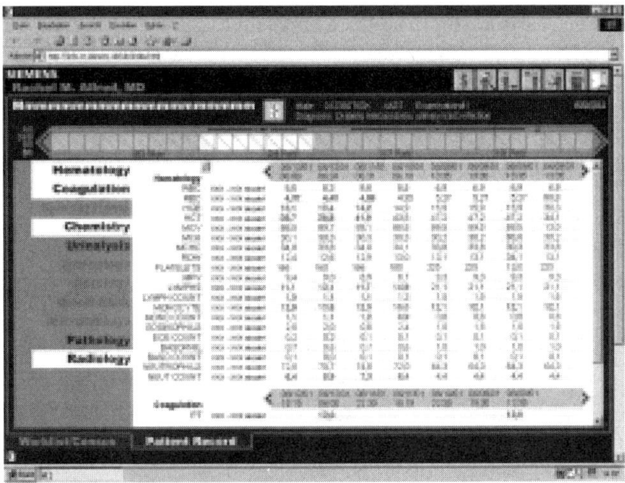


Figure 3.34: Screen shot of an application component for the presentation of results (here: chemistry).

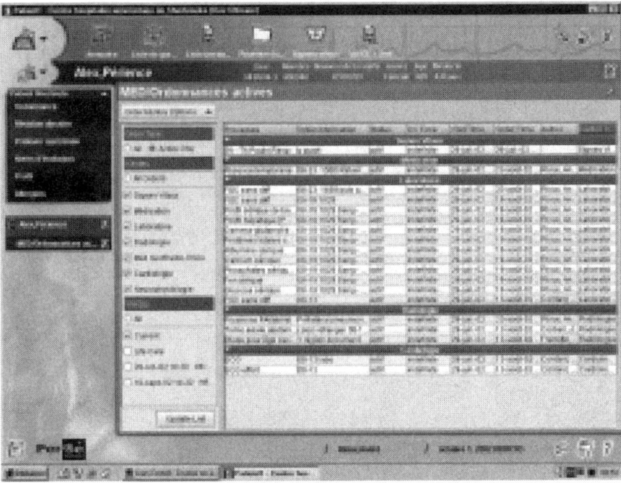

Figure 3.35: Application component, listing new results (top) as well as unsigned orders (bottom) for a selected patient.

Application components for order entry and result reporting are usually closely connected to those of medical and nursing documentation, in order to obtain patient data for the order, and to store the patient-oriented results in the patient record. They can also be closely connected to the application components of the service units, which makes updating service catalogs or scheduling examinations easier. Application components for order entry and result reporting should also allow or be at least closely connected to application components for the ordering of drugs, medical equipment, and transportation and maintenance services.

Application components for *ward management* usually support the assignment of patients to beds and rooms. These components must be connected to the patient management system in order to get information about newly admitted patients, or even to allow the direct admission of the patient on the wards by the nurses. Often, transfer and discharge of patients are also possible. Application components for ward management must be closely connected to those for medical and nursing documentation, as documentation is often linked to administrative events such as admission or discharge.

Application components that provide clinical knowledge (often called *knowledge servers*) offer access to medical and nursing knowledge to healthcare professionals (e.g., medical and nursing guidelines and standards, reference databases, scientific papers, drug databases). Figure 3.36 presents an example.

Application components that comprise functionality for medical documentation, nursing documentation, order entry and result reporting, and ward management are sometimes also called *clinical information systems*.

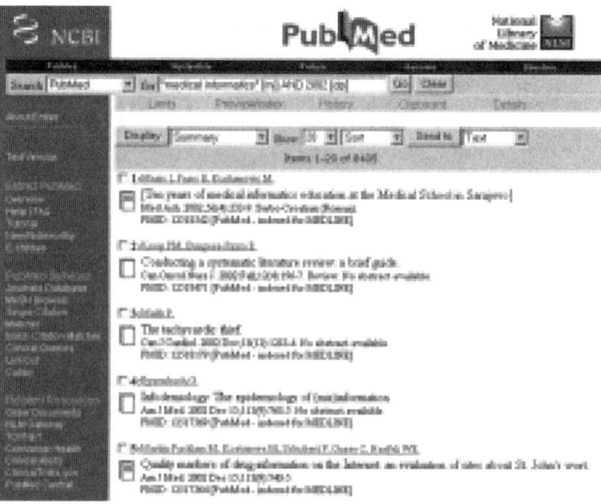


Figure 3.36: Screen shot from a clinical knowledge server, offering clinical references.

## Application Components in Outpatient Units

Outpatient care means patient care during one or several short visits in outpatient departments in a hospital. In most cases, those visits are related to previous or future inpatient stays in the same hospital.

An application component for outpatient units has to support appointment scheduling (Figure 3.37), printing of receipts or other documents, medical documentation (with special emphasis on the different documentation requirements of different clinical areas), work organization support (e.g., task lists), billing, and other management functions.

These functions are similar to functions needed in general practitioners' offices. Therefore, software products used in general practitioners' offices are sometimes also implemented in outpatient units in hospitals. These products are attractive, as they offer specific documentation modules for different medical areas (e.g., graphical tools for the documentation of dermatological status for dermatologists). In addition, the software products for billing can also often be transferred easily and cheaply.

However, application components for outpatient care must be the same or at least closely connected to the application components on the ward in order to support the close cooperation of inpatient and outpatient care. This is often difficult when software products from general practitioners' offices are used. Therefore, software products from vendors with experience in the area of hospital information systems may be better from an integration point of view. However, in this case, the functionality may not be as broad as when software products from vendors who specialize in the general practitioners' area are used.

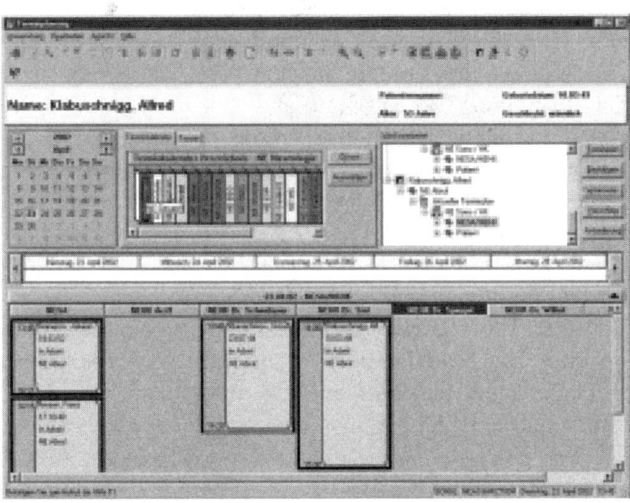


Figure 3.37: Screen shot of an application component for scheduling in an outpatient unit.

## Application Components in Diagnostic Service Units: Radiological Units

As an important diagnostic service unit, the radiology unit and the application components used there will be presented.

In diagnostic radiology, in- and outpatients are examined. A patient is usually treated on a ward or in an outpatient unit. When radiological examinations are needed, the ward or outpatient unit orders them and schedules an appointment. The examination itself may then be done using an analog technology (e.g., x-ray) or digital technology (e.g., computed tomography, magnetic resonance imaging). The tools that generate images are called modalities. Based on the generated images, a specialist in radiology creates a report, which is then presented (sometimes together with selected pictures) to the ordering physician. Application components for diagnostic radiological units, therefore, comprise functions for departmental management, including report writing, image storing, and communication.

Application components for departmental management are often called *radiological information systems* (RISs). They should offer functions for appointment scheduling, organization of examinations and staff (work-flow management, working lists), provision of patient data and examination parameters, and creation of reports. There are different vendors for such specialized radiological information systems.

In the case of analog pictures, application components for image storing and communication (so-called *archive management systems*) support the archiving of analog pictures (often stored in own picture archives), and their retrieving and lending.

In contrast, digital images are stored in so-called *picture archiving and communication systems* (PACS). The application components that realize the PACS must allow the storage, management and presentation of large amounts of data (Figures 3.38 and 3.39) and their quick communication from the storage media to the attached workstations for the diagnosing specialists or for the ordering departments. Those software products also comprise means for image processing and are often offered by vendors, which also offer physical data processing components such as storage, networks, and modalities.

It is clear that the functionality of RIS and PACS components should be closely connected. They should also have a tight connection to patient administration, clinical documentation, order entry and result reporting, and therapeutic service units (such as surgical units), in order to allow quick access to reports and imaging pictures from other units.

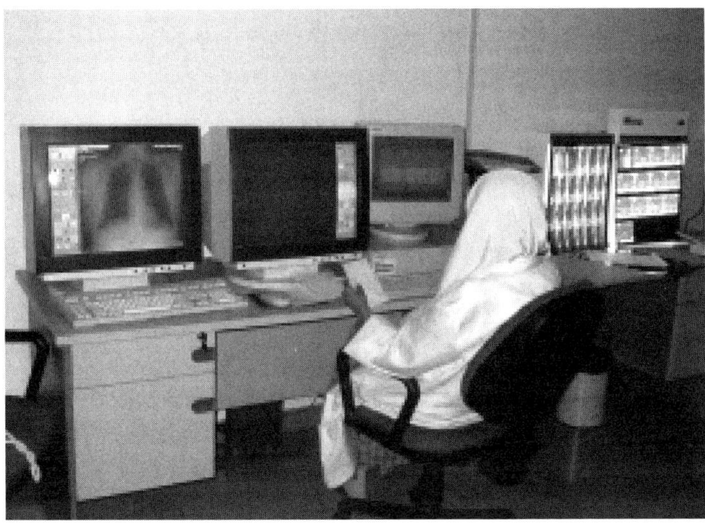

Figure 3.38: Presentation of radiological images at a radiological unit using a PACS.

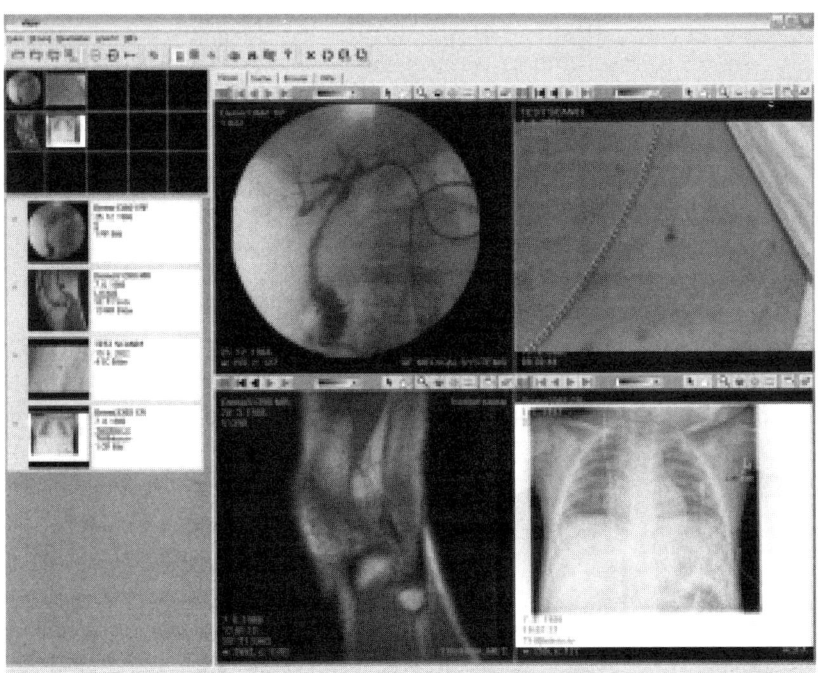

Figure 3.39: Screen shot from a PACS application component, presenting different archived images of a patient.

## Application Components in Diagnostic Service Units: Laboratory Units

During laboratory examinations, only specimens of patients (e.g., blood sample, tissue sample) are used. Appointments are therefore not necessary. Depending on the type of laboratory, different examination technologies are used (e.g., chemical analysis of blood samples, microscopical analysis, and tissue samples). Chemical analysis is usually done by automated equipment. Depending on the order, the sample is usually automatically distributed to various analytical devices, which are regularly checked for their precision in order to conform to quality management requirements. In addition, the laboratory physician checks all results of a sample for plausibility (so-called validation).

Application components in laboratory units are often called *laboratory information systems* (LISs). A laboratory information system must be able to support the management of the whole procedure of analysis: the receipt of the order and the sample, the distribution of the sample and the order to the different analytical devices, the collection of the results, the validation of results, the communication of the findings back to the ordering department, as well as general quality management procedures. The validation of laboratory results is more effective when patient-related clinical data (e.g., recent diagnoses, drug medication) are accessible to the laboratory physician. Laboratory information systems, therefore, should be closely connected to the application components on the ward and outpatient units as well as to those for order entry and result reporting. Laboratory information systems are usually also sold by specialized vendors.

## Application Components in Therapeutic Service Units: Intensive Care Units

Seriously ill patients are treated in intensive care units. The patients are generally in an unstable state, and within seconds may enter into a life-endangering situation. Thus, the detailed and complete presentation of all vital parameters (e.g., blood pressure, pulse, breathing frequency) is required for a successful therapy. This is only possible when automated monitoring devices continuously measure and record various parameters (Figure 3.40). In addition, parameters that can point to the initial deterioration of the patient's status should be automatically detected and should lead to the immediate alerting of the treating healthcare professionals.

Application components in intensive care units are also called *patient data management systems* (PDMSs). This term should not be confused with the term patient management system (PMSs). PDMSs are specialized to automatically monitor, store, and clearly present a vast amount of patient-related clinical data. In this area, the requirements for the permanent availability of the application components and their data is of highest importance in order to guarantee the patient's safety. After referral to a regular ward, a short summary of the therapy on the intensive care unit should be created and communicated to the application components on the ward. In addition, a connection to the application components for order entry and result reporting is necessary. PDMSs are sold both by specialized vendors and by vendors that also offer automated monitoring tools.

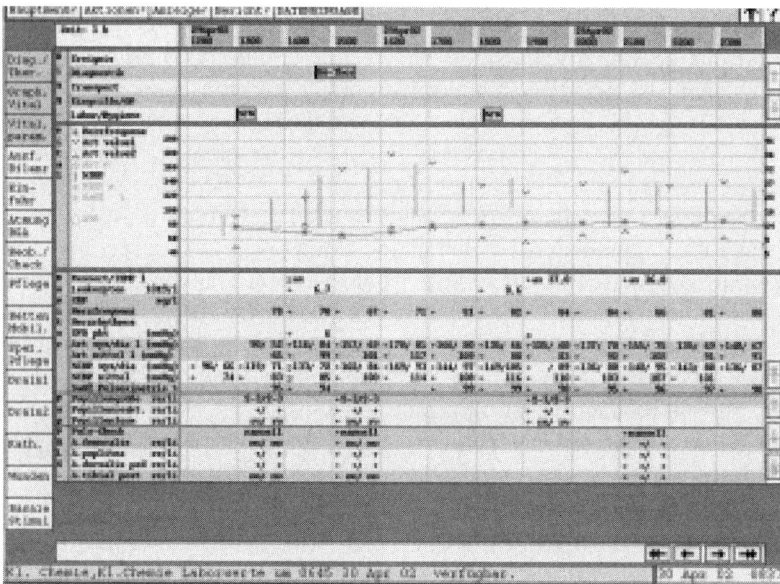

Figure 3.40: Screen shot of an application component for an intensive care unit, showing, among other parameters, heart frequency, lab results, and blood pressure.

## Application Components in Therapeutic Service Units: Operating Rooms

In operating rooms, invasive procedures are performed. Usually, patients stay in the OR for only a few hours. During this time, they are prepared for the operation, the operation is performed, and finally, for a period of time after the operation, the patients' state is monitored.

Application components usually support operation planning and operation documentation. Components for operation planning are also called *operation planning systems*. They allow assigning of operation date and time, and therefore should be available on the wards as well as in the offices and management units of the operating rooms. Depending on the planned operations, an operation plan can be created for a day or a week. The data necessary for efficient planning are the diagnoses of the patient, the planned operation, the surgeons and other staff involved, the planned time for operation, and the available operating rooms. Therefore, application components for operating rooms should be closely connected to those for medical documentation.

During each operation, a vast amount of data have to be documented, including the members of the operating team, the operative procedure, the date and time, duration of the operation, materials used, and other necessary data to describe the operation and its results. Application components that support this operation documentation are also called *operation documentation systems*. Usually, the planning data are taken from the operation planning systems to be updated and completed during and after the operation. Based on these data, an operation report can be created, which may be completed with further comments of the surgeons. Therefore, word processing capability is needed. Operation data needed for billing must be communicated to the administrative application components. The operation documentation system should also allow extensive data analysis (e.g., operation lists for junior surgeons). It should replace the often-used operation book, where all operations are documented by hand. Due to the close connection between operation planning and operation documentation, vendors mostly offer software products supporting both functions.

*Operation management systems* are application components that combine operation planning systems and operation documentation systems.

## Application Components for Hospital Administration

One major goal of administrative application components is the documentation and billing of all accountable services. The types of data needed and the details of billing depend on the country's healthcare system.

Application components for hospital administration support functions such as financial accounting, controlling and budgeting, cost-performance accounting, equipment inventory, and materials management. A close connection is needed to the application components on wards and outpatient units as well as to those in service units, in order to obtain, for example, billing data and legally required diagnoses and procedure codes. Some of the software products implemented here are not specific to hospitals, but are also used in other areas outside health care where similar administrative functions have to be supported.

## Application Components for Integration of Application Components

Depending on the HIS architectural style, specialized application components may be used to support communication between the different application components described above. Different types of such application components are discussed in detail in section 3.7.

## Typical Physical Data Processing Components

When you analyze data processing components from the users' point of view, you can identify, for example, pencil and paper, folders, telephones, mobile phones, typewriters, fax machines, and even cars (e.g., when used for transportation of reports) as typical paper-based components, and personal computers, laptops, servers, organizers, and palmtops as typical computer-based components.

Data processing components (Figure 3.41) have different properties, that is, they can be characterized by

- their location,
- their mobility (mobile or stationary tool), and
- the installed application components.

Figure 3.41: Typical paper-based data processing components.

Examples of typical computer-based data processing components in a hospital are

- a stationary personal computer for the staff of a hospital administration department, where an application component for administration, a word processing component, and an email system are installed to support financial accounting;
- a server managing the electronic patient record data (Figure 3.42);
- a terminal computer where a laboratory application component is installed for laboratory staff;

- a mobile computer used on a ward for information access and order entry (Figure 3.43); and
- a mobile personal digital assistant (PDA), supporting personal organization and the writing of notes.

The *infrastructure* of a hospital information system can be described by the overall number of main data processing components, or by the average number of data processing components per unit (for example, two personal computers per ward) or per staff member.

The infrastructure of a given hospital information system can comprise primarily paper-based data processing components, primarily computer-based data processing components, or a mixture of both. Typically, you will find such a mixture in hospitals (Figure 3.44).

For example, a typical scenario could be the following: The infrastructure for a 1500-bed university hospital may comprise about 2000 personal computers and 3000 telephones. At least two personal computers are usually installed in each ward and outpatient unit (in intensive care units, there is one computer for each patients' room). Every physician may have access to a personal computer. One personal computer may also be available in each operating room and for each member of the administrative staff. At least two telephones may be available in each unit, and a mobile phone or pager for approximately half of the staff members (mainly physicians).

Figure 3.42: A server room for the electronic patient record system and other clinical application components.

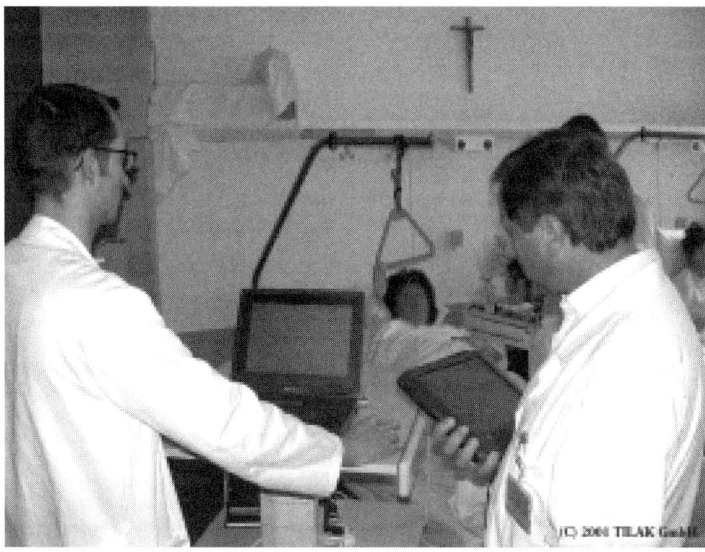

Figure 3.43: Using a mobile terminal during physician's rounds on a ward.

Figure 3.44: A typical HIS infrastructure on a ward, comprising computer-based as well as paper-based information processing tools.

## *Healthcare Professional Workstations*

Very specific information processing tools in hospitals are the so-called *healthcare professional workstations* (HCPW) (Figures 3.45 and 3.46). These healthcare professional workstations consist of a (mobile or stationary) personal computer, connected to the hospital's computer network, together with the application components installed and the hospital functions supported. Healthcare professional workstations usually provide extensive functionality, which is needed by healthcare professionals. They are typically located on a ward, in an outpatient unit, or in a physician's office. A healthcare professional workstation typically offers the following functions:

- admission, discharge, transfer of patients (ADT);
- access to the electronic patient record (explained later in this section);
- order entry of examinations, drugs, meals, materials;
- access to medical knowledge (reference databases, clinical guidelines, drug lists, etc.);
- e-mail and Internet access;
- text processing and statistical functionality.

Thus, a healthcare professional workstation supports most of the typical hospital functions presented in section 3.2.

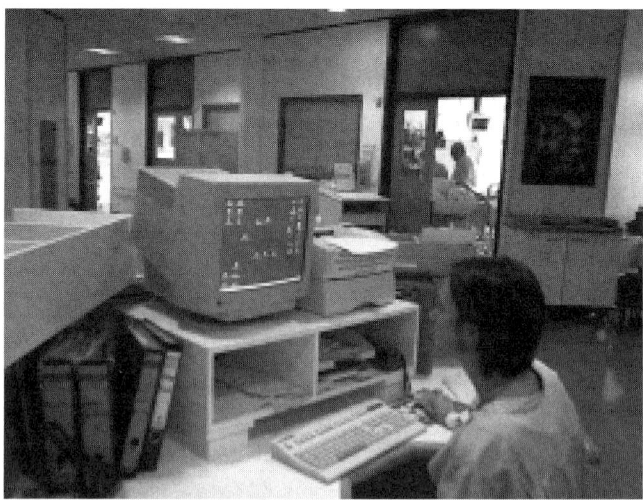

Figure 3.45: A healthcare professional workstation on a neurological intensive care ward.

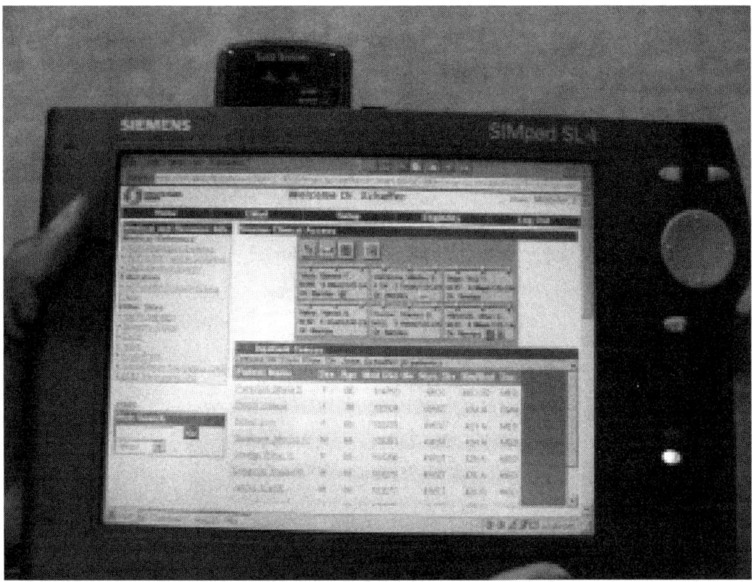


Figure 3.46: The main screen of a (mobile) healthcare professional workstation, showing patient lists on the lower and upper right, and available functionality on the left.

## *Electronic Patient Record Systems*

A patient record in general is composed of all data and documents generated or received during the care of a patient at a healthcare institution.

Nowadays, many documents in the paper-based patient record are computer printouts, such as laboratory results, or discharge summaries typed into a text processing system. The portion of documents created on a computer will further increase. Thus, it seems natural to strive for a patient record that is partly or completely stored on electronic document carriers: the electronic patient record (EPR) (Figures 3.47 and 3.48).

The EPR is thus a complete or partial patient record stored on an electronic storage medium. Given this definition, every computer-based application component with clinical documentation functionality contains at least a partial EPR.

Electronic patient records can be accessed more quickly, are available at different places at the same time, cannot get lost, and need less archiving space. In addition, depending on the user (e.g., physicians, nurses, administrative staff), documents and data can be selected and presented in different forms: there are different "views" on the data. And, assuming a sufficient degree of internal structuring, data may be combined and presented in different ways for particular tasks (mean values may be calculated, progress charts drawn, summaries generated, etc.). This promotes the multiple use of data, the deliberate exchange of information, and the efficiency of documentation as a whole.

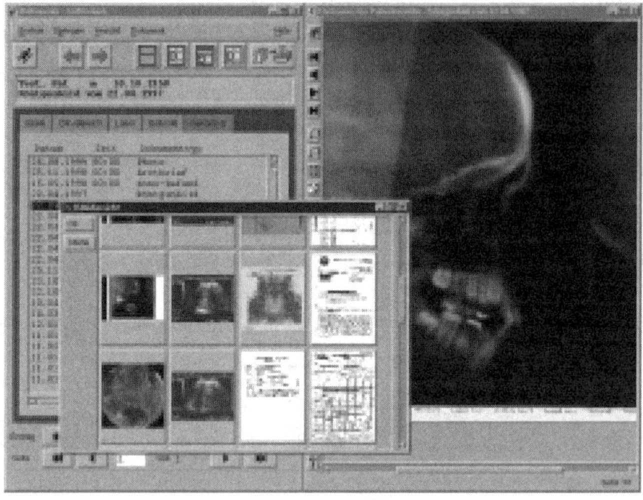

Figure 3.47: Screen shot from an electronic patient record of a patient, comprising both documents and images.

Despite of all these advantages, there are also some disadvantages of an EPR. First, it creates a strong dependence on complex technology. There are serious questions, for example, about the record's availability at any time and place that it is needed, and about the staff's ability to handle it with the skills necessary to exploit its potential and achieve reliable results. Other questions concern the costs: The introduction and operation of a comprehensive EPR is quite expensive. Its introduction might only be economical if it leads to the complete replacement of paper-based record archives. Until today, however, this is hampered in many countries by a host of organizational and legal problems.

Thus, whether EPRs can be handled as easily and flexibly as paper-based records, or whether they are even more useful than paper-based records, will depend to a large extent on the design of the application components implementing them.

Most of the EPRs today are still supplementing and sometimes duplicating the paper-based record. In this sense, every computer-based application component for clinical documentation contains a partial EPR. Despite the growing proportion of electronic documents, the “paperless hospital” still seems to be a remote ideal today. There might be a continuing need for some paper-based documents.

Introducing a comprehensive EPR requires long-term systematic management. Particularly in the case that the paper-based record is to be replaced, this should be done in a stepwise process. The first step in the introduction of an EPR is to provide carefully selected documents of particular importance in electronic form. Frequently, the information contained in clinical basic data-set documentation can be exploited to produce a useful overview of a patient's hospital contacts, problems, and healthcare activities, by way of an index to the patient record.

In a more advanced phase, the EPR should be accessible from all areas of a hospital. This requires a pervasive, hospital-wide network with adequate transmission capacity. There must be networked healthcare professional workstations in all wards, outpatient clinics, physicians' offices, operating rooms, etc. Finally, to build a complete electronic archive, all remaining paper-based documents have to be scanned and coded.

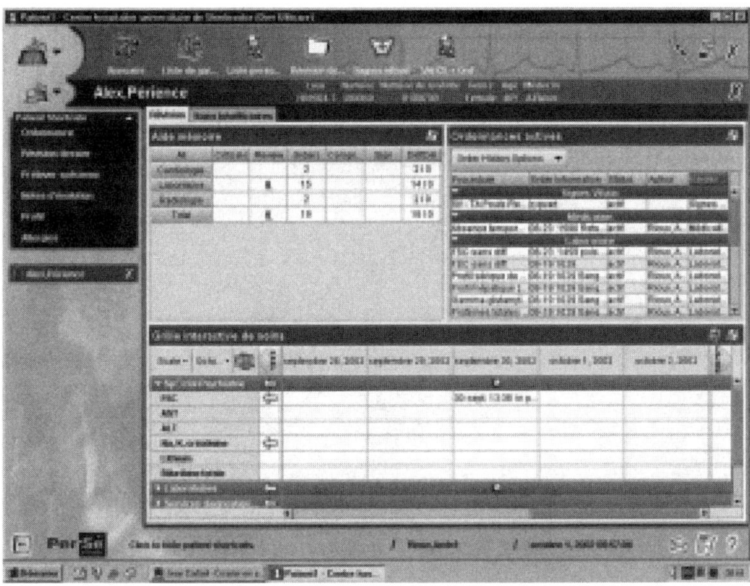


Figure 3.48: Screen shot from the electronic patient record of a patient, showing open procedures on the right, and executed procedures on the bottom.

Health-related patient data are most sensitive and must be protected from unauthorized access. Normally, only healthcare professionals involved in the treatment of patients should be able to access patient data. Only those data that are of potential importance for optimal patient care should be available. For example, for a surgical patient, earlier psychiatric stays may not be relevant for the current treatment.

Electronic patient records, when insufficiently designed, may make data access too easy and may thus violate data protection. Thus, the clear authentication of the user is very important. It is usually done by individual logging, using user name and password. However, the use of *healthcare professional cards* that contain authentication information may in the future facilitate this login. Such a card can also be used to enable the healthcare professional to sign an electronic document using his or her digital signature.

## *Exercises*

### Exercise 3.5.1: HIS Infrastructures

Look at Figures 3.49, 3.50, 3.51, and 3.52, taken at a ward of the Plötzberg Medical Center and Medical School (PMC). Describe the individual information processing tools that you see. Then summarize the typical HIS infrastructure for a ward in this hospital.

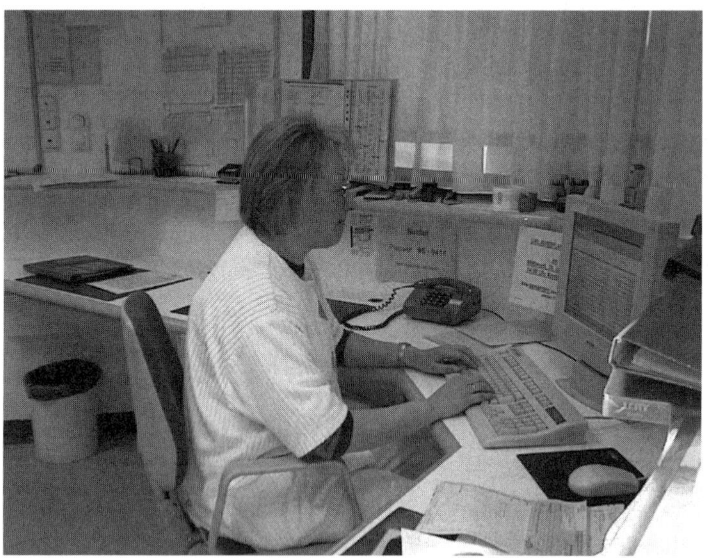

Figure 3.49: At an ophthalmology unit (1).

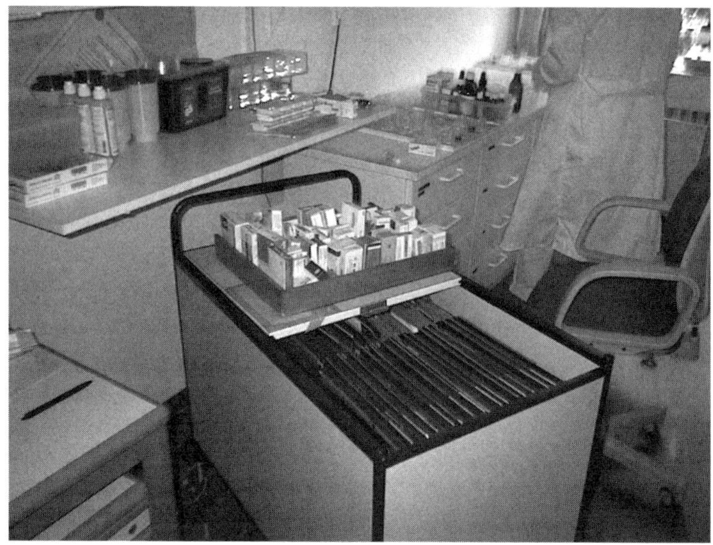

Figure 3.50: At an ophthalmology unit (2).

Figure 3.51: At an ophthalmology unit (3).

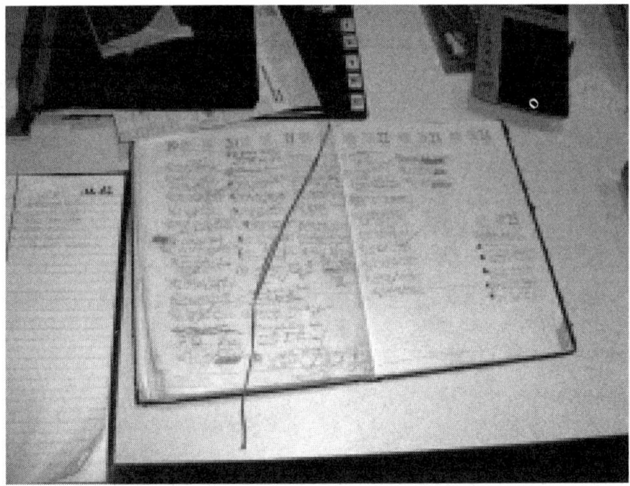

Figure 3.52: At an ophthalmology unit (4).

### Exercise 3.5.2: A Paperless Hospital

Look at Figure 3.53 and compare the HIS infrastructure with those from the ophthalmology unit in exercise 3.5.1. What is the main difference? Do you think a completely paperless hospital is really an aim that can be and should be achieved?

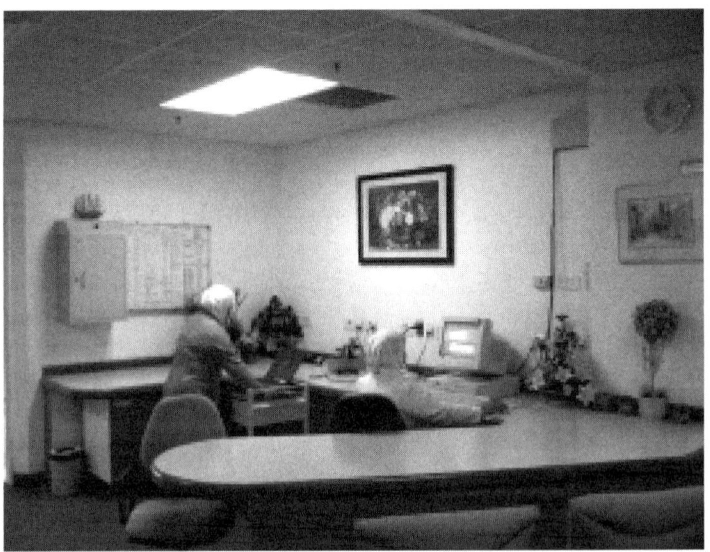

Figure 3.53: A ward in a "paperless" hospital.

### Exercise 3.5.3: Mapping Application Components and Hospital Functions

Look at the typical (computer-based) application components presented in this section. Match them with the hospital functions presented in Figure 3.21 (section 3.3). Which application components can be matched to which functions?

### Exercise 3.5.4: Functionality of Healthcare Professional Workstations

Look at the typical application components (section 3.5) and hospital functions (section 3.2). Now look at a typical healthcare professional workstation as described above: Which hospital functions does it support? Which application components should be installed on it?

### Exercise 3.5.5: Healthcare Professional Workstations and the 3LGM

Healthcare professional workstations are specific information processing tools. How would you model them within a 3LGM-model of a hospital information system? Look at the definition of healthcare professional workstation to solve this exercise.

## *Summary*

Typically, at the logical tool layer, an HIS comprises dedicated application components to support information processing in patient administration units (e.g., patient management systems), wards (e.g., medical and nursing documentation systems, order entry systems, ward management systems, knowledge servers), outpatient units, diagnostic service units (e.g., radiological information systems, laboratory information systems), therapeutic service units (e.g., patient data management systems, operation planning and documentation systems), and hospital administration units. At the physical tool layer, we can distinguish between paper-based (e.g., telephone) and computer-based (e.g., computer) data processing components.

Healthcare professional workstations offer extensive functionality for different healthcare professional groups with the help of different application components installed on one personal computer.

An electronic patient record in general comprises all data and documents that are generated in electronic form during patient care. Introducing a comprehensive electronic patient record requires long-term systematic management and should be done in a stepwise manner.

## 3.6 Architectures of Hospital Information Systems

We now describe typical architectures of HIS. We characterize the "anatomy" of a hospital with respect to its information processing and its information and communication technology (i.e., to the hospital's subsystem HIS).

After reading this section, you should be able to answer the following questions:

- What do typical architectural styles at the logical tool layer of HIS look like?
- What do typical architectural styles at the physical tool layer of HIS look like?

### *Typical HIS Architectures*

As defined in section 2.3, the architecture of an information system describes its fundamental organization, represented by its components, their relationships to each other and to the environment, and the principles guiding its design and evolution. The components of an HIS comprise hospital functions, business processes, and information processing tools.

Let us first look at the functionality of an HIS: With regard to the overall functionality of an HIS, there is nearly no difference between individual HISs, as the hospitals' goals and thus the hospitals' functions are in general the same. All functions presented in the Heidelberg reference model for hospital functions (see Figure 3.21 in section 3.3) should thus be supported by any HIS. Remember, from our point of view, these hospital functions can be supported by paper-based or computer-based information processing tools.

However, there are significant differences in HIS architectures with respect to the types and relationships of information processing tools used. We will find equivalent architectures and summarize them into *architectural styles*. The definition of architectural styles of HISs will help to describe real HIS architectures, to compare them, and to assess them.

We first look at typical HIS architectural styles at the logical tool layer, and later look at HIS architectural styles at the physical tool layer. In the following, we concentrate on the computer-supported part of HISs.

### Architectural Styles at the Logical Tool Layer

Computer-based application components of HISs may have a database system (see section 3.4), that is, a database together with a database management system. In most cases, patient-related data are stored in these database systems. We will use the number of database systems in an HIS as the basis to distinguish possible architectural styles at the logical tool layer of HISs: the $DB^1$ and the $DB^n$ architectural styles.

### $DB^1$ Architectural Style

If an HIS (or a sub-information system) comprises only one application component containing a database system, we call this the $DB^1$ architectural style. In this case, all patient-related data are stored in exactly one database system.

In the simplest case, the overall HIS consists of one computer-based application component, which contains the one and only database system. There could be, for example, an application component that supports patient management and all administrative functions. The other hospital functions (such as clinical documentation) will surely also be realized, not through computer-based but rather through paper-based application components. A graphical representation of such a $DB^1$ architectural style is presented in Figure 3.54.

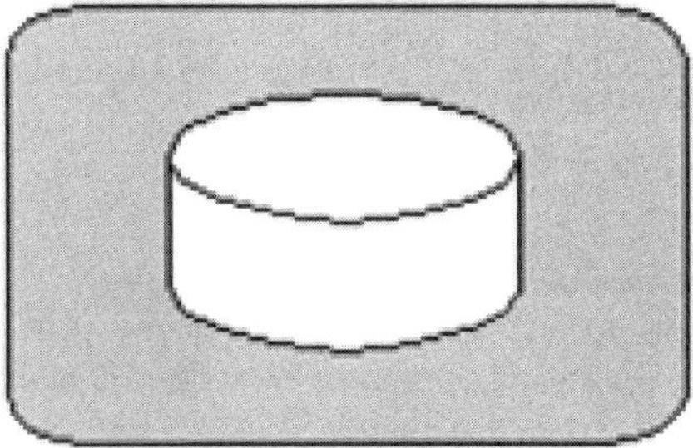

Figure 3.54: $DB^1$ architectural style with one computer-based application component, using 3LGM symbols. The gray rectangle denotes the computer-based application component that contains a database system (denoted by the cylinder).

Usually, however, one application component is not sufficient to support the different hospital functions. As information and communication technology increasingly intrudes in health care, more and more computer-based application components will be needed. For example, the radiology department may not be satisfied with its paper-based application components and, therefore, may introduce a radiological application component that supports patient admission, scheduling, billing, and documentation. A laboratory unit and an outpatient unit, for example, may also introduce departmental application components on their own.

Figure 3.55 presents this architectural style in a schema.

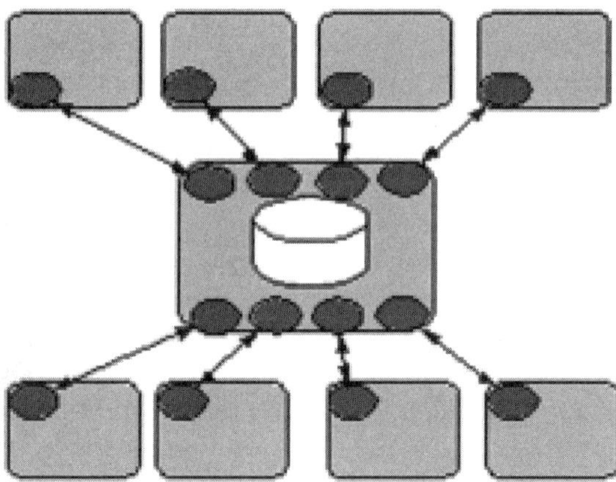

Figure 3.55: DB[1] architectural style with multiple computer-based application components, using 3LGM symbols. Only one computer-based application component (in the center) contains a database system.

The precondition for the DB[1] architectural style is now that the different computer-based application components all work only with the database system of the central application component. This is only possible when the database schema of the central application component is known, together with the methods that are available to access and store data. This is usually the case only when standards are used, when the software products of the application components originate from the same company, or when they are all self-developed by a hospital.

This DB[1] architectural style was the basis for the realization of some very successful computer-supported HISs in the 1970s and 1980s (e.g., DIOGENE of the University Medical Center of Geneva[34]). Those HISs first started with mostly self-developed computer-based application components that facilitated easily connecting them in a DB[1] architectural style.

Later, the self-development of software products became too expensive, and so commercially available software products were used. However, standards are needed when software products from different vendors are connected in a DB[1] architectural style. The different application components for HIS must provide standardized interfaces in order to access the database system of another vendor and to refrain from having one's own database

34. Borst F, Appel R, Baud R, Ligier Y, Scherrer JR. Happy birthday DIOGENE: a hospital information system born 20 years ago. Int J Med Inf 1999 Jun; 54(3): 157-67.

system. One of those standards is HISA,[35] which provides the beginnings of a standardization of the contents of database systems (database schemas). However, this is only at the beginning stages and has not yet led to the broader support of this standard by different vendors.

The $DB^1$ architectural style therefore can be found mostly in HIS or in its sub-information systems using application components that are based on homogeneous software products (either self-developed or purchased from the same vendor). When application components from different vendors are used, the so-called $DB^n$ architectural style can usually be found.

### $DB^n$ Architectural Style

In modern HISs, based on commercial software components of many different vendors, we can normally find the $DB^n$ architectural style. This means that several application components contain their own database systems. Figure 3.56 presents this architectural style.

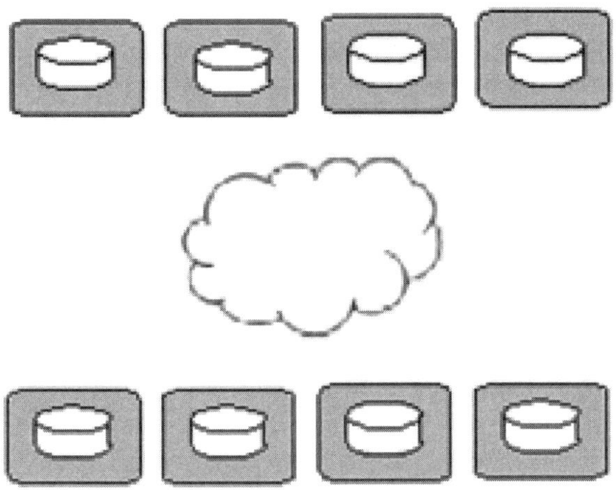

Figure 3.56: $DB^n$ architectural style with multiple computer-based application components, each with its own database system, using 3LGM symbols. The cloud in the center indicates that some as yet unknown means is needed to link the components.

As a consequence of this architectural style, patient-related data are stored redundantly in database systems of different application components. For example, administrative patient data (such as patient identification number, name, sex, date of birth, address) and administrative case data

35. CEN TC251. N-97-024, Healthcare Information System Architecture Part 1 (HISA) Healthcare Middleware Layer—draft. Report no. PrENV12967-1 1997E. Brussels: European Commitee for Standardisation. http://www.centc251.org.

(such as case identifier, date of admission, admitting ward) may be stored in different application components, such as patient management systems, laboratory information systems, and radiology information systems.

Therefore, in this architecture, great emphasis has to be placed on the integrity of redundant data. For example, the architecture must define which system is the responsible source for which data elements. It may be useful to state, for example, that administrative patient data may be created and changed only by the patient management system (however, the other components may locally store and use a copy of these data).

In the case that the different computer-based application components are not at all connected, and data storage is organized completely independently, there is no way to guarantee data consistency. This form of the $DB^n$ architectural style normally has negative consequences for data quality and information management. It may lead to redundant data entry and inconsistent data. Thus, this HIS style usually indicates that information management has to be improved.

Therefore, the logical consequence is to directly connect those application components that may need to exchange certain patient-related data. Figure 3.57 presents this subtype of the $DB^n$ architecture.

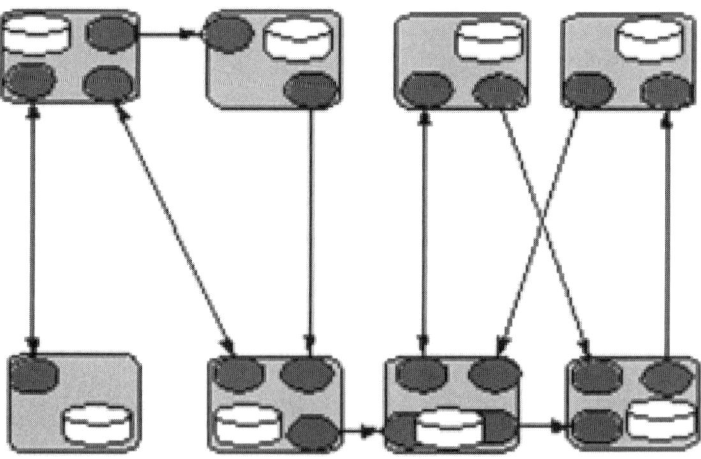

Figure 3.57: $DB^n$ architectural style with multiple computer-based application components, using 3LGM symbols, with several bidirectional communication interfaces. This representation is also called a "spaghetti" architectural style.

For example, if administrative patient data are needed in the patient management system, in the radiological information system, and in the laboratory information system, direct communication interfaces between these components seem to be a possible solution. For example, a communication interface that allows the transfer of patient data between the patient management system and the radiological information system may be introduced. This will lead to several bidirectional communication interfaces (*"spaghetti" architectural style*). All these different interfaces must be supported and managed. As the number of application components rises, the number of interfaces grows nearly exponentially. The maximum number of communication interfaces between $n$ application components ($n \geq 2$) is $\sum_{x=1}^{n-1} x$.

To reduce this large number of interfaces, one can use more intelligent methods and tools to organize and realize the interoperability of application components—i.e., "middleware" approaches. The concept of middleware describes those software components of a computer-supported information system that serve for the communication between application components. Details are presented later in section 3.7.

For example, most hospital information systems following the DB$^n$ architectural style use a message queue manager, also known as a *communication server*. A communication server is an application component that is responsible for supporting asynchronous communication between other application components. This subtype of the DB$^n$ architecture (*"star" architectural style*) is presented in Figure 3.58.

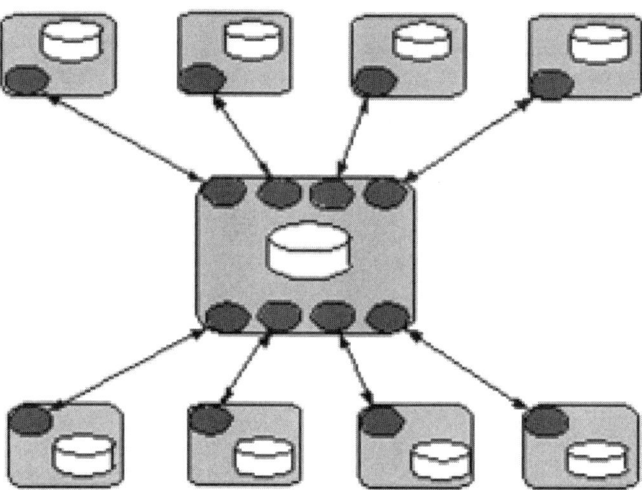

Figure 3.58: DB$^n$ architectural style with multiple computer-based application components, using 3LGM symbols, connected by a specific application component for communication (the communication server). This representation is also called the "star" architectural style.

By using a communication server, no direct interfaces between application components are needed. Interfaces are needed only between the application components and the communication server. The number of interfaces that must be managed can consequently be low—ideally, only *n* interfaces exist for *n* application components.

Details on communication servers and communication standards are presented in section 3.7.

## Architectural Styles at the Physical Tool Layer

The number of computer-based physical data processing components can (even in smaller hospitals) easily amount to a three- or four-digit number. Typical architectural styles at the physical tool layer in the computer-supported part of hospital information systems can be described independently of the architectural style at the logical tool layer: the mainframe-based architecture and the client-server architecture.

The *mainframe-based architecture* consists of one or multiple (networked) mainframe systems to which various terminals are attached. The terminals can be used to access the application components that are installed on the mainframe system. The terminals do not have their own data processing facilities or local memories. This architectural style is rather old; however, it is now discussed again in the form of network computing (NC). In this architecture, the network computer accesses a Web-based application server (terminal server) where all applications are installed. The network computers have, similar to the terminals, no memory and no data processing unit ("thin client").

The other typical architectural style is the *client-server architecture*. In this architecture, various central servers are usually interconnected by a network. These servers can be, for example, application file servers (storing different application components) or database servers (storing data of different application components). Both server types may be combined in one (physical) server. A variety of workstations are connected to this network. The server offers services that can be accessed by the workstations as clients. The workstations are usually typical personal computer systems with their own memory and data processing units. They can offer access to application components installed on the application file server as well as to locally installed application components.

The low costs of hardware has led to an increased use of the client-server architecture in hospitals, with various clients and servers distributed over different units. However, this has engendered high costs for maintenance and support of the servers and of the clients, and has made data security and server availability difficult to guarantee. To solve this problem, the different servers are now often re-centralized in one unit (mostly the ICT department), hoping to reduce costs for server maintenance. A collection of servers in one area also allows for the improvement of data security and availability (e.g., by clustering servers). In addition, hard disks and floppy disks are often removed from the personal computers as clients, thus leading to network computers, in order to reduce costs for maintenance and support of clients. In summary, a re-centralization of information processing on the physical tool layer is now often seen as a means to reduce costs and to improve the quality of information processing at the physical tool layer.

## Some Further Remarks

The architectural styles that have been presented are valid both for hospital information systems and for sub-information systems. In reality, a pure architectural style will normally be found only when looking at sub-information systems. For example, in a radiology unit you may find some servers and attached clients on which a radiology application component and a picture archiving and communication system (PACS) component using a bidirectional communication link are installed. When looking at the architecture of a complete HIS, you will usually find a mixture, for example, of $DB^1$ and $DB^n$ architectures.

You can get an impression of a certain HIS architecture by studying its strategic information management plan (explained in detail in section 0). You can also see its infrastructure there (e.g., number of application components and computer systems). Regarding the computer-based part of HIS, we now observe distributed architectures, at the logical tool layer, with respect to autonomous application components in a $DB^n$ architecture, as well as at the physical tool layer, with respect to servers and clients, connected by a computer network.

All architectural styles have their own specific advantages and disadvantages. Chapter 4 presents quality criteria for hospital information systems that can be used to assess different architectures.

## *Example*

### Example 3.6.1: Communication Between Application Components

Figure 3.59 describes in detail, in the context of a radiological examination, the communication among a patient management system, an order entry system on a ward, a radiological information system (RIS), a picture archiving and communication system (PACS), and an electronic patient record (EPR) system in an architecture based on a communication server.

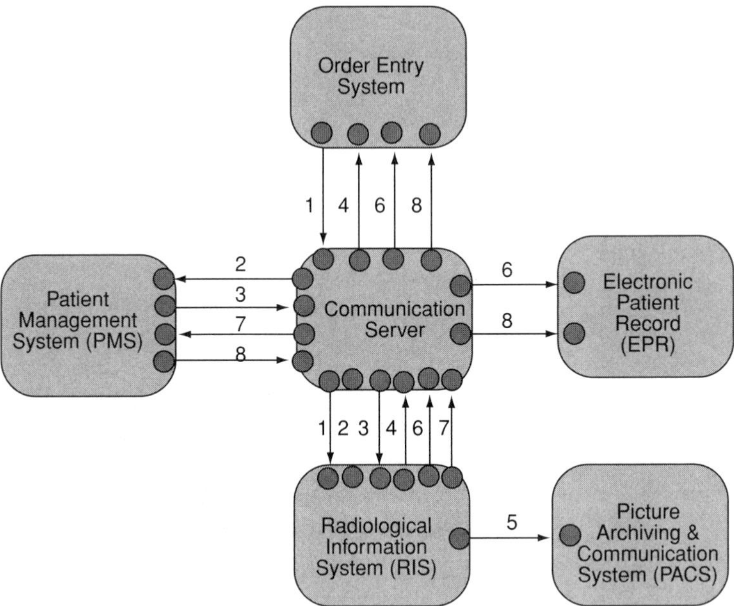


Figure 3.59: The communication between different application components in the context of a radiological examination, using 3LGM symbols.

Explanation of the steps of communications:

1. Request for an appointment for a given patient (including the patient identification number (PIN), a requested radiological examination, and a proposed date) is entered into the order entry system and sent to the RIS.
2. The RIS checks the date. When it is okay, a request for patient data (based on the known PIN) is sent from the RIS to the PMS.
3. The PMS sends patient data (such as name and birth date) to the RIS.
4. The RIS sends an appointment acknowledgment back to the order entry system on the ward.
5. The RIS generates a work list with patient data and requested radiological examination and sends it to the PACS.
6. After the examination is completed, the result report is written in RIS and then sent to the order entry system. The order entry system automatically prints the report on a ward printer. In addition, the result report is sent to the electronic patient record system for archiving.

7. The executed radiological examinations are coded in the RIS and then sent to the patient management system for service documentation and billing.
8. If, during the whole process, a change of patient administrative data is documented in the PMS, this change is communicated to all of the other computer-based application components.

## *Exercises*

### Exercise 3.6.1: HIS Architecture in a Strategic Information Management Plan

Take an HIS strategic information management plan of a given hospital. Answer the following questions concerning HIS infrastructure and architecture:

- What is the HIS infrastructure?
- What kind of paper-based and what kind of computer-based information processing tools are used in the hospital?
- What is their availability and distribution?
- How many healthcare professional workstations are used in which areas of the hospital?
- What functionality for which healthcare professional groups do the healthcare professional workstations offer?
- What is the general HIS architecture?
- What is the architecture at the logical tool layer in the computer-supported part?
- What is the architecture at the physical tool layer in the computer-supported part?

### Exercise 3.6.2: HIS Architectural Styles

Look at the different architectural styles on the logical and physical tool layers described in section 0. Which architectural styles at the logical tool layer are typically matched to which architectural styles at the physical tool layer? Discuss your findings.

### Exercise 3.6.3: Communication Server

Imagine that you want to model the information system's architecture of a given hospital. You expect that there may be a communication server that organizes the communication between most of the computer-based application components.

(a) How can you find out whether there is a communication server in the given HIS? Is a site visit on various wards useful to find a communication server?

(b) Where will you model the communication server in your HIS model: at the domain layer, at the logical tool layer, or at the physical tool layer? Take into account the definition of communication servers as given in the text. Explain your answer.

(c) What can happen when you overlook a communication server? How will your model change? Which (wrong) architectural style would you model?

### Exercise 3.6.4: An Architectural Style at the Logical Tool Layer

Look at Figure 3.60. It shows a specific representation of the $DB^n$ architectural style. Describe this architectural style. How is it distinguished from the $DB^1$ architectural style? How is it different from the other possible representation of the $DB^n$ architectural style presented in Figure 3.58? What are its advantages and disadvantages?

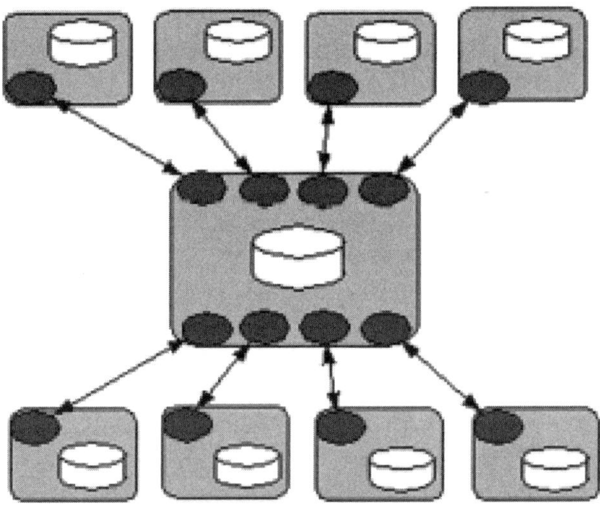

Figure 3.60: $DB^n$ architectural style with multiple computer-based application components, connected by a specific application component, using 3LGM symbols.

### Exercise 3.6.5: Architecture of a Sub-Information System

Imagine you want to model the architecture of a sub-information system (e.g., nursing information system) as part of the overall hospital information system. Is it possible that the architectural style of the sub-information system is different from that of the overall HIS? Explain your answer.

### Exercise 3.6.6: Anatomy and Physiology of Information Processing

If the architecture of an HIS can be compared to the anatomy of information processing, what could the physiology of information processing be? It may help to look up the terms in an encyclopedia.

## *Summary*

As far as the overall functionality of hospitals is concerned, not many differences exist among HISs. However, there are significant differences in HIS architectures. At the logical tool layer, we can distinguish between $DB^1$ and $DB^n$ architectural styles, depending on the number of application components containing a database system. Representations of the $DB^n$ architectural style are the "spaghetti" architectural style and the "star" architectural style.

Typical architectural styles at the physical tool layer comprise the mainframe-based architecture and the client-server architecture.

Today, distributed architectures can usually be found at the logical and physical tool layers. In distributed HISs, it is the task of information management to guarantee the integrity of data and integration of the various components.

# 3.7 Integrity and Integration Within Hospital Information Systems

As most hospital information systems have distributed architectures, and contain various application components and physical data processing components, special emphasis has to be placed on the integration of those components. In this section, we discuss integrity and integration within hospital information systems as well as methods and tools to achieve them.

After reading this section, you should be able to answer the following questions:

- Which main conditions of integrity within hospital information systems exist, and how can they be supported?
- Which qualities of integration within hospital information systems can be distinguished?
- What methods and tools exist for the integration of distributed information systems?
- What special methods and tools exist for the integration of a hospital information system?

## *Integrity*

In a hospital information system, integrity in the broadest sense is understood to mean the correctness of the data. This correctness can be understood in different ways. Thus, for every given type of correctness (that is, integrity), conditions are to be formulated. The fulfillment of these conditions then indicates a certain type of integrity within a given HIS. Two main aspects of integrity are formal integrity and content integrity.

### Formal Integrity

In a hospital information system, formal integrity comprises object identity and referential integrity, which both have great significance.

Generally speaking, it is expected that *object identity* is guaranteed by every database. This concept comes from object-oriented programming and means that an object has an existence that is independent of its value. Thus two objects may look the same, that is, have the same value, but be different. Applying this to the representation of entity types in a database leads to the requirement that the representation of every entity must be uniquely identifiable. In a hospital information system, this is especially important for entity types like "patient" and "case" since all medical data need to be assigned to a particular patient and his or her cases.

Experience has shown that the object identity of the entity type patient can be guaranteed only when every patient receives a unique number, the *patient identification number (PIN),* during his or her first visit to the hospital. This PIN has to be used in all parts of the hospital information system for the identification of the patient. It should also be used during future visits. The PIN should have no internal meaning. That is, it is created continuously and is usually numerical. Past attempts to generate a PIN from data collected from the patient, e.g., from the date of birth and the name, have led to considerable problems that absolutely need to be avoided. Problems arise because, for example, if a date of birth is corrected, the PIN must also be changed. In this case object identity could be compromised.

Similar actions should be taken for cases. A case identifier, which should also have no apparent meaning, should be assigned for every case. A case identifier cannot change, as opposed to the PIN, whose relation to a patient must be corrected after a misidentification has taken place. However, after the correction of a misidentification of a patient, it may be necessary to assign a particular case identifier to a different patient. If it is always ensured, within the hospital information system, that a case identified with a case identifier is always assigned to the correct patient, then the case identifier can be used as a distinguishing identifier for the patient. In the part of the hospital information system that is not supported by computers, for example, forms requesting laboratory testing, the case identifier is used to uniquely identify a patient. Then, for example, the laboratory information system can use its database system to relate the case identifier to the PIN, and thereby find the patient. It must be assumed, though, that the actual assignment of the case identifier to the PIN was communicated to the laboratory information system.

The correct assignment of entities, for example, of cases to a certain patient, or results from the cases, is referred to as *referential integrity* (see the UML diagram in Figure 3.61). Object identity is needed for referential integrity.

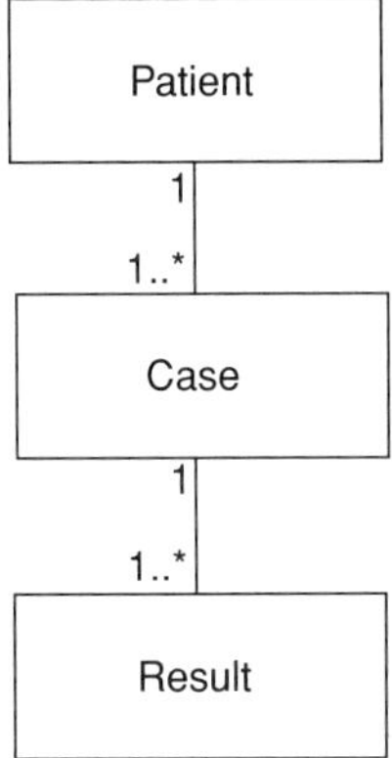


Figure 3.61: Assignment of results to cases, and of those cases to a particular patient, in a data model.

The assignment of the PIN and the case identifier is the task of the patient management system (compare section 3.5), which must have direct access to a database that holds data allowing the reidentification of all past patients and cases in the hospital. This central *patient database* is usually a component of the patient management system.

The ensuring of object identity for patients and cases is the basic assumption for a hospital information system, regardless of whether it is computer supported or not. Without object identity there is no referential integrity, and without referential integrity it cannot be ensured that results can be related back to the correct patient. Without the correct distribution of the PIN and case identifier, the installation of communication networks and computer systems is practically useless.

### Transaction Management to Ensure Formal Integrity in the $DB^n$ Architectural Style

Transaction management is required to ensure the formal integrity of a database. It makes sure that a database in a state where all conditions of integrity are met will remain in this state even after changes are performed on the database.

The *2-phase commit protocol* was developed for transaction management in $DB^n$ architectures. In the initial phase, this protocol checks if the transaction can be carried out by all affected databases. The changes are actually carried out only in the second phase. For carrying out the protocol, the database systems must be tightly coupled by synchronous communication, and the database schemata of all involved database systems must be known. For an application component in a hospital information system, this means that an interface must be provided where both changes as well as the cancellation of these changes are possible. This is not the case for commercial application components available today. Generally, the database schema is also not known.

Due to these reasons, the 2-phase commit protocol to ensure formal integrity in hospital information systems has usually not yet been implemented. To nevertheless guarantee integrity, the following measures are taken.

For every redundantly stored entity type, an application component is determined whose database system serves as the *master database system* for this entity type. Thus, data about entities of this type can only be inserted, deleted, or changed in this master database system. Typically, it is the case that data about entities of type "patient" (that is, patient administrative data) and of type "case" can be created, deleted, or changed only in the patient management system.

Transactions in a master database system are carried out without regard to whether the corresponding operations can also be (immediately) carried out in the other affected database systems. Patient admission is thereby carried out through the patient management system independent of, for example, if the radiology information system is capable of inserting corresponding data about a patient or case into its database system at the same point in time. The radiology information system is therefore obliged to catch up on database operations at a later point in time.

## Content Integrity: Medical Data Dictionaries

Content integrity requires that the same data that are used in different application components in a hospital actually are interpreted in the same way. This can be supported by *medical data dictionaries* (MDDs).

MDDs are central catalogs of medical concepts and terms that offer the possibility of representing the semantic relationships among all data stored in a hospital information system, and of linking that local vocabulary to internationally standardized nomenclatures and knowledge sources. MDDs can be independent application components or part of the existing application components.

An MDD is normally composed of a system of medical concepts and terms, an information model, and a knowledge base. Which system of medical concepts and terms is used for an MDD depends on the goal of the MDD. If only a few or only in-house application components are to be integrated, an internally developed system (e.g., the Medical Data Dictionary of HELP Systems PTXT[36]) often stands behind the system of medical concepts and terms. If you would like to access various external knowledge sources, e.g., to start a literature search from a clinical workstation, generally acknowledged systems of concepts and terms have to be used (e.g., nomenclatures such as SNOMED[37] or more complex networks of medical concepts and terms like the UMLS metathesaurus[38]). These sources are also often integrated into the in-house MDD. The linking of the systems of concepts and terms with the application components is partially realized through so-called terminology servers and terminological services (e.g., GALEN[39]).

## *Integration*

*Integration* is a union of parts making a whole, which as opposed to its parts, displays a new quality. We speak of an *integrated hospital information system* if we want to express that it is a union that represents more than just a set of independent components. Rather, the components, in a sense, work together. It is assumed here that the application components at the logical tool layer as well as the corresponding components at the physical tool layer are linked, or networked, together through interfaces. Different types of cooperation can lead to different qualities of integration:

## Data Integration

*Data integration* is guaranteed in a hospital information system when data that have been recorded are available wherever they are needed, without having to be reentered. Thus, each data item needs to be recorded, changed, deleted, or otherwise edited just once—even if it is used in several application components. Data integration is a prerequisite for the multiple use of data. In the $DB^n$ architectural style, it requires communication interfaces in the computer-supported part of HIS, and ways to print out data (e.g., labels,

36. Huff SM, Cimino JJ. Medical data dictionaries and their use in medical information system development. In: Prokosch HU, Dudeck J. Hospital Information Systems. Amsterdam: Elsevier; 1995. pp. 53-75.
37. Systemized Nomenclature of Medicine (SNOMED). College of American Pathologists. http://www.snomed.org.
38. Unified Medical Language System (UMLS). National Library of Medicine (NLM). http://www.nlm.nih.gov/research/umls.
39. OpenGalen. http://www.opengalen.org.

order entry forms) or scan data in order to provide communication between the computer-supported and the paper-based part of HIS.

Assume your child was treated in the pediatrics department and a detailed patient history was collected and saved. Now, the child has to go for a hearing examination at the ear, nose, and throat department of the same hospital. If the patient history needs to be collected again because the document from the pediatrics department cannot be accessed, there is no data integration. Data integration is possible even when data items are physically stored redundantly.

## Access Integration

*Access integration* is guaranteed when the application components needed for the completion of a certain task can be used where they are needed. If, for example, the patient management system is needed for patient admission, then the patient management system should be available at all workstations where a patient admission has to take place: central admission areas, wards, outpatient units, the radiological outpatient unit, emergency department, etc.

## Presentation Integration

*Presentation integration* is guaranteed when different application components represent data as well as user interfaces in a unified way. So, for example, different application components at a workstation should display at nearly the same place on the interface the name of the patient who is currently being processed, and icons for patients should code gender with the same colors.

## Contextual Integration

High quality of the hospital information system is realized when data, access, and presentation integration are available at the workstation of a staff member. Still, however, the patient context may get lost through the change from one application component to another. *Contextual integration* means that the context is preserved when the application component is changed, e.g., at a healthcare professional workstation. Or, more generally, the aim is that a task that has already been executed once for a certain purpose need not be repeated again in the hospital information system, in order to achieve the same purpose.

Assume that one application component for the presentation of laboratory results (LABRES) and one application component for the documentation of nursing measures (NURS) exist on a ward on one healthcare professional workstation for use by nurses. When the newest results for patient Fritz Mayer need to be analyzed, Fritz Mayer's administrative data need to be searched for in LABRES. That means the patient must be identified in LABRES. Following this, the patient's results can be displayed. Now, if nursing measures for Fritz Mayer need to be documented with NURS, then patient identification should be immediately displayed in NURS, without forcing the nurse to search for him again. Thus, in this example, the selection of the patient is a task that must not be repeated if performed once, even when changing the application component.

In the literature, this type of integration is also referred to as *visual integration*, where, however, emphasis is put on the fact that the integration of application components within a graphical user interface is dealt with.

## *Methods and Tools for System Integration in Distributed Systems*

Methods and tools are necessary for the integration of hospital information systems with a $DB^n$ architectural style. Informatics offers general solutions for the *system integration* of so called distributed systems. These solutions will be explained in this section. In addition, various dedicated solutions, especially for hospital information systems, have been developed in medical informatics which will be explained later.

### Federated Database System

A federated database system is an integrated system of autonomous (component) database systems. The point of integration is to logically bring the database schemata of the component database systems to a single database schema, the *federated database schema*, in order to attain data integration even when there is redundant data in information systems with a $DB^n$ architectural style. This virtual federated database schema should be able to be accessed as though it were a real database schema.

Middleware methods as described below can be used for the implementation of a federated database system.

When a federated database system has been implemented for a given set of component database systems, software products can be developed that can have read access and, if applicable, write access on the corresponding data described by the federated database schema. This means that the developer of this software product must be aware of the federated database schema during development. Generally speaking, this method requires a standardized federated database schema. Such standards, unfortunately, are not currently available for hospital information systems.

## Middleware

The term *middleware* describes the software components of a computer-supported information system that serve for the communication between application components.

### Communication for Function Calls and Message Exchange

Middleware components for *remote procedure call (RPC)* or *remote function call (RFC)* enable the execution of a procedure that can run on a remote computer through a process that is running on a local computer. *Synchronous communication* is thereby carried out, meaning that the process in the initiating application component, following the initialization of communication with another application component, is interrupted as long as response data from the partner are obtained. Through one application component, e.g., for outpatient management at a healthcare professional workstation, a procedure of the patient management system can be carried out with which a patient admission can be done. The Open Systems Foundation (OSF)[40] is making an effort through the definition of a *distributed computing environment (DCE)* to come up with the standardization and expansion of the functionality of RPC and RFC.

*Asynchronous communication* means that the process in the initiating application component, following the initialization of communication with another application component, does not have to be interrupted while awaiting response data from the communication partner. This form of communication occurs through the sending of messages. Methods and tools are necessary for *message queuing*. The tool that is used is generally called a *queue manager*, and in hospital information systems, a *communication server*. We will return to the communication server later in this section. Besides supporting the sending of messages from the sender to the receiver, a queue manager also supports the distribution of a single message to numerous receivers (multicasting).

### Communication for Database Access

If the main topic of concern of the application component on the remote server is the database system, and if the main point of concern for communication is to insert data, change data, or read data in the database of a database system, then special methods and tools based on the standard query language (SQL) are available. SQL-drivers offer interfaces to different database management systems and are responsive to an *application programming interface (API)*. A standard for such API is described by *open database connectivity (ODBC)*.[41]

---

40. The Open Group, http://www.opengroup.org.

41. Microsoft Corporation, http://www.microsoft.com.

**Middleware in Distributed Object Systems**

If the application components at the logical tool layer of an information system are understood as objects that (in the sense of object-oriented programming) offer services and are distributed in various computers, then we are referring to a *distributed object system*. Depending on the situation, an object can be a *server* that offers services to other objects, or it can be a *client* that uses services of other objects.

For such distributed object systems, the object management group (OMG)[42] has proposed a *common object request broker architecture* (CORBA).[43] The object request broker (ORB) carries an index of all services provided by the objects that are part of the current architecture. The index is updated at run time, so that the ORB can support an object demanding a certain service (client) by selecting the most suitable offering object (server).

The OMG has set up (branch-)specific working groups *(domain task forces, DTFs)* through which the services for an application area are standardized. Software manufacturers can manufacture objects as products such that they realize these services in a standardized form. For example, the DTF CORBAmed was implemented for the medical area (details will be given later in this section).

Existing application components *(legacy systems)* that were not implemented as objects can also be fit into a CORBA architecture. They can be encapsulated in a wrapper that lets them appear as an object that is compatible with CORBA.

CORBA's competition is currently the products or architectural styles OLE and COM/DCOM.[41]

## Hypertext Markup Language (HTML)

In the Internet, user interfaces of application components are described with the *hypertext markup language (HTML)*. These interfaces, through an HTML browser, can be displayed and used on a given hardware or operating system platform. In addition, it is possible to use various different application components on one healthcare professional workstation that could be installed on different servers.

In this way, it is possible to simply and elegantly provide access integration. Data, presentation, and contextual integration, however, cannot be reached in this way alone.

42. Object Management Group (OMG). http://healthcare.omg.org.

43. Object Management Group (OMG). CORBA—Common Object Request Broker Architecture. http://www.corba.org, http://www.omg.org.

## *Methods and Tools for Integrating Hospital Information Systems*

For the integration especially of hospital information systems, specific methods and tools have been developed on the basis of the general methods and tools for distributed systems discussed in the previous paragraph. We will discuss communication servers and communication standards, CORBAmed, and CCOW.

## Data Integration for the $DB^n$ Architectural Style Through Message Exchange (Communication Servers and Communication Standards)

### Communication Servers

For supporting asynchronous communication between application components, queue managers are referred to as *communication servers* in hospital information systems. The communication server stands at the center of the logical tool layer of a hospital information system (compare Figure 3.58 in section 3.6). This architectural principle can be found in most hospital information systems with the $DB^n$ architectural style.

At the logical tool layer, a communication server is an application component. Corresponding software products are offered by different manufacturers.

Generally speaking, a communication server serves for the asynchronous sending, receiving, and buffering of messages. It can also be used to monitor the traffic between application components. An application component can relay or send a message to the communication server over its communication interface. The communication server will then relay the message to the one address or many addresses (multicasting) specified by the sender when these application components are ready to receive. In the meantime, the communication server buffers the sent messages in a queue (message queuing).

In the case that the receiving application component is awaiting messages in a different form than the sending application component sends, the communication server can translate the sent message.

The communication server is in this way a tool with which *asynchronous communication* can efficiently be supported in a large hospital information system. With this technology, a higher level of autonomy, expandability, and constrainability can be reached.

With the communication server software available today, message sending can also be done as *synchronous communication.* For this, the communication server is configured so that the sending application component is blocked from the time that it sends a message to the time that it receives a response message.

### Communication Standards

Independent of whether synchronous or asynchronous communication is taking place and whether a communication server is used, a consensus must exist about the syntax and semantics of the messages that are to be exchanged between the two communicating application components. Costs of the implementation and running of communication links can be significantly reduced when communication standards are put in place.

Two important communication standards in health care are HL7 and DICOM.

*Health Level 7 (HL7)*

HL7[44] is the most implemented communication standard in hospital information systems for the transfer of patient- and case-based messages, excluding image data. HL7 describes with which events, and with which structure, messages are exchanged between application components.

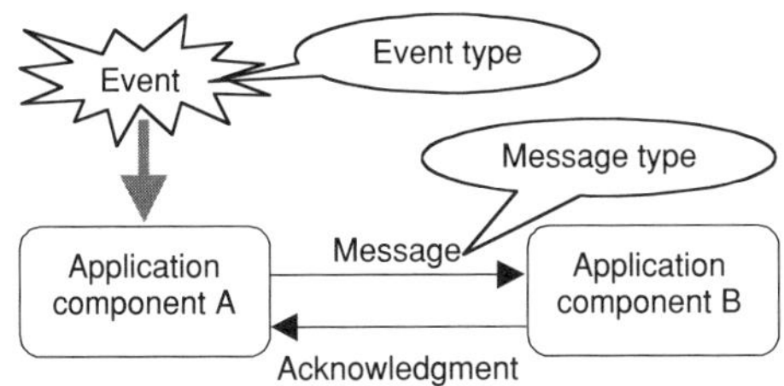


Figure 3.62: Event-driven communication with HL7.

HL7 assumes that a message is sent from application component A (Figure 3.62) to another application component B through the occurrence of an event. The message type that is used for the message depends on the occurring type of event. It describes the structure of the sent message and determines the meaning of the individual parts of the message. Following the arrival of the message, application component B confirms the receipt of the message through a receipt message that is sent back to application component A. If a communication server such as in Figure 3.60 is used to send a message from the patient management system PMS to the laboratory system LABSYS, then the communication server first takes over the role of the receiving application component B. As a second step, the communication server as the sending application component A sends the message to LABSYS, which takes over the role of B.

44. Health Level Seven. HL 7. http://www.hl7.org.

HL7 possesses an extensive catalog of event types. For example, A01 stands for the admission of a patient, A02 stands for the transfer to another organizational unit within the hospital, A03 stands for the discharge of a patient, or R01 for the completion of an examination result.

Message types are assigned to event types. For example, if the laboratory system in the laboratory of a hospital registers the occurrence of an event of type R01, then it can send a message of message type ORU (unsolicited transmission of an observation message).

Despite this standardization, the use of "plug and play" equipment is often not possible due to various reasons. On the one hand, HL7 leaves users with freedoms with regard to the definition of terms to be conveyed. In this case, consensus must exist between the communicating application components, whether, for example, the choices "male," "female," "other," and "unknown" for gender should be documented as "m," "f," "o," and "u," with "0," "1," "2," and "3," or in some other fashion. On the other hand, manufacturers of software products sometimes offer HL7 interfaces to their products that can't send or receive all required event types and/or all necessary message types. In this case, a thorough analysis is necessary before deciding on a purchase. For existing implementations, there furthermore exists the problem of the comparison of catalogs. In this case, for example, it is necessary in an application component for material use documentation to have an up-to-date copy of the material catalog from the materials industry. Interfaces that serve the corresponding HL7 event and message types are often not offered by software manufacturers.

When a message was constructed in accordance with the previous explanations, it is left up to the particular implementation how communication between the physical data processing components will occur. A message can then, for example, be written in a text file or can be transported by a disk or through an FTP file transfer. The exchange format and protocol on the physical tool layer is to be decided on in every single communication link.

Current developments are leaning toward using the markup language *eXtended Markup Language* (XML),[45] which is already being widely used in the Internet for the definition of message types and the formulation of messages. Through its "tag/value" concept, XML offers the possibility to determine the meaning of parts of messages (e.g., <date of birth> indicating the date of birth: <date of birth>19500317</date of birth>). In contrast, in "classic" HL7, the meaning is determined by order and position (e.g., birth date is on the 4th place in '|123456789|2718787|Müller^Hans||19500317|M'). In this fashion, not only is the flexibility of HL7 enlarged, but the importance of the language in sight of the ability to describe facts in a hospital is greatly expanded.

45. Extended Markup Language (XML). http://www.xml.org.

*Digital Imaging and Communications in Medicine (DICOM)*
The *National Electrical Manufacturers Association* (NEMA) developed the communication standard *Digital Imaging and Communications in Medicine* (DICOM)[46] for the transfer of images. With DICOM, images from radiological examinations, for example, can be sent from their digital modalities to the result workstations or into the PACS. But also data describing the originating requests, for example, from the radiology information system (RIS), can be sent to the required digital modalities, and the results from the RIS with the images from the PACS to the intensive care unit. In contrast to HL7, DICOM not only defines a message format, but also couples it closely with exchange formats.

In the future, it can be assumed that RIS, PACS, and all image viewing systems in a digitized unit for diagnostic radiology in a hospital will communicate based on DICOM.

The application component RIS is also dependent on messages from the patient management system and must also send, for example, billing data there. As discussed above, this communication should be carried out on the basis of HL7. Orders from wards and outpatient units will also most likely reach radiology as HL7 messages, whereas the results and images will come back as DICOM messages. The common initiative *Integrating the Healthcare Enterprise* (IHE)[47] of the Healthcare Information and Management Systems Society (HIMSS) and Radiological Society of North America (RSNA) has taken on the task of settling this complex interplay.

## Access and Presentation Integration on the Basis of Distributed Object Systems (CORBAmed)

The exclusive use of message-oriented methods described in the last section is not sufficient to get access and presentation integration in a hospital information system with a $DB^n$ architectural style. For access and presentation integration, the CORBA architectural style as described above offers excellent mechanisms for the use of functions and services of one application component through another application component. The domain task force CORBAmed[48] which is set up for health care by the Object Management Group (OMG), has the goal of defining standardized object oriented interfaces for the use of services and functions between application components in health care. CORBAmed works closely with the working groups of HL7 and DICOM.

46. National Electrical Manufacturers Association (NEMA). DICOM—Digital Imaging and Communication in Medicine. http://medical.nema.org.
47. IHE. Integrating the Healthcare Enterprise. http://www.rsna.org/IHE/index.shtml.
48. Corba Med, the Healthcare Domain Task Force of the OMG. http://cgi.omg.org/corbamed.

The CORBAmed working group is involved with, among other things, the standardization of services

- for the identification and description of patients (patient-centered services),
- for supporting healthcare professionals (provider-centered services),
- of clinical information services (enterprise information services), and
- of administrative information services (administration-centered services).

CORBAmed is expected to fundamentally change the architecture of hospital information systems. Traditional hospital information systems often have a department-oriented structure on their logical tool layer, whereas CORBAmed promotes a more service-oriented structure. This fits well into current developments in hospital organization. To provide an even more competitive level of patient care, it is discussed in hospitals whether the present structure, oriented toward departments, shouldn't be replaced by a treatment process-oriented structure in which interdisciplinary teams are responsible for the care of the patient.

## Contextual Integration with CCOW

Contextual integration requires the synchronization of application components at the workstation. The *clinical context object workgroup* (CCOW)[49] has developed standards for the synchronization of even independently developed application components on a computer at a healthcare professional workstation. In one of the first versions of the standard, a process, referred to as *Patient Link,* is described for the synchronization of application components with regard to a chosen or identified patient. When the user of an application component changes the chosen patient at the workstation, all other application components on the given workstation follow in this change. This is amended through a process that passes the data about user authorization to the other application components when the user has logged in at an involved application component. In this way, the annoying multiple user logins for different application components can be eliminated.

## *Integrating Hospital Information Systems into Health Information Systems*

For the integration of a hospital information system in a healthcare region, the application components of the hospital have to have communication

---

49. Clinical Context Object Workgroup (CCOW), http://www.hl7.org/special/Committees/ccow_sigvi.htm.

links with the application components of other institutions of the healthcare region through appropriate communication interfaces.

The following two problems in particular exist through this crossing of hospital's boundaries:

- Encryption: Those messages transferred during communication in the context of notifications, teleconsultations, or teleconferences, and for the global use of patient records, have to be protected from unauthorized third party access. Encryption procedures that are sufficiently secure and can be obtained as commercial encryption software exist for these cases. A problem in this case, however, is the correct identification of the respective communication partner. A remedy in this case could be electronic identification. In health care, the so-called healthcare professional card (HPC) is currently being tried out, which uniquely identifies a specific healthcare professional.
- Patient identification: We have already determined that patient-based communication within a hospital is only possible when a patient is uniquely identified and a patient number as well as a case identifier are assigned (object identity) upon admission. This is only possible when all application components that are used for admission have access to the central patient database. Only under certain conditions, for example when the different institutions of a region legally build one unit, is it possible to assign patient and case identification numbers from one central location in a unified way. This difficult process of uniting patient-based documents especially hinders the building of a global patient record. For notifications, teleconsultations, and teleconferences, patient identification is also possible through the personal agreement of the involved people. The improvement of patient identification can be reached through the structure of the so-called *master patient index* (MPI). Manually or semiautomatically found relationships of patient identification numbers from different institutions are saved in one regional MPI and are made available to all institutions in the region.

Up to now we thought of communication links between application components in different institutions as a means for providing access to patient data that is stored in the hospital. Besides this, Internet technology also enables the direct usage of a hospital's application component at a remote site. The use of the HTTP protocol, for example, enables a physician who has set up his own practice to easily and cost-effectively access an electronic patient record in a hospital. This record may include the images that are managed there, for example, in the diagnostic radiology department.

## *Exercises*

### Exercise 3.7.1: Patient Identification Number

Discuss the significance of the patient identification number (PIN) to achieve integrity inside a hospital information system. Why should the PIN not have an internal meaning? What could happen when the PIN contains the date of birth or other patient characteristics?

### Exercise 3.7.2: Object Identity

Explain why object identity, especially with regard to patients and cases, is the precondition for patient-centered information processing. Take an electronic patient record system as an example.

### Exercise 3.7.3: Communication Standards

Look at Figure 3.59 (in section 3.6) and try to find out which communication standard (HL7 or DICOM) may be used for each of the described communication links.

## *Summary*

Within distributed hospital information systems, special emphasis has to be placed on the integration of the various components.

Integrity in the broadest sense means how correct data are. We differentiate formal integrity from content integrity. Formal integrity encompasses object identity (every entity is uniquely identifiable, e.g. the patient by a PIN) and referential integrity (the correct assignment of entities). To ensure formal integrity, it is useful to have a master database system for each entity type. Content integrity means that the same data are also interpreted the same way in various application components. Content integrity can be supported by medical data dictionaries, which are central catalogs of medical concepts and terms.

Integration means making a whole of various parts, and this whole displays a new quality. Integration within distributed hospital information systems encompasses the following types: Data integration means that data that have been recorded once are available where they are needed, without having to be reentered. Access integration is guaranteed when the application components needed for the completion of a certain task can be used there where they are needed. Presentation integration is present when different application components represent data as well as user interfaces in a unified way. Finally, contextual integration means that the context is preserved when the application component is changed.

Generally, there are various methods for system integration in distributed systems. A federated database system is an integrated system of autonomous (component) databases systems, having a virtual federated database schema in common. The term *middleware* describes the software components that serve for the communication between application components. Such middleware concepts comprise, e.g., RPC/RFC, components for database access, or special architectures such as CORBA. Finally, HTML offers a way to display and use interfaces on any given hardware or operating system platform.

Within hospital information systems, there are already specific methods and tools for the integration of distributed HIS. Data integration can be supported by communication servers and communication standards. A communication server is an application component that serves for the asynchronous sending, receiving, and buffering of messages. Main communication standards used in health care are HL7 (for the transfer of patient- and case-based messages) and DICOM (for the communication of images). Access and presentation integration are supported by CORBAmed, which standardizes object-oriented interfaces for the use of services and functions between application components in health care. Contextual integration is supported by the CCOW standards for the synchronization of independently developed application components on one computer.

When hospital information systems have to be integrated within a healthcare region, two main problems exist: The encryption of the messages, and the unique patient identification.

# 3.8 Example

### Example 3.8.1: Healthcare Professional Workstations Supporting Hospital Processes

In this example, typical activities and processes during a patient's stay in the Plötzberg Medical Center and Medical School (PMC) are described by means of a fictional example.[50] It is demonstrated which clinical business processes are typical, and in which way business processes in hospitals can be supported by healthcare professional workstations. This example presents

50. This text is based on the report "Medical Information Processing In Hospitals By Using Integrated Clinical Workstations—Conceptual Design" of the project "Innovative Data Processing Techniques in Hospitals" from the Department of Medical Informatics, University of Heidelberg, in cooperation with SAP AG and with the contribution of Andersen Consulting. In this project, processes in hospitals had already been defined in 1991 in order to specify the functionality of information processing tools. We would like to especially acknowledge the work of Christoph Isele and Jochen Pilz in the preparation of this example.

the more dynamic view as compared to the description of the hospital functions in section 3.2.

## Patient Treatment at a Physician's General Practice

Dr. Schroeder, a physician in general practice, diagnoses the patient Karl Hofmann, 62 years old, with a transient ischemic attack and suspected stenosis of the arteria carotis interna, based on a scotoma on the left side. He would like to hospitalize Mr. Hofmann for further examination and treatment.

Figure 3.63: In the patient administration department, during admission of a patient.

While Mr. Hofmann is in the doctor's consulting room, Dr. Schroeder calls the nearest hospital, the PMC, for the purpose of setting up a date for admission. Due to the nature of the medical problem, he is put through to the neurology department. The physician carrying out the admission knows that 7 days of treatment will have to be planned. He can see from the electronic synoptic chart of beds occupied displayed on his workstation that a bed will be vacant next Tuesday. He proposes that date for hospitalization.

Dr. Schroeder agrees. The physician performing admission enters Mr. Hofmann's name, date of birth, and the diagnosis for hospitalization under the assigned date. On the basis of these data, it can be clarified over the telephone that Mr. Hofmann had already been under medical care at the PMC at an earlier time. For identification, access is gained to the data of the patient management system (PMS) and the electronic patient record system (EPR) where Mr. Hofmann's former stays in the hospital are documented.

## Patient Admission to the Hospital

By the time of the patient's arrival at the PMC, the data of the most important documents (findings from the doctor's practice) are transmitted to the hospital by electronic data exchange.

### Administrative Admission

Mr. Hofmann arrives at the PMC on the assigned date. The employee in the patient administration department gathers from the chart of occupied beds displayed on her workstation that a reservation has been made and she admits Mr. Hofmann to the neurology department as a new patient (Figure 3.63).

On the patient's admission to the hospital, a magnetic card is filled out so that Mr. Hofmann can easily, rapidly, and positively be identified during his stay and so that he can avail himself of services such as making telephone calls.

Based on the contract of treatment concluded upon admission, measures for reimbursement of hospital charges by the health insurance plan may be initiated through the centralized computer-based patient management system.

After completion of the administrative admission, Mr. Hofmann is taken to his ward.

### Nursing Admission

On the ward, Mr. Hofmann is welcomed by the nurse Mrs. Weber. He tells her that he would like to have a single room. The healthcare professional workstation on the ward is connected to the communication network of the hospital. Mrs. Weber can see from the synoptic chart displayed on the monitor that a single room is available. She transfers Mr. Hofmann from the reserved bed to the bed in the single room.

The nurse then takes Mr. Hofmann through the ward. She shows him where the patients' bathroom is, and where he can get refreshments or a snack between meals.

The multifunctional patient terminal at the bedside includes a telephone. Under the corresponding number, Mr. Hofmann's name now appears on the telephone list.

Then, Mrs. Weber carries out the nursing admission. By using the nursing care planning and nursing care documentation functions of her healthcare professional workstation, the patient's state of health and other clinical observations are documented (Figure 3.64). Problems concerning nursing are noted, and for Mr. Hofmann nursing objectives and nursing measures are included in care planning. It is noted that Mr. Hofmann has false teeth and limitations in movement.

For part of nursing care planning, the nursing standards of the ward (hospital) can be used, while further measures specifically for Mr. Hofmann are noted. In the course of admission for nursing care, the habits of Mr. Hofmann are recorded as well, and later on will also be include in the patient's care plan.

Figure 3.64: Nurses preparing a nursing care plan at the healthcare professional workstation.

## Medical Admission

At the beginning of the medical admission, Dr. Schumacher, the attending neurologist, screens the information the patient has brought along with him (Figure 3.65). The most important data from the medical history and the essentials on the previous treatment of hypertension are noted in the patient's chart. Dr. Schumacher reviews the results of the last examination and sets up a current therapy plan.

Dr. Schumacher enters the patient history into the electronic patient record. In doing so, he is supported by the specific hardware of his healthcare professional workstation. The patient history sheet is displayed on the monitor. The physician can directly fill in the fields shown on the monitor. The system transcribes the handwriting and displays the entry on the patient history sheet.

# Decision Making, Planning, and Organization of Patient Treatment

## Presentation of Information and Knowledge

For compiling the patient history and for further planning of the patient's treatment, the documents received from the referring physician can be clearly presented on the display unit of the workstation. Reference books containing information on drugs and other medical information are integrated into the healthcare professional workstation. They assist the physician in gathering information on the therapy prescribed by the referring physician, in continuing the treatment of additional diseases (diabetes, hypertension), and in ordering, in the current case, further examinations for the purpose of determining the diagnoses. During compilation of the medical history, Dr. Schumacher may address direct inquiries to the aforementioned information services.

Figure 3.65: Recording findings from the physician's patient history in the healthcare professional workstation.

## Decision Making, Care Planning, and Patient Information

During the physician's round, Dr. Schumacher is going to instruct that, as a nursing procedure, regular blood pressure measurements should be taken based on the information he has on hand regarding the patient's hypertension (Figure 3.66).

He also orders a salt-free and diabetic diet for Mr. Hofmann.

For the current medical problem, Dr. Schumacher prescribes the administration of heparin from the standard spectrum of therapies that, in conjunction with the regular checking of coagulation factors, shall be carried out as a therapeutic measure.

As for further examinations, he reviews the spectrum of services offered by the service units. The selection is first automatically reduced to those measures deemed suitable in view of the current diagnosis. Dr. Schumacher orders a sonographic examination for the assessment of the stenosis, a computer-assisted tomogram for exclusion of infarction, and a blood test to analyze blood lipid concentration and coagulation factors.

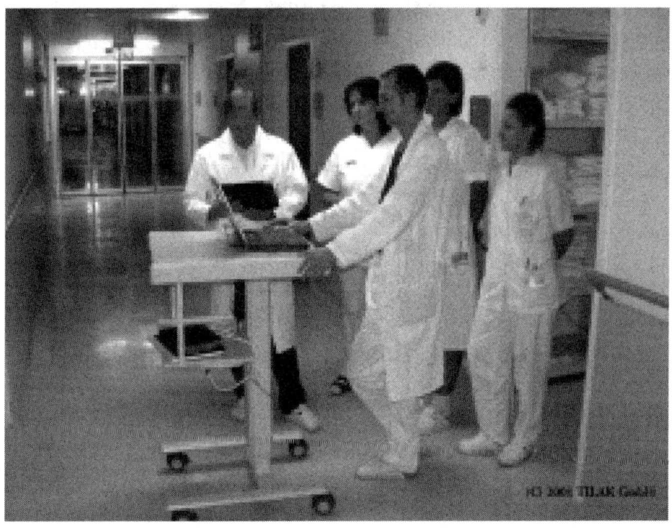

Figure 3.66: A physician reviewing data and entering orders at the ward's mobile healthcare professional workstation during the physician's round.

The nurse, Mrs. Weber, selects the "planning of meals" function on her healthcare professional workstation and enters Mr. Hofmann's request. The selection is restricted as a result of the diet that has been ordered, and the choice of food is automatically adapted to the requirements of diabetes and hypertension.

At a time arranged with the kitchen, an order based on the schedule data is generated concerning the diet and is passed on to the kitchen through the communication system.

## Execution of Diagnostic or Therapeutic Procedures

In the morning, the nurse prepares Mr. Hofmann's medication. She reads the name of the drugs and the prescribed dosages from the medical documentation on the healthcare professional workstation and, at the same time, documents their dispensing.

After instructions having been given by the physician, Mrs. Weber can see from the synoptic chart for the ward displayed on her workstation that a series of further measures have been ordered for her patient. She discusses how they are to be carried out with Dr. Schumacher. Those measures frequently recurring at regular intervals are supported by the documentation function of the healthcare professional workstation. The patient's blood pressure will be monitored and recorded using the documentation function.

The nurse prepares the catheter and the syringe for heparinization. Dr. Schumacher inserts the catheter to which he connects the automatic syringe containing the prescribed dose.

## Order Entry and Communication of Findings

During the period for which the checking of coagulation factors has been ordered, a request for a blood test will automatically be generated every day through the documentation system. The laboratory that will carry out the examination is assigned automatically in accordance with internal reservations.

The nurse generates a label with the patient identification (Figure 3.67) and the order number for the laboratory. A request for carrying out the order is automatically passed on to the laboratory through the communication system.

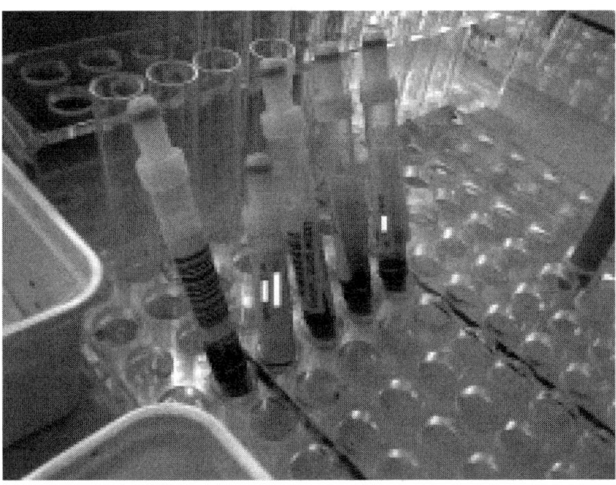

Figure 3.67: Machine-readable labels on blood samples.

For the laboratory test, a blood sample is taken from the patient, marked with the above label, and sent to the laboratory. A note is made using the documentation function of the healthcare professional workstation.

The sonographic and CT examinations are also requested by using the communication function. On this occasion, dates are set up with the performing service units for carrying out the examinations.

The results (texts and images) of the examinations are received from the lab and imaging department and are placed in the electronic patient record and in the physician's (electronic) mailbox. In this mailbox, all the findings that have not yet been read will be highlighted. Thus Dr. Schumacher is currently informed about which findings arrived on the ward and which were taken note of. A note is made automatically in the patient record that the results have arrived, and the time they are read is noted. The laboratory results can be displayed in various ways, e.g., displaying the time line of selected lab parameters.

## Decision Making, Planning, and Organization of Patient Treatment

The findings of the requested examinations for assessment of the stenosis, the sonographic result, and the computed tomography report can be displayed simultaneously. As far as the CT result is concerned, Dr. Schumacher can view a reference x-ray image selected by the radiologist on the monitor (Figure 3.68).

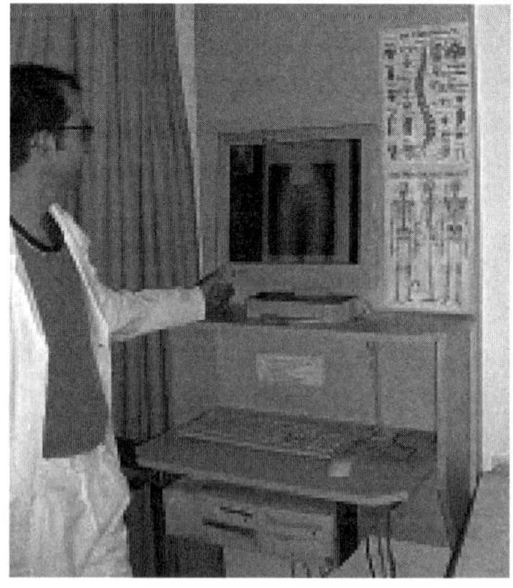

Figure 3.68: A physician reviewing digital radiological images in an examination room.

Following the interpretation of the examination results, Dr. Schumacher decides that the stenosis should be removed by vascular surgery. For support in his decision-making process, he can refer to a series of similar examples.

For localization of the stenosis he orders a digital subtraction angiography for Mr. Hofmann. Due to the specific nature of the problem, Dr. Schumacher contacts the radiology department himself. He also enters the date for Mr. Hofmann's angiography into the electronic radiological appointment book.

Stress and excitement about the forthcoming procedure leads to an increase in Mr. Hofmann's blood pressure, a circumstance realized by Dr. Schumacher during his ward round from the profile of blood pressure values shown on the portable display unit forming part of the healthcare professional workstation. He therefore increases the dose of the antihypertensive drug. This change in medication is recorded, via the portable display unit, in the medical documentation system and will be taken into account during the next dispensing of medicine.

## Order Entry and Scheduling

For scheduling of the surgical procedure, Dr. Schumacher contacts the Department for Vascular Surgery of the PMC and discusses Mr. Hofmann's case with the surgeon, Dr. Schoenberg, on the basis of the electronic patient record comprising the text documents, pictures, and sound documents to which both doctors may gain access from their workplaces. In addition, the documentation referring to the patient is made available by the neurologist to his colleague in the Department for Vascular Surgery.

They both agree on a date for the procedure. The patient data are displayed for Dr. Schoenberg on her monitor, and by using the management of resources function she makes the reservations for a bed and operating room.

Dr. Schumacher orders, as an administrative measure, the transfer of Mr. Hofmann on the agreed date. Recording of this transfer automatically takes place in the central patient management system, after acceptance of the transfer by Dr. Schoenberg. As a result, Mr. Hofmann's bed in the neurology department is marked as vacant from the date of transfer. The successful handling of the patient's transfer is documented by attributing the status "prepared" to the measure concerned.

## Referral to Another Department

On the date of transfer, Dr. Schumacher reviews both Mr. Hofmann's therapy and state of health. He can clearly present the values determined for coagulation factors, blood pressure, and diabetes control on the monitor. In the documentation displayed on the monitor, a special marking indicates the rise in blood pressure. Dr. Schumacher alters the limiting value in the reference function for blood pressure since a reduction of pressure to the normal value might compromise a sufficient supply of blood to the brain.

During his ward rounds, Dr. Schumacher confirms the transfer scheduled for that day. Thereafter, all the services provided to the patient are ceased and documented for billing purposes. Information about the services is transmitted to the department that is continuing treatment. Mr. Hofmann keeps the same telephone number that he had on his original ward. A transfer service is requested for taking him to the department performing further treatment.

The nurse generates a final report on nursing care, which she completes and signs, using her healthcare professional card for authentication.

The final report on nursing, the epicrisis (on the treatment given by then), and other essential documents are automatically made available to the department continuing treatment.

## Discharge From Hospital

After the procedure engendered no complications, Mr. Hofmann remains in the surgical department for a few more days of observation. The physician in the neurology department is informed about the outcome of the operation and the progress of recovery.

The patient is discharged from the PMC a short time later. His discharge is documented in the electronic patient record. Mr. Hofmann returns the patient card, and the services registered thereon are entered into the workstation.

Before leaving the hospital, Mr. Hofmann calls on the neurology department where the dates for postoperative care are set up. By way of the healthcare professional workstation, a (standard) plan for aftercare is proposed to Dr. Schumacher that he, together with Mr. Hofmann, adapts to the latter's requirements and desires.

Mr. Hofmann goes to the central office for patient admission and patient discharge, where he is given, upon leaving the hospital, a bill for those services that have to be reimbursed by the patient himself.

After completing the measures requested for Mr. Hofmann and documentation of the results, Dr. Schumacher writes a discharge report that is automatically generated. He completes the documents and electronically signs them.

Immediately after the patient's discharge from the hospital, the information relevant for further treatment, as well as a treatment plan, are electronically transmitted to Dr. Schroeder, the referring physician.

All of the information required for billing is automatically extracted from the documented patient data. An invoice of the services supplied is made out for the cost-reimbursing institution.

The administrative sector is also supported in converting the diagnosis on discharge into a code. This code, the master information on the patient, and other relevant data are compiled automatically and, through the communication system, are passed on to the patient records department.

After completion of the case, the patient is removed from the list of current patients, and the electronic patient record is archived—transmitted to an unalterable and indelible optical bulk storage location.

Should Mr. Hofmann be readmitted to the PMC for treatment at a future time, access to the electronic patient record can be gained again through the healthcare professional workstation.

## 3.9 Exercises

### Exercise 3.9.1: Hospital Functions and Processes

Look at the process presented in example 3.8.1. Match the different steps of a patient's stay in a hospital with the hospital functions presented in section 3.2.

### Exercise 3.9.2: Multiprofessional Treatment Teams

Look at the process presented in example 3.8.1. Describe the different healthcare professionals who are involved in patient care. What are their roles in the multiprofessional treatment team? Which healthcare professional groups are also important for patient care but not explicitly mentioned in the process description?

### Exercise 3.9.3: Information Needs of Different Healthcare Professionals

Look at the process presented in example 3.8.1. What are the most important information needs of the different healthcare professionals involved?

## 3.10 Summary

The typical main hospital functions are patient admission, planning, and organization of patient treatment, order entry and communication of findings, execution of diagnostic and therapeutic procedures, clinical documentation, administrative documentation and billing, and patient discharge and referral to other institutions. These hospital functions are typically supported by the functions handling patient records, work organization and resource planning, and hospital administration.

HIS models are used to support the description, management, and operation of HIS. A good model adequately supports information managers in these tasks. According to their different purposes, different metamodels (models of models) exist for HIS. We can, for example, refer to functional metamodels, technical metamodels, organizational metamodels, data metamodels, and business process metamodels.

A metamodel for modeling hospital information systems is the three-layer graph-based metamodel (3LGM). It is used to describe the static view of an HIS over three layers: the domain layer, the logical tool layer, and the physical tool layer.

Typically, an HIS comprises dedicated application components to support information processing in patient administration units, wards, outpatient units, diagnostic service units, therapeutic service units, and hospital administration units.

At the logical tool layer, we can distinguish between $DB^1$ and the $DB^n$ architectural styles, depending on the number of application components containing a database system. Typical architectural styles at the physical tool layer are the mainframe-based architecture and the client-server architecture. Today, distributed architectures on the logical and physical tool layers can usually be found.

Within distributed hospital information systems, special emphasis has to be placed on the integration of the various components. Integrity of data in the broadest sense means how the correct data are. We differentiate between formal integrity (object identity and referential integrity) and content integrity (supported by medical data dictionaries). Integration is a union of parts making a whole. We can distinguish data integration, access integration, presentation integration, and contextual integration. Methods and tools for system integration in distributed systems comprise federated database systems, middleware, and HTML. Special methods and tools for integrating hospital information systems comprise communication server and communication standards (for data integration), CORBAmed (for access and presentation integration), and CCOW (for contextual integration).

When hospital information system have to bc integrated within a healthcare region, two main problems occur: the encryption of the messages and the unique patient identification.

# 4 What Are Good Hospital Information Systems?

## 4.1 Introduction

Quality in general is the ability to meet all the expectations of the purchaser of goods or services, or, in other words, the degree to which a set of inherent characteristics fulfills requirements, where "requirements" means need or expectation.[51]

Three major approaches to quality assessment are quality of structures, quality of processes, and outcome quality.[52] In the context of health care, the concept of *quality of structures* means the human, physical, and financial resources that are needed to provide medical care (e.g., educational level of staff, availability of medical equipment). *Quality of processes* describes the quality of activities carried out by care providers (e.g., adherence to professional standards, appropriateness of care). Finally, *outcome quality* describes the effects of patient care, that is, the changes in the health status of the patient (e.g., mortality, morbidity, costs). While quality of structures influences quality of processes, quality of processes in turn influences outcome quality.

Those concepts can be transferred to hospital information systems. In this context, quality of structures refers to the availability of technical or human resources needed for information processing (e.g., number and availability of computer systems and other ICTs, i.e., the HIS infrastructure). Quality of processes deals with the quality of the information processes that are necessary to meet the user's needs. Outcome quality describes whether the goals of information management have been reached, or, in a broader sense, to what extent the hospital information system contributes to the goals of the hospital.

---

51. ISO. International Standard ISO 9000:2000. Quality management systems—Fundamentals and vocabulary. Geneva: International Organization for Standardization, International Electrotechnical Commission; 2000. http://www.iso.org.

52. Donabedian A. Explorations in quality assessing and monitoring, Vol 2: The criteria and standards of quality. Ann Arbor: Health Administration Press; 1982.

These quality concepts for hospital information systems can help to identify and solve problems concerning information processing. In other words, quality characteristics may help to describe HIS diseases (the problems), the corresponding HIS diagnoses (identification of the problems), and adequate HIS therapies (solution of the problems).

It may not be so difficult to describe what a bad hospital information system means. But what are characteristics and features of a good hospital information system? In this chapter, we introduce some of the most essential ones.

After reading this chapter, you should be able to answer the following questions:

- Which facets of quality have to be considered in hospital information systems?
- What are the characteristics of the quality of structures of HIS, and how can they be assessed?
- What are the characteristics of the quality of processes of HIS, and how can they be assessed?
- What are the characteristics of outcome quality of HIS, and how can they be assessed?
- What does information management have to balance in order to increase the quality of a hospital information system?

## 4.2 Quality of Structures

In the context of health care, the concept of quality of structures includes the human, physical, and financial resources that are needed to provide medical care (e.g., educational level of staff, availability of medical equipment). In the context of hospital information systems, the quality of structures refers to the availability of technical or human resources needed for information processing (e.g., infrastructure of the information system, computer knowledge of staff). It comprises quality characteristics of data, of information processing tools, and of component integration.

After reading this chapter, you should be able to answer the following questions:

- What criteria for quality of data exist?
- What criteria for information processing tools exist?
- What criteria for the integration of components exist?

### *Quality of Data*

Data that are stored and processed in a hospital information system should adhere to certain criteria for data quality, such as

- correctness (e.g., correct patient name),
- integrity (see section 3.7),
- reliability (e.g., no element of uncertainty with regard to the patient's name),
- completeness (e.g., no administrative data on the patient are missing),
- accuracy (e.g., patient data are as detailed as necessary),
- relevancy (e.g., no irrelevant data such as number of grandchildren are stored),
- authenticity (e.g., the authorship of a discharge report is clear and indisputable),
- availability (e.g., recent lab results are available on the ward),
- confidentiality and security (e.g., the diagnoses of a patient are only accessible to the treating healthcare professionals), and
- safety (e.g., data are is secure from being lost in case of technical failures).

When databases are involved, the common *normal forms* of databases should also be taken into account.

## *Quality of Information Processing Tools*

The quality of information processing tools can be separated into quality of application components and the quality of data processing components. The quality of information processing tools can usually be assessed using system analysis, evaluation, and assessment methods. In general, only a missing or erroneous information processing tool should attract attention.

## Quality of Application Components

Computer-based application components are controlled by *application programs*, which are adapted *software products*. These software products have to have a certain quality. The main characteristics of this *software quality* have been defined by ISO 9126.[53] The objective of this standard is to provide a framework for the evaluation of software quality. ISO 9126 sets out six quality characteristics with corresponding subcharacteristics:

- Functionality: Are the required functions available in the software?
- Reliability: How reliable is the software?
- Usability: Is the software easy to use?

53. ISO. International Standard ISO/IEC 9126-1. Information technology—Software product evaluation—Quality characteristics and guidelines for their use. Geneva: International Organization for Standardization, International Electrotechnical Commission; 2001. http://www.iso.org.

- Efficiency: How efficient is the software?
- Maintainability: How easy is it to modify the software?
- Portability: How easy is it to transfer the software to another environment?

ISO 9241[54] specifically deals with *software ergonomics*. It contains 17 parts. Part 10 of this standard deals with dialogue principles for user interface design. A high level of software ergonomics is very important in HIS because healthcare professionals spend only a smaller amount of their working time at computers, they are not trained computer workers, and they often have to use various application components. In addition, staff turnover is very high, so the software products should be easy to learn and to use.

The dialogue principles of ISO 9241 are as follows:

- Suitability for the task: Does the user interface support the user in fulfilling his tasks effectively and efficiently?
- Suitability for learning: Is the user being supported to learn and use the user interface?
- Suitability for individualization: Can the user interface be adapted to the tasks and to the individual skills and needs of the user?
- Conformity with user expectations: Is the user interface consistent and adapted to the characteristics of the user (e.g., his knowledge, skills, and expectations)?
- Self-descriptiveness: Is each step of the user interface understandable for the user by providing direct feedback or explanation?
- Controllability: Can the user, after having initiated the first step, control the flow and speed of tasks?
- Error tolerance: Can the task be completed if obviously wrong input is entered by the user, with either little or no effort to correct it?

Many of those quality criteria also can be applied to paper-based information processing tools (Figure 4.1).

54. ISO. International Standard ISO 9241. Ergonomics requirements for office work with visual display terminals (VDTs). Geneva: International Organization for Standardization, International Electrotechnical Commission; 1993. http://www.iso.org.

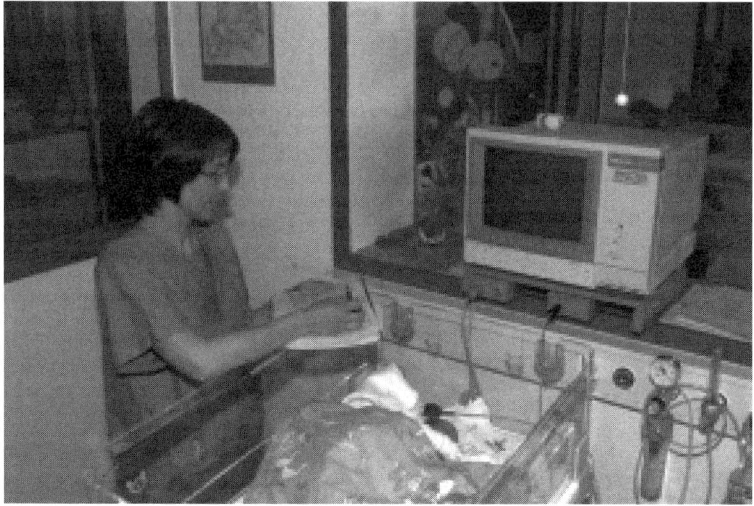

Figure 4.1: Paper-based documentation at the patient's bedside, using an easy-to-use, stable, mobile, paper-based information processing tool.

## Quality of Data Processing Components

The quality of physical information processing tools can be described by the following characteristics:

- Appropriateness (e.g., not dominating the physician-patient relationship),
- Availability (e.g., mobile tool that is not restricted to a certain place),
- Multiple usability (multipurpose, e.g., personal digital assistant),
- Efficiency (e.g., low cost for purchase and support),
- Flexibility (e.g., can be modified easily),
- Stability and reliability,
- Security (e.g., supporting basic data security, data safety, as well as electrical safety),
- Harmlessness (e.g., not harming the user or the patient),
- Usability (e.g., easy to use, user friendly), and
- Standardization (e.g., standardized form for order entry).

In addition, several country-specific regulations concerning the quality of medical-technical equipment have to be considered, especially in service units such as operation rooms.

Many of those quality criteria also can be applied to paper-based information processing tools (compare Figures 4.2 und 4.3).

Figure 4.2: A bed as a flexible tool, also supporting information processing tasks.

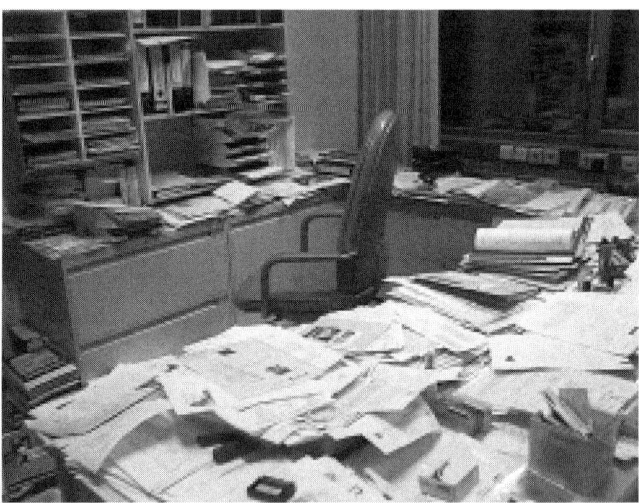

Figure 4.3: In a senior physician's office, "special" organization of work using paper-based tools.

## *Quality of Component Integration*

HIS architecture should ensure that the different computer-based and paper-based information processing tools can be smoothly and efficiently coordinated, in order to provide a maximum quality of information processing.

Quality of component integration can comprise various characteristics, such as data integration, access integration, presentation integration, and contextual integration. They have been presented in detail in section 3.7.

In general, the systematic management of the HIS can help to achieve a component integration that is able to support the main functions of a hospital. Methods and tools for integrating components within distributed hospital information systems have also been described in section 3.7.

Besides the diverse aspects of integration quality, two other aspects will be discussed here that are also related to the quality of component integration: adaptability and flexibility of the HIS, and controlled redundancy of data.

## Adaptability and Flexibility

In general, the hospital information system should be sufficiently flexible to adapt to the changing needs of the hospital. For example, it should be easy to add new computer-based application components to the information systems, and application components should be easily replaceable by other (advanced) application components. A star-based architecture with a communication server (see section 3.6) supports the exchanging or adding of new computer-based application components. Additionally, the available bandwidth of the network infrastructure should be easily extendable to match the increasing volume of communication.

## Controlled Redundancy of Data

Usually, redundant data storage should be avoided. However, there are reasons why redundant data storage is unavoidable, mostly because commercial software products that have their own database system and that use the same patient data are bought. For example, most application components need patient administrative data. In a communication-based (not database-centered) architecture, this data redundancy can be systematically managed if one administrative application component with its master database system (see section 3.7) has to distribute new or updated patient administrative data to the other application components. All of those other application components may redundantly store patient data in their database systems.

Sometimes, data redundancy is valuable. For example, data may be stored redundantly in different sites in order to avoid data loss in case of systems failures. Or patient data may be available in the electronic patient record, but also as copy in a microfiche archive or in a paper archive. Also, data may be duplicated on different hard discs in a specific database server (e.g., using redundant array of independent discs [RAID] technology), allowing reconstruction of data when a hard disc fails.

But this data redundancy must be systematically managed. In particular, it must be clear which component is the master source of the data, when data copies are made, for which purpose they are made, and in which case changes of the master data are communicated to the data copies. Only a thorough planning, monitoring, and directing of data redundancy in a hospital information system can avoid the proliferation of data and the uncontrolled, chaotic storage media redundancy.

## *Exercises*

### Exercise 4.2.1: Diagnoses and Therapy of Quality of Structures

Various quality criteria for the structures of hospital information systems have been presented. Discuss how you can diagnose an insufficient quality of structures: Which method could you use to assess each of the mentioned quality criteria? Then explain how you could deal with an insufficient quality of structures: What can be done to improve the different aspects of the quality of structures?

### Exercise 4.2.2: Quality of Information Processing Tools

Various quality criteria for the quality of information processing tools have been presented. They primarily focus on computer-based components. Discuss how those criteria can be applied to paper-based information processing tools.

## *Summary*

Criteria for quality of structures of hospital information systems comprise quality of data, quality of information processing tools, and quality of component integration.

- Quality of data comprises issues such as correctness, integrity, reliability, completeness, accuracy, relevance, authenticity, availability, confidentiality and security, and safety.
- Quality of information processing tools comprise quality of application components (such as software quality and software ergonomics), and quality of data processing components (such as usefulness, appropriateness, availability, multiple usability, etc.).
- Quality of component integration comprises adaptability and flexibility of the HIS and controlled redundancy of data.

## 4.3 Quality of Processes

In general, quality of processes describes the quality of activities carried out by care providers (e.g., adherence to professional standards, appropriateness of care). In the context of hospital information systems, quality of processes deals with the quality of the information processes that are necessary to meet the user's needs.

Criteria for quality of processes in HIS comprise efficiency of information logistics, leanness of information processing tools, single recording and multiple usability of data, controlled transcription of data and no media cracks, and patient-centered information processing.

The quality of processes can be assessed using system analysis and evaluation methods, especially by methods for analyzing and optimizing business processes where various methods and tools exist.

After reading this chapter, you should be able to answer the following question:

- What are the characteristics of the quality of processes of HIS, and how can they be assessed?

### *Efficiency of Information Logistics*

Information processing should be as efficient as possible. It should not contain unnecessary steps (e.g., documentation of data that are never used again), should be as parallel as possible, should allow the multiple usability of data, and should avoid redundant activities (e.g., transcription of data).

In general, information logistics (see section 2.4) should be organized as efficiently as possible (compare Figure 4.3):

- The right information: Is the information correct, reliable, and valid? For example, is the patient identification on the lab result correct?
- At the right time: Is the information available when the healthcare professional needs it (*just in time*)? For example, are the recent lab results available during the physician's round?
- At the right place: Is the information available wherever the healthcare professional needs it? For example, is nursing documentation available at the patient's bedside as well as in the ward office?
- To the right people: Is the information available only to the healthcare professional needing it? For example, are the diagnoses of a patient only available to the treating healthcare professionals? Is data protection guaranteed?
- In the right form: Is the information available in a usable format for the healthcare professional? For example, can information personally be filtered (*personal filtering*), not overwhelming the healthcare professional with too much information (*information overload*)?

### *Leanness of Information Processing Tools*

The user wants to use as few application components and data processing components as possible for a given task. Thus for each task, there should be as many different tools as necessary but as few as possible. For example, during nursing documentation, how many information processing tools does a nurse have to use (e.g., an application component for care planning, another application component for report writing, and the paper-based record for order entry)? The fewer the information processing tools that have to be used for one task, the easier it is for the staff. In addition, information processing tools should not dominate the processes. For example, the communication between healthcare professional and patient as well as within the healthcare professional team may not be good if it is supported by powerful computer systems with large screens. Thus, information processing tools should stay more in the background.

### *Single Recording, Multiple Usability of Data*

Application components often need the same data. For example, patient administrative data or basic medical data are needed by many different application components. To avoid duplicate data entry, which is inefficient and prone to error, data should be recorded only once, even when they are used by different application components and stored in different databases. One prerequisite is data integration (compare section 3.7). Multiple usability of data is one of the most important benefits computer support can bring to information systems.

### *Controlled Transcription of Data, No Media Cracks*

Transcription of data should be avoided. Transcription means the transfer of data from one storage device to another storage device, e.g., to transfer patient diagnoses from the patient record to an order entry form, or to copy data from a printout into a computer-based application component (Figures 4.4 and 4.5). Transcription usually leads to the duplication of data. This has to be avoided as it is time-consuming and possibly erroneous. Transcription is usually combined with a change of the storage media (*media crack*), but can also include the transfer from paper to paper.

Figure 4.4: Example of a transcription (1).

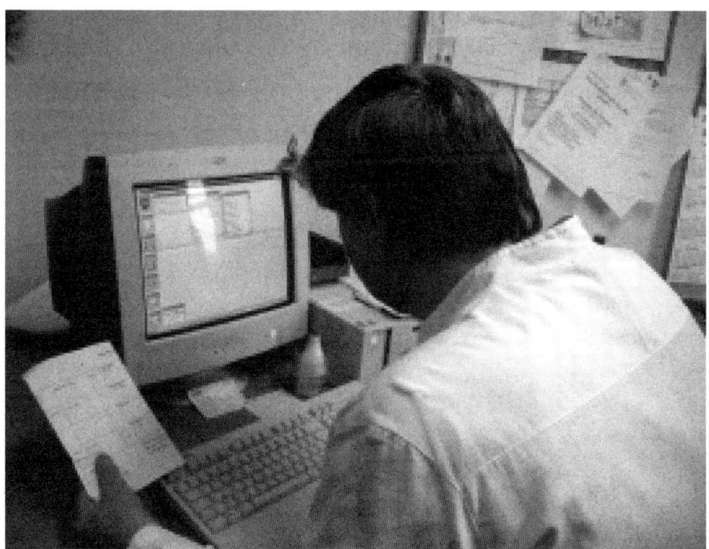

Figure 4.5: Example of a transcription (2).

## *Patient-Centered Information Processing*

The degree of highly specialized and distributed patient care creates a great demand for integrated information processing among healthcare professionals and among healthcare institutions (compare section 0). Information processing therefore should center on the patient (not on the institution). This means, for example, that all relevant data about a patient should be made available to any healthcare professional involved in the care of the patient. The availability of an electronic patient record system that stores all data about a patient is usually the precondition for real patient-centered information processing.

## *Exercises*

### Exercise 4.3.1: Diagnoses and Therapy of Quality of Processes

Various quality criteria for the quality of processes of hospital information systems have been presented. Discuss how you would assess the different aspects of an insufficient quality of processes. Which method could you use to assess each of the cited quality criteria? Then explain how you could deal with an insufficient quality of processes: What can be done to improve the different aspects of the quality of processes?

### Exercise 4.3.2: Transcription of Data

Look at Figures 4.4, 4.5, 4.6, and 4.7. They show four examples of transcriptions. Answer the following questions:

- In which process may this transcription take place?
- Which data may be transcribed?
- Which tools are involved? Is the transcription associated with a media crack?
- Which negative consequences may this transcription have?
- What can be done to avoid the transcription or to avoid errors?

Figure 4.6: Example of a transcription (3).

Figure 4.7: Example of a transcription (4).

### Exercise 4.3.3: Leanness of Information Processing Tools

Explain how the leanness of information processing tools, as described above, is correlated with the transcription of data and media cracks.

### Exercise 4.3.4: Quality of Processes

Have a look at Figure 4.8, an extract from a simplified UML activity diagram process model of the process "ordering meals" from the Plötzberg Medical Center and Medical School (PMC). Which of the criteria for quality of processes is not fulfilled? How could the process be changed (e.g., by using other information processing tools) to improve the quality of processes?

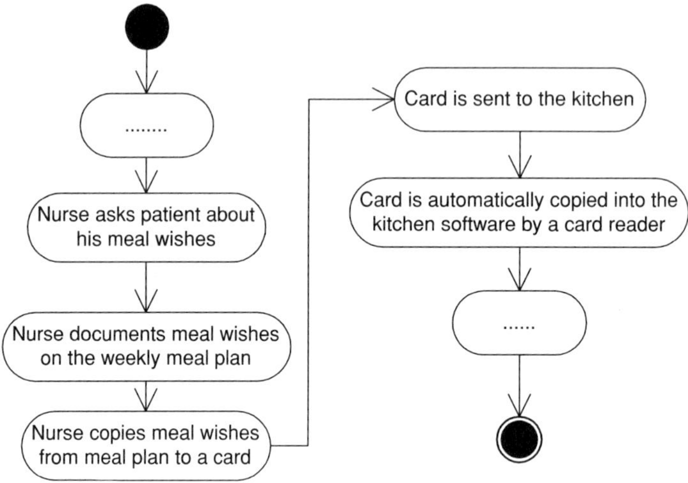


Figure 4.8: Extract from the business process "meal ordering."

### *Summary*

The criteria for quality of processes of hospital information systems are

- efficiency of information logistics (e.g., correctness and completeness, just-in-time information, availability, personal filtering);
- leanness of information processing tools;
- single recording, multiple usability of data;
- controlled transcription of data, no media cracks;
- patient-centered information processing.

## 4.4 Outcome Quality

In general, outcome quality describes the effects of patient care, that is, the changes in the health status of the patient (e.g., mortality, morbidity, costs). In the context of hospital information systems, outcome quality describes whether the goals of information management have been reached, or, in a broader sense, to what extent the hospital information system contributed to the goals of the hospital and to the expectations of different stakeholders.

Quality of outcomes thus means whether the hospital information system finally fulfills the needs of its different user groups and thus supports efficient and effective patient care. Outcome quality describes the measurable value of the HIS for the hospital and its various stakeholders. Despite good quality of structures and processes, it is not proven that the hospital information system contributes to the aims of the hospital or the expectations of the stakeholders. Quality of structures and quality of processes is just a prerequisite for outcome quality.

The outcome quality of HIS can be assessed using system analysis and evaluation methods such as assessment studies.

After reading this chapter, you should be able to answer the following question:

- What are the characteristics of outcome quality of HIS, and how can they be assessed?

## *Fulfillment of the Hospital's Goals*

For the hospital as an enterprise, the hospital information system should contribute to

- quality improvement,
- patient satisfaction, and
- cost reduction

as general aims of all hospitals. Additional hospital aims include

- fulfillment of legal requirements,
- support of clinical research, and
- being a specialized medical competence center.

Furthermore, each individual hospital wants to attain further specific goals, in which the HIS can participate. For example:

- Efficient communication with other health providers (e.g., quick communication of discharge reports to the next health provider).
- All patient-related information is available during patient's stay.
- A comprehensive electronic patient record should be established.
- The use of personal mobile information processing tools should be extended.
- User interface design should be optimized to reduce the necessary teaching time.
- Patients should be able to access the content of "their" electronic patient record.
- Medical research should be able to exploit the data stored in the electronic patient record.

## *Fulfillment of Information Management Laws*

In each country, different laws affect health information processing, addressing, for example, organization of health care, financing of health care, and health statistics. Those laws must be taken into account by information management.

An important part of these laws deal with data protection. Health-related patient data are most sensitive and must be protected from unauthorized access. Normally, only those healthcare professionals involved in the treatment of patients should be able to access patient data. And only those data that are of potential importance for optimal patient care should be stored. For example, for a surgical patient, earlier psychiatric stays may not be relevant to the surgeon. The information system should be designed in such a way that data protection (as defined by the national laws) is guaranteed.

For example, in the United States, the Health Insurance Portability and Accountability Act (HIPAA) of 1996 deals with standards for electronic data interchange, protection of security and confidentiality of electronic health information, and unique identifiers for providers and patients.[55] In Germany, laws on the organization of health care (SGB V[56]), on its financing (KHG,[57] BPflV[58]), on data protection (BDSG[59]), on digital signatures (IuKDG[60]), and on hospital statistics have to be taken into account in information management.

## *Fulfillment of the Expectations of Different Stakeholders*

As well, distinct stakeholders have specific expectations. The following user needs should be addressed:

---

55. Health Insurance Portability and Accountability Act (HIPAA). http://www.cms.gov/hipaa.

56. Basler D, Sander A. Fünftes Buch Sozialgesetzbuch V (SGB V). Editio Cantor; 2002. Also: http://www.sozialgesetzbuch.de/gesetze/index.php.

57. Jung K (eds). Krankenhausfinanzierungsgesetz (KHG). Stuttgart: Kohlhammer; 1985. Also: http://www.bmgesundheit.de/downloads-gesetze/gesetzlichekranken-versicherung/soli/khg.htm.

58. Tuschen KH, Quaas M. Bundespflegesatzverordnung (BpflV). Stuttgart: Kohlhammer; 2001.

59. Gola P, Schomderus R, Ordemann H-J. Bundesdatenschutzgesetz (BDSG). C.H. Beck; 2002. Also: http://jurcom5.juris.de/bundesrecht/bdsg_1990/gesamt.pdf.

60. Informations-und Kommunikationsdienstgesetz (IuKDG). http://www.iid.de/rahmen/iukdgbt.html.

- Patient: Availability of up-to-date medical knowledge gives the staff more time for the patient, as they don't waste time on unnecessary documentation tasks or inflexible information processing tools.
- Relatives: The patient can easily be found in the hospital, and information for home care is made available.
- Physicians: Test results are available at the physician's rounds, so that not time is lost with insufficiently designed information processing tools. Multiple usability of data, the availability of the whole patient record, simple and standardized forms for data entry, and access to new medical knowledge are important.
- Nurses: Easy procedures for scheduling and order entry, availability of bedside documentation tools, support of ward organization, and easy access to nursing guidelines and to nursing knowledge are provided.
- Administrative staff: Up-to-date administrative information and efficient tools to support billing and financial budgeting are available.
- Hospital management: Easy access to complete and up-to-date information on the quality of patient care and on its costs is provided.

## *Exercises*

### Exercise 4.4.1: Diagnoses and Therapy of Outcome Quality

Various quality criteria for the outcome quality of hospital information systems have been presented. Discuss how you can diagnose insufficient outcome quality. Which method would you use to assess each of the cited quality criteria? Then explain how you would deal with insufficient outcome quality. What can be done to improve the different aspects of outcome quality?

### Exercise 4.4.2: National Laws for Information Processing

As described above, information processing has to take into account the different laws of the respective country. Find out (e.g., using information from the Internet, from publications, or from other lectures) which laws are important for your country with regard to information processing. Briefly describe the content of the laws.

## *Summary*

The criteria for outcome quality of hospital information systems are

- fulfillment of the hospital's goals,
- fulfillment of the information management laws, and
- fulfillment of the expectations of different stakeholders.

## 4.5 Balance as a Challenge for Information Management

Besides quality criteria, optimal balance is also a determinant of the quality of the hospital information system. This is a particular challenge for information management, as it must weigh the different—and possibly contradicting—goals of the hospital. The solution will require the ability of those responsible for information management to carry through with their goals, and the willingness of the affected stakeholders to compromise. Above all, an appropriate organization of strategic information management is required. Systematic information management is discussed in Chapter 5.

After reading this section, you should be able to answer the following question:

- What does information management have to balance in order to increase the quality of a hospital information system?

### *Balance of Homogeneity and Heterogeneity*

The collection of information processing tools (both on the logical and on the physical tool layer) should be as homogeneous (i.e., comparable in appearance and usability, for example using tools from the same vendor) as possible and as heterogeneous as necessary. In general, a homogeneous set of information processing tools makes training and support of users easier and thus leads to reduced costs for the HIS. However, in reality, we usually find a very heterogeneous set of tools at both the logical and the physical tool layer. Why?

At the logical tool layer, we need application components for the support of the hospital functions (see section 3.2). Maximum homogeneity, at least for the computer-supported part of the hospital information system, can easily be reached when just one computer-based application component exists that is implemented through a single software product from a single manufacturer. Normally, this can be realized only when the hospital produces its own software. As this is not economically feasibly for hospitals, diverse software products are purchased, which can lead to a very heterogeneous HIS. This is especially true when products are chosen from different manufacturers. These products might please the various stakeholders of the hospital (which will all have optimal support for *their* tasks), but they will make integration, operation, and user support much more difficult. These difficulties are often overlooked by the concerned stakeholders. In this situation, it is the task of information management to ensure and support an appropriate compromise between the hospital's need for economical homogeneous information processing and the needs of the various stakeholders.

At the physical tool layer, the heterogeneity is often the consequence of the evolution of the HIS, comprising different generations of computer systems and application components. This could be prevented only if all components are regularly completely exchanged, which is generally not sensible.

Heterogeneity is not always bad. Moreover, heterogeneity is appropriate to a certain degree. But when heterogeneity of information processing tools is not systematically managed, it can lead to the uncontrolled proliferation of tools and to unnecessary costs. The better all stakeholders are involved in strategic information management through an appropriate organization, the more this situation can be avoided.

## *Balance of Computer-Based and Paper-Based Tools*

It is the task of information management to manage information processing in such a way that the goals of the hospital can best be reached. So, for a hospital whose goal is to provide very personal and humane treatment, it might be sensible, for example, to abstain from the use of technology and especially computers as much as possible for all immediate physician-patient contact. It is possible to write notes on the ward with paper and pen rather than using electronic tools, depending on what best supports the hospital's functions. For a hospital whose goals it technological leadership, it might be appropriate to proceed in the opposite direction.

That is, the optimum of computer support is not defined by the maximum; rather, it evolves through the various goals of the hospital and its stakeholders as well as through the hospital functions to be supported.

## *Balance of Data Security and Functionality*

The data saved in a hospital information system are worth protecting. Every patient must be confident that his or her data won't be made available to a third party. To ensure this, the appropriate laws of the particular country are to be adhered to. However, hospital information systems are not just purely technical, but rather are socio-technical systems. This means that people are also part of the information system and are therefore also responsible for data security and protection.

A hospital information system should implement strict access control methods to ensure that unauthorized access is impossible. However, this can lead to hindrances in the execution of hospital function. For example, it may occur that a medication cannot be prescribed in an emergency when the attending physician belongs to another hospital department and therefore doesn't have the right to read the clinical-chemical result or to order a medication. This can, in an extreme case, even lead to a life-threatening situation. Thus, an access control system that is strict and adapted to predefined tasks and roles in a department can hinder the cooperation between healthcare professionals and other departments. This would be unfortunate, as it is the job of information management to build the HIS such that cooperation is supported. Consequently, following a thorough risk analysis, it should be weighed whether access control measures in certain situations should be less strict for medical staff, thereby strengthening their own level of responsibility.

Similar risks should be considered in determining how long data should be kept. Healthcare laws, research needs, and lawsuit requirements should be addressed. So, for example, following the expiration of the storage period, if documents are destroyed, it could be difficult to prove that the hospital carried out a correct medical process in the event of a lawsuit. The resulting consequences would be requests for damage compensation and possibly punishment. However, long-term storage of data may be costly and space-consuming (e.g., archive room, disk storage capacity). Risk management must be carried out with strong support from hospital management.

### *Balance of Functional Leanness and Functional Redundancy*

*Functional leanness* describes a situation where one hospital function is supported by one and only one application component; the opposite is *functional redundancy* which results in additional costs both for investment and maintenance. But as discussed with controlled data redundancy (compare section 4.2), functional redundancy is not always bad. For example, patient admission may be supported by application components other than the patient management system and the application component for the delivery room's management. Even if this conflicts with functional leanness, it may be suitable to have a more convenient graphical tool in the clinical area and a faster and text-oriented tool for specialized administrative staff. Thus it is the management's task to check carefully where and why there is functional redundancy, because unmanaged functional redundancy may lead to *functional oversaturation* and unnecessary costs.

As a consequence, these checks may lead to the necessity of declaring an application component to be *superfluous.* Don't hesitate to remove those components; otherwise the HIS will become *logically oversaturated.*

### *Summary*

Besides quality criteria, which should be fulfilled as well as possible, an optimal balanced situation is also a determinant of the quality of the hospital information system. This is a particular challenge for information management. These criteria comprise:

- Balance of homogeneity and heterogeneity: The collection of information processing tools (at both the logical and the physical tool layer) should be as homogeneous as possible and as heterogeneous as necessary.
- Balance of computer-based and paper-based tools: The optimum of computer support is not defined through the maximum; rather, it evolves through the various goals of the hospital and its stakeholders as well as through the hospital functions to be supported.
- Balance of data security and functionality: Risk should be weighed for the determination of how data security is achieved, and how long data should be kept.
- Balance of functional leanness and functional redundancy: Functional redundancy results in additional costs both for investment and maintenance, but there may be reasons to have redundant functionality.

## 4.6 Examples

The following examples present various attempts to describe quality criteria for HIS.

### Example 4.6.1: The Baldrige Healthcare Information Management Criteria

This example is taken from the Malcolm Baldrige National Quality Award Program[61]:

> Describe how your organization ensures the quality and availability of needed data and information for staff, suppliers/partners, and patients/customers. Within your response, include answers to the following questions:
>
> a. Data Availability
>
> (1) How do you make needed data and information available? How do you make them accessible to staff, suppliers/partners, and patients/customers, as appropriate?
>
> (2) How do you ensure data and information integrity, reliability, accuracy, timeliness, security, and confidentiality?
>
> (3) How do you keep your data and information availability mechanisms current with healthcare service needs and directions?
>
> b. Hardware and Software Quality
>
> (1) How do you ensure that hardware and software are reliable and user friendly?
>
> (2) How do you keep your software and hardware systems current with healthcare service needs and directions?

61. National Institute of Standards and Technology, Baldrige National Quality Program. http://www.baldrige.org.

**Example 4.6.2: The Davies CPR Award of Excellence**

The Computer-Based Record Institute (CPRI, now CPRI-HOST) established the Davies Recognition Program[62] in 1994 to recognize exemplary implementations of computer-based patient records (CPRs). The rationale was to foster wider adoption in the industry by highlighting and sharing lessons learned from organizations that have successfully used computer-based records to improve healthcare delivery. The first awards were granted in 1995, and a total of 13 organizations have been recognized in the first six years of the program through 2000.

The award is organized into four sections:

*Management*

- CPR planning: Assess the planning process for the CPR system, the relationship between system planning and the business strategy of the healthcare organization, and the business case used to justify and guide the investment.
- Implementation: Assess the approach to implementation and evolution of the CPR system, and the key factors that contributed to success.
- Operations: Assess the management of ongoing operations of the CPR system.
- Evaluation of management of the CPR effort.

*Functionality*

- Targeted processes: Describe the clinical, administrative, and financial processes and the goals for supporting those processes that drove the functional design of the CPR system.
- Information access: Describe the extent to which information managed by the CPR system meets critical organizational needs.
- Decision support: Describe the extent to which the CPR system provides tools for supporting clinical decisions at the point of care and for improving clinical practice and care delivery. The mix and specifics of decision support capabilities may differ according to the setting and organizational objectives.
- Work flow and communication: Assess the extent to which the CPR supports the work and work flow of care delivery and local and cross-setting communications between and among healthcare professionals and patients, support staff, and other departments.
- Other operational and strategic activities: Describe the extent to which the CPR supports other key organizational activities, as relevant.

---

62. Nicholas E. Davies CPR Recognition Award of Excellence Program. http://www.cpri-host.org/davies/index.html.

- User satisfaction, productivity, and effectiveness: Assess the overall success of the implemented CPR in supporting essential users of the system and care delivery processes of the organization.

*Technology*

- Scope and design of CPR system: Describe the scope and technical design of the CPR system, including software applications and tools used to implement and operate the system.
- Security and integrity: Describe the strategy and approaches for managing, maintaining, and enabling audits of system security, data confidentiality, and integrity in support of the standards and business objectives of the healthcare organization. Compliance with HIPAA security and privacy requirements should be addressed.
- Standards: Describe the adoption of standards to facilitate data standardization and data sharing within the healthcare organization and with external organizations and parties.
- Performance: Assess how the technology for the CPR system has supported its end-users such that it (1) ensures that the CPR system meets desired levels of performance necessary to support key users and business processes on a reliable, sustained basis, and (2) supports advances in technology and growth and organizational changes in the business of the healthcare organization.

*Value*

- Success in meeting expectations of the business case.
- Success in achieving desired change in targeted processes.
- Success in meeting other corporate objectives.

### Example 4.6.3: The JCAHO Information Management Standards

The Joint Commission on Accreditation of Healthcare Organizations (JCAHO)[63] is an independent, not-for-profit organization. It evaluates and accredits more than 19,500 healthcare organizations in the United States, e.g., hospitals, healthcare networks, ambulatory care units, long-term-care facilities, and laboratories. Accreditation means to certify that an institution meets predefined quality standards. JCAHO standards are nationally recognized as those that are conducive to providing a high standard of patient care. External evaluation is done at regular time intervals (e.g., three years). To comply with the standards, organizations usually develop a strategic information management plan.

63. Joint Commission on Accreditation of Healthcare Organizations (JCAHO), http://www.jcaho.org.

JCAHO has defined standards that must be fulfilled to achieve accreditation. Those standards comprise, for example, aspects of patient care, data security, and staff management. Since 1994, 10 information management standards have been introduced. Standards 1 to 6 are planning standards, and standards 7 to 10 deal with standards and scoring guidelines using the different types of information that must be linked to provide useful information for management's decision-making processes.

The information management standards are as follows:

1. The hospital plans and designs information management processes to meet internal and external information needs that are appropriate for the hospital's size and complexity.
2. Confidentiality, security, and integrity of data and information are maintained.
3. Uniform data definitions and data capture methods are used whenever possible.
4. Decision makers and other appropriate staff members are educated and trained in the principles of information management.
5. Transmission of data and information is timely and accurate, and the formats for disseminating data and information are standardized.
6. Adequate integration and interpretation capabilities are provided.
7. The hospital defines, captures, analyses, transforms, transmits, and reports patient-specific data and information related to care processes and outcomes.
8. The hospital collects and analyzes aggregate data to support patient care and operations.
9. The hospital provides systems, resources, and services to meet its needs for knowledge-based information in patient care, education, research, and management.
10. Comparative performance data and information are defined, collected, analyzed, transmitted, reported, and used consistently with national and state guidelines for data set parity and connectivity.

The information management standards are further divided into several sub-sections. For example, the subsections of information management standard number 7 comprise the following criteria: entries are made in patient records as soon as possible after the event; all entries are authenticated: operative reports are written or dictated immediately after surgery; and so on.

### Example 4.6.4: The KTQ Information Management Standards

Cooperation for Transparency and Quality in Hospitals (KTQ)[64] is a voluntary accreditation program for German hospitals. It has been developed since 1997 by the German hospital federation, the German medical association, and German health insurance institutions.

KTQ focuses on the quality of patient care and presents criteria for six main areas: patient care that is oriented to the needs of the patient, staff development and staff integration, patient and staff safety, information management, hospital management, and quality management. The aim is to support continuous quality improvement by offering criteria that can be used both for self-assessment and external assessment of the quality of patient care in a hospital.

The main information management criteria (which are then further explained) are as follows:

- Regulations for management, documentation, and archiving of patient data exist.
- Documentation of patient data is complete, correct, and reproducible.
- Regulations exist to guarantee that patient data are available whenever they are needed.
- Regulations exist for information transfer within and between hospital departments.
- Central information offices of the hospital have up-to-date information.
- The hospital regularly informs the public.
- Data protection is guaranteed.
- A sufficient information technology infrastructure is available.

## 4.7 Exercise

### Exercise 4.7.1: Quality Criteria for Hospital Information Systems

In the examples in section 4.6, different aspects of HIS quality are described. Analyze how they correspond to the quality criteria for structures, for processes, and for outcomes as described in Chapter 4. Which can be matched, and which cannot? Why?

64. Kooperation für Transparenz und Qualität im Krankenhaus (cooperation for transparence and quality in the hospital), http://www.ktq.de.

## 4.8 Summary

Three major approaches to quality assessment are typically distinguished: quality of structures, quality of processes, and outcome quality. Quality characteristics may help to describe "HIS diseases," find "HIS diagnoses," and derive adequate "HIS therapies."

In the context of hospital information systems, quality of structures refers to the availability of technical or human resources needed for information processing. It comprises quality of data, quality characteristics for information processing tools, and quality of component integration. The quality of structures can usually be assessed using system analysis methods (e.g., 3LGM) and evaluation methods.

Quality of processes deals with the quality of the information processes that are necessary to meet the user's needs. It comprises efficiency of information logistics, leanness of information processing tools, single recording and multiple usability of data, controlled transcription of data without media cracks, and patient-centered information processing. The quality of processes can be assessed using system analysis and evaluation methods, such as methods for analyzing business processes

Outcome quality describes whether the goals of information management have been reached, or, in a broader sense, to what extent the hospital information system contributes to the goals of the hospital and to the expectations of different stakeholders, taking into account information management's laws. Outcome quality can be assessed using system analysis and evaluation methods such as assessment studies.

It is a particular challenge for information management to take into account those criteria where only an adequate balance is a determinant of the quality of a hospital information system. Those criteria comprise the balance of homogeneity and heterogeneity, the balance of computer-based and paper-based tools, the balance of data security and functionality, and the balance of functional leanness and functional redundancy.

# 5 How to Strategically Manage Hospital Information Systems

## 5.1 Introduction

Information management is defined as the management of all components of a hospital information system: the management of information, of application components, and of physical data processing components. We now look at the management of hospital information systems and discuss typical goals and tasks as well as tools and methods for information management in hospitals.[65]

After reading this chapter, you should be able to answer the following questions:

- What does information management in hospitals mean in detail?
- How is information management in hospitals typically organized, and what are the responsibilities of a chief information officer (CIO)?
- Which tasks and methods are related to strategic HIS planning, and what is the strategic information management plan?
- Which tasks and methods are related to strategic HIS monitoring?
- Which tasks and methods are related to strategic HIS directing?

## 5.2 Strategic, Tactical, and Operational Information Management

In this section, we present in more detail the tasks of information management in hospitals. After reading this section, you should be able to answer the following questions:

- What does information management encompass?
- What are the three main scopes of information management?

---

65. This chapter is based on Winter AF, Ammenwerth E, Bott OJ, Brigl B, Buchauer A, Gräber S, et al. Strategic Information Management Plans: The Basis for Systematic Information Management in Hospitals. Int J Med Inform 2001; 64(2-3): 99-109.

- What are the tasks of strategic, tactical, and operational information management in hospitals?

## *Information Management*

The concept *management* can stand for an institution or for an enterprise function. As an institution, management comprises all organizational units of an enterprise that make decisions about planning, monitoring, and directing all activities of subordinate units. As an enterprise function, management comprises all leadership activities that determine the enterprise's goals, structures, and activities.

We can distinguish between (general) management dealing with the enterprise as a whole and management dealing with distinguishable units of the enterprise. The management of the business unit information processing is called *information management.* In general, information management should contribute to fulfill strategic enterprise goals. Information management encompasses

- the management of information
- the management of application components, and
- the management of physical data processing components whether computer-based or not.

Information management plans the information system of an enterprise and its architecture, directs its establishment and its operation, and monitors its development and operation with respect to the planned objectives. Different management levels have different perceptions and interests. With respect to its scope, information management can be divided into strategic, tactical, and operational management, which all comprise as main tasks planning, monitoring, and directing.

- *Strategic information management* deals with the enterprise's information processing as a whole and establishes strategies and principles for the evolution of the information system. An important result of strategic management activities is a strategic information management plan, which includes the direction and strategy of information management and the architecture of the enterprise information system.
- *Tactical information management* deals with particular enterprise functions or application components that are introduced, removed, or changed. Usually these activities are done in the form of projects. Such tactical information management projects are initiated by strategic information management. Thus, strategic information management is a vital necessity for tactical information management. The re-

sult of tactical information management projects is the enterprise information system.

- *Operational information management* is responsible for operating the components of the information system. It cares for its smooth operation in accordance with the strategic information management plan.

This separation is essential, because each of these information management levels has different perspectives, and therefore uses different methods and tools. For example, strategic information management focuses on strategic information management plans (compare section 5.4). Tactical management needs, for example, methods for project management, user requirements analysis, and software development or customizing. Operational management requires methods and tools for topics, which range from intra-enterprise marketing of services to help desk and network management.

Figure 5.1 present the relationships among strategic, tactical, and operational information management. Details are given in the next sections.

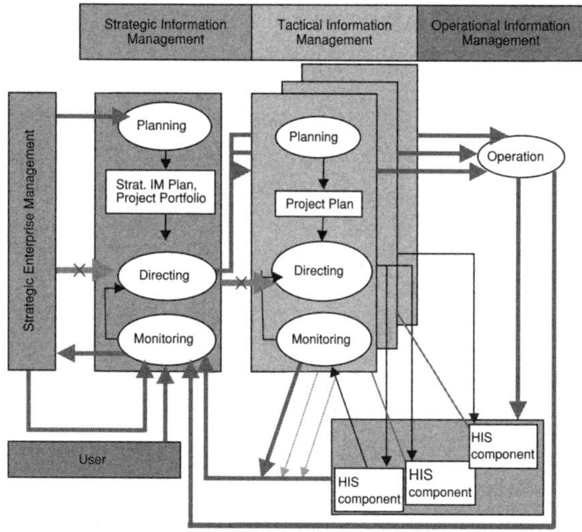


Figure 5.1: Relationship among planning, directing, and monitoring during strategic, tactical, and operational information management.

Management comprises only those tasks that are nonexecutive. Therefore, operational tasks (such as operating a computer server) are not part of management's tasks. However, those operational tasks have to be planned, directed, and monitored. This is carried out by operational information management.

Figure 5.2 presents a three-dimensional classification of information management activities. It shows the three main objects of information management (information, application components, and physical data processing components), the three main tasks (planning, directing, monitoring), and the three scopes (strategic, tactical, operational).

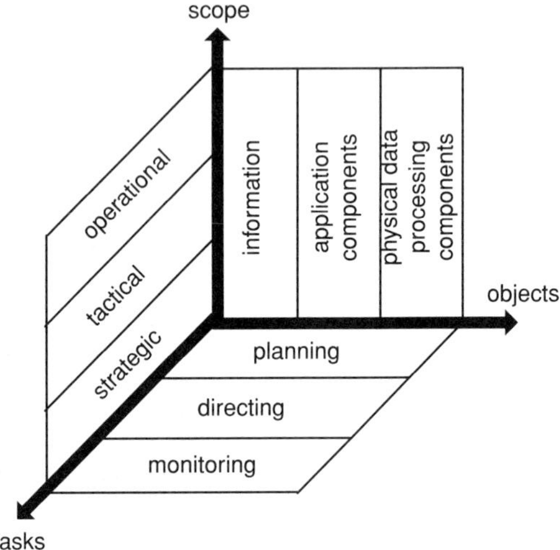


Figure 5.2: Three-dimensional classification of information management activities.

## *Information Management in Hospitals*

We can now apply the defined management concepts to the enterprise "hospital." *Information management in hospitals* is the management of hospital information systems. The tasks of information management in hospitals are

- planning the hospital information system and its architecture;
- directing its establishment and its operation; and
- monitoring its development and operation with respect to the planned objectives.

Information management in hospitals is performed in an environment full of influencing factors. For example, decisions made by the hospital's management directly influence information management (e.g., a decision to increase completeness of diagnoses coding). New legal regulations have an effect on information management (e.g., a law enforcing the introduction of a new billing system based on patient grouping). Users of the hospital information system with their attitudes, comments, demands, and fears also influence information management. On the other side, information management itself may affect, for example, the management of the enterprise (e.g., information management may propose to introduce a hospital-wide, multiprofessional electronic patient record system; this must in turn lead to strategic enterprise activities such as process reorganization).

Figure 5.3 presents this relationship between HIS management and HIS operation, and the influencing factors.

We now look at the activities of strategic, tactical, and operational information management in hospitals.

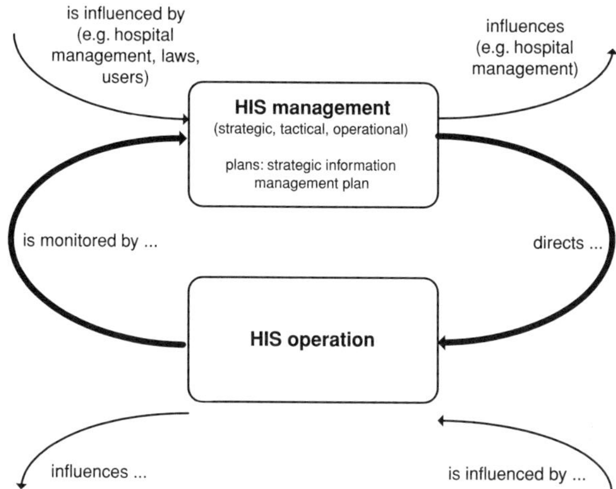


Figure 5.3: Strategic, tactical, and operational information management in hospitals, HIS operation, and their relationships.

## *Strategic Information Management*

Strategic information management deals with the hospital's information processing as a whole. It depends strictly on the hospital's business strategy and strategic goals and has to translate these into an appropriate information strategy. The *planning* activities of strategic information management result in a specific strategic information management plan, describing the HIS with its supported functions, its architecture, and its organization. An important component of strategic information management is the *strategic information management plan*. This plan includes the direction and strategy of information management and gives directives for the construction and development of the hospital information system by describing its intended architecture. A proposal for the structure and content of strategic information management plans is presented in section 5.4. The strategic information management plan is the basis for strategic *project portfolios*. They contain concrete projects, which implement the objectives of the strategy, and shall be revised regularly. For example, the strategic information management plan might contain the introduction of healthcare professional workstations on all wards within the next five years to provide healthcare professionals with the right information, in the right place, at the right time. The strategic project portfolios could then contain individual projects, for example, on clinical documentation, order entry, and patient record archiving.

*Directing* as part of strategic information management means to transform the strategic information management plan into action, that is, to systematically manipulate the hospital information system to make it conform to the strategic plan. The system's manipulation is usually done by the initiation of projects of the strategic project portfolio. The projects deal with the construction or further development and maintenance of components of the hospital information system. Planning, directing, and monitoring these projects are the tasks of tactical information management. Operational management will then be responsible for the proper operation of the components. An example of strategic directing would be to initiate a project for the introduction of online access to clinical guidelines via healthcare professional workstations.

*Monitoring* as part of strategic information management means continuously auditing HIS quality as defined by means of its strategic information management plan's directives and goals. Auditing should determine whether the hospital information system is able to fulfill its tasks efficiently, that is, whether it can offer efficient information and knowledge logistics. For example, it should be verified

- that doctors and nurses in a ward get recent laboratory findings in an adequate form and in time,
- that up-to-date therapy information and information on medication interactions are available at the physician's workplace even during nights and weekends,
- that hospital management is able to get valid and sufficient information about the economic situation of the hospital.

The management's task is to install "sensors" to audit the information system's quality (compare Chapter 0). Management has to receive information from the current projects, from operational management, from users, and from the various stakeholders. Additional information can be gained through evaluation projects.

Monitoring results are used as input for the directing tasks of information management, which could for example initiate further projects. Monitoring results will also give feedback to update the strategic information management plan, which could for example lead to further activities of strategic management.

Strategic information management and its strategic information management plan are the vital requirements for tactical and operational information management in a hospital.

## *Tactical Information Management*

Tactical information management deals with particular enterprise functions or application components. It aims to introduce, remove, change, or maintain components of the hospital information system. This could be an application component for patient admission or for clinical documentation. Related activities are usually performed within projects; they have to be initiated as part of an information strategy, which is formulated in the project portfolio of a strategic information management plan as drawn up by the strategic information management. The result of tactical information management projects is the enterprise information system.

The organization of the operation and maintenance of information processing tools is part of operational management. However, if problems occur during the operation of HIS components (e.g., frequent user complaints about a medical documentation system), appropriate projects may be executed by tactical information management (e.g., introducing a better version of the documentation system). Typically, those tactical information management projects comprise a planning phase, a running phase (which could be, for example, system analysis, evaluation, selection, providing, or introduction), and a termination phase (Figure 5.4).

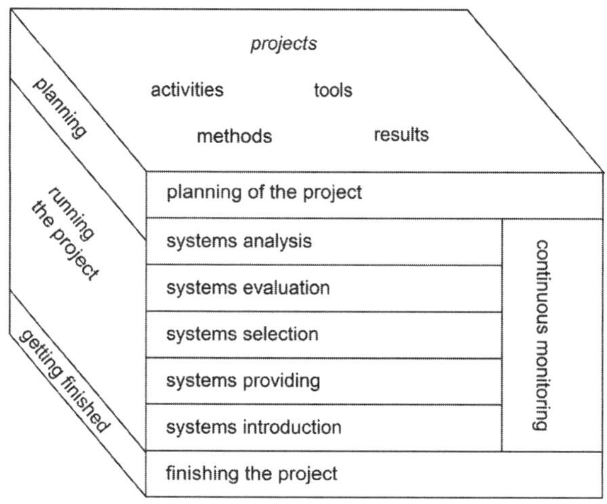


Figure 5.4: Typical phases of tactical information management projects.

*Planning* in tactical information management means planning projects and all the resources needed for them. Even though tactical information management projects are based on the strategic plan, they need a specific tactical project plan. This plan has to describe the project's subject and motivation, the problems to be solved, the goals to be achieved, the tasks to be performed, and the activities to be undertaken to reach the goals.

*Directing* in tactical management means the execution of such tactical information management projects in hospitals, based on a project plan. Therefore, it includes typical tasks of project management such as resource allocation and coordination, motivation, and training of the staff, etc.

*Monitoring* means continually checking whether the initiated projects are running as planned and whether they will produce the expected results. Monitoring results influence project planning, as a project's plan may be updated or changed according to the results of the project's monitoring in a given situation.

## *Operational Information Management*

Operational information management is responsible for operating the components of the hospital information system. It has to care for its operation in accordance with the strategic information management plan.

*Planning* in operational information management means planning organizational structures, procedures, and all resources such as finances, staff, rooms, or buildings that are necessary to ensure the faultless operation of all components of the hospital information system. For example, operational information management may require the installation of a messaging infrastructure that enables the quick transmission of users' error notes to the responsible services. These resources need to be available for a longer period of time. Therefore, they should be allocated as part of a strategic information management plan. Moreover, planning in this context concerns the allocation of personnel resources on a day-to-day basis (e.g., planning of shifts for staff responsible for user support or network management).

*Directing* means the sum of all management activities that are necessary to ensure proper responses to operating problems of components of the hospital information system, that is, to provide backup facilities, to operate a help desk, to maintain servers, and to keep task forces available for repairing network components, servers, personal computers, printers, etc. Directing in this context deals with engaging the resources planned by the strategic information management plan in such a way that faultless operation of the hospital information system is ensured. Operational information management does not mean to exchange a server, but to organize the necessary services for its maintenance.

*Monitoring* deals with verifying the proper working and effectiveness of components of the hospital information system. For example, a network monitoring system may regularly be used to monitor the availability and correct working of network components (compare Figure 5.5).

Figure 5.5: Monitoring of the server of a hospital information system.

## *Example*

### Example 5.2.1: Typical Projects of Tactical Information Management

Typical tactical information management projects in hospitals comprise

- analysis of the structure and processes of order entry in order to select a new computer-based application component to support this function;
- further development of a medical documentation system in order to support new legal demands on diagnoses-related patient grouping and billing;
- introduction of a clinical knowledge server in order to improve knowledge logistics;
- introduction of application components for documentation in operating rooms, including diagnoses documentation, procedure documentation, and report writing;
- replacement of an application component for report writing in outpatient units;

- design, implementation, and introduction of an application component to support the management of patient care standards;
- assessment of the effects and costs of a healthcare professional work-station;
- assessment of the user acceptance of a new application component for an intensive care unit.

## *Exercises*

### Exercise 5.2.1: Relationships Between Tasks of Information Management

Look at Figure 5.3 and find examples of factors influencing HIS operation.

### Exercise 5.2.2: Typical Projects of Tactical Information Management

Look at Figure 5.4 which shows typical phases of information management projects. Match the typical tactical information management projects from example 5.2.1 to those typical project phases.

### Exercise 5.2.3: Diagnostics and Therapy of HIS

Planning, monitoring, and directing of hospital information systems to a certain extent can be compared to health and the diagnostics and therapy of diseases. Discuss similarities and differences.

## *Summary*

Information management in hospitals is a complex task. To reduce complex-ity, we distinguish among strategic, tactical, and operational information management. Each of these information management levels has different perspectives and uses other methods and tools.

The tasks of information management are

- planning of a hospital information system and its architecture;
- directing its establishment and its operation; and
- monitoring its development and operation with respect to the planned objectives.

Strategic information management deals with the hospital's information processing as a whole. Its planning activities result in a specific strategic information management plan. Its directing activities transform the strategic plan into action through the initiation of projects. Its monitoring comprises continually auditing the HIS quality as defined by means of the strategic plan's directives and goals.

Tactical management deals with particular enterprise functions or application components that are introduced, removed, or changed. Usually these activities are done in the form of projects. Its activities comprise planning projects and all resources needed for them, the execution of such projects, and continually monitoring whether the initiated projects are running as planned.

Operational information management is responsible for operating the components of the hospital information system.

## 5.3 Organizational Structures for Information Management

Organizational structures for information management in hospitals differ greatly among hospitals. In general, each hospital should have an adequate organization for strategic, tactical, and operational information management, depending on its size, its internal organization, and its needs.

Organizational structures can be described at the overall hospital level (e.g., a chief information officer, a central ICT department), and at the departmental level (e.g., specific information management staff for a certain department, a certain outpatient unit).

After reading this section, you should be able to answer the following questions:

- How is information management in hospitals typically organized on the strategic, tactical, and operational level?
- What are the responsibilities of a chief information officer (CIO)?

### *Typical Organizational Structures for Strategic Information Management*

It is generally useful to centralize responsibilities for information management in one role. This role is usually called *chief information officer* (CIO).[66] The CIO bears the overall responsibility for the strategic, tactical, and operational management of the information system and the budgetary responsibility, and has the authority for all employees concerned with information management. The specific position of the CIO demands dedicated professional skills. In addition to more general executive and managerial competencies, business and economic competencies are required as well as innovative competencies and medical informatics competencies.

---

66. The CIO is also often called vice president (or director) of information systems (or information services, information management, information and communication technology, information resources), or chief of information services.

Depending on the size of the hospital, the role and the tasks of a CIO may be performed by one dedicated person (e.g., a full-time health informatics specialist) or by a high-ranking member of the hospital's board (e.g., the chief executive officer, CEO). Some of the tasks of the CIO may also be performed by an *information management board*. Such a board can often be found in larger hospitals (Figure 5.6). Members should include one representative from the hospital's board of directors, representatives from the main departments and user groups, and the director of the ICT department. If no dedicated CIO position exists, the president of this board can be regarded as the CIO of the hospital.

The CIO should report directly to the CEO or the hospital's board of directors and, therefore, should be ranked rather high in the hospital's organizational hierarchy, optimally as a member of the top management team of the hospital. The CIO's role should be a strategic one that comprises the following tasks of strategic information management:

- make or prepare all relevant strategic decisions on the HIS, especially with respect to infrastructure, architecture, and information management organization;
- align the hospital's business plan with the information management plan;
- establish and promote the strategic information management plan;
- initiate and control projects for tactical information management;
- initiate HIS evaluation studies and adequate HIS monitoring activities;
- identify and solve serious information management problems;
- report to the CEO or the hospital's board of directors.

The CIO's membership in the top management team should provide the possibility to influence the hospital's strategies using information technology as a strategic resource. Therefore, business knowledge and the ability to effectively communicate with other business managers, for example the chief financial officer (CFO) or the chief operating officer (COO), is important for a CIO. Nevertheless, reality often differs greatly from this image. Whether the role of the CIO is a strategic one or a more tactical or even operational one depends on internal hospital factors such as the CIO's top management membership, the internal communication networks among top executives and the CIO, the top management's strategic knowledge about ICT, the hospital's strategic vision of ICT, and on the personal skills of the CIO.

Figure 5.6: An information management board meeting. Participants are (from the left): the vice director of administration, the vice director of nursing, the director of the medical informatics department as chairman, the head of the center for information management, the medical director, and the vice head of the center for information management.

## *Typical Organizational Structures for Tactical and Operational Information Management*

With regard to the responsibilities for tactical and operational management, it is sometimes not useful and often not feasible to totally centralize these services. Especially in larger hospitals, they are performed in cooperation between central units and the decentralized staff.

There is usually at least one central unit or department (often called the department for medical informatics, hospital computing center, or ICT department) for the computer-supported part of the HIS. This unit takes care of the tactical and operational information management of those parts of the HIS with hospital-wide relevance (e.g., the administrative systems, the healthcare professional workstations, the telecommunication system, and the computer network). In larger hospitals, there may be subdivisions with respect to tasks (e.g., different units for desktop management, user support, clinical systems, or networking). The head of those central units is typically the CIO.

In addition, there may also be information management staff located in the individual departments of the hospital. This staff may be dedicated health informaticians or specially skilled users. These local information managers have responsibilities for tactical and operational information management with regard to their department, but in accordance with the central information management unit. For example, they may (with support from the central unit) introduce a hospital-wide application component in their department and operate it. On the other hand, they will also take care of additional information needs of their departments, for example, by introducing a dedicated departmental system. However, this should be done only in accordance with the strategic information management plan.

To guarantee the continuous working of the most important components of an HIS, it is helpful to draw up a concept for operational information management. Such a concept should clarify the following:

- Which components have to be supported?
- What tasks comprise operational support?
- Who is responsible for the operational support?
- What should be the intensity of operational support?

Typically, three levels of operational support can be distinguished. *First-level support* is the first address for all user groups with any kind of problem. It may consist, for example, of a central 24-hour-hotline that is responsible for the management of user accounts and first trouble shooting, or of decentralized information processing staff. When the first-level support cannot solve the problems, it hands them over to the *second-level support*, a specially trained informatics staff in the central information management department who are usually responsible for the operation of the specific application components. The *third-level support*, finally, addresses the most severe problems that cannot be solved by the second-level support. It can consist, for example, of specialists from the vendor of an application component.

Table 5.1 presents objects, responsibilities, tasks, and the intensity that should be defined as part of the operational management concept for the computer-supported part of an HIS. As an example, a concept for operational management in a hospital could clarify

- that central servers and networks are supported by the central information management department, which offers first- and second-level support 24 hours a day. A hotline is created that guarantees response time in less than one hour. Third-level support (see Figure 5.7) is provided for certain application components by the vendors of the respective application software products.
- that workstations are supported by the local technical staff in each department. They offer first- and second-level support during the day. They are available by pager.

Table 5.1: Dimensions to be considered for operational information management of the computer-supported part of hospital information systems.

| *Dimension* | *Facets* |
|---|---|
| Objects | Decentralized application components (e.g., in departments) |
| | Central application components (e.g., patient management system) |
| | Workstations |
| | Decentralized servers |
| | Central servers |
| | Networks |
| | Backbone |
| Responsibility | Local (in departments) |
| | Central (in departments for information processing) |
| | Vendors |
| Task | First-level support (problem taking, problem analysis, problem solving, user training) |
| | Second-level support (training courses, regular operation, data protection) |
| | Third-level support (software development, problem solving, contact with vendors) |
| Intensity | Availability (e.g., 24 hours/day, 7 days/week) |
| | Presence (e.g., locally, by pager, by hotline) |
| | Timeliness (e.g., answering time < 2 hours) |

Figure 5.7: An immediate support center for third-level support of a vendor.

## *Example*

### Example 5.3.1: Organizational Structures for Information Management in a Hospital

Figure 5.8 presents the overall organization of information management at the Plötzberg Medical Center and Medical School (PMC).

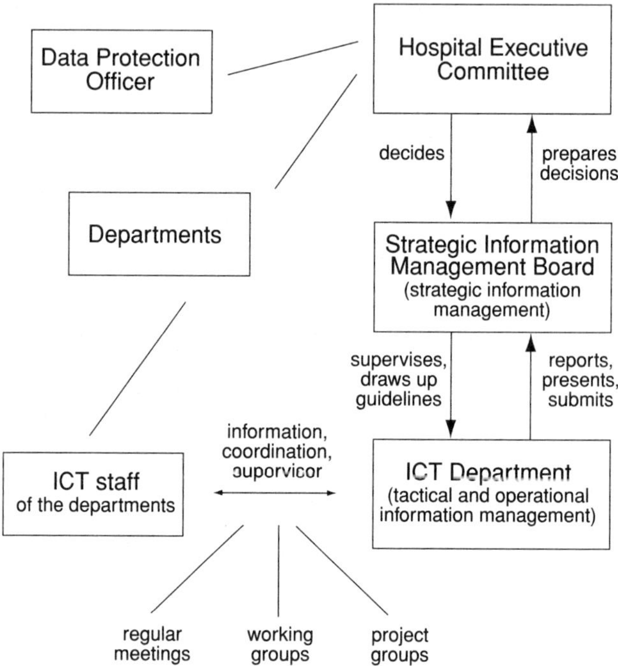


Figure 5.8: Organization of information management at the Plötzberg Medical Center and Medical School (PMC).

## *Exercises*

### Exercise 5.3.1: Information Systems Managers as Architects

Information systems managers can be partly compared to architects. Read the following statement and discuss similarities and differences between information system architects and building architects:

> "We're architects.... We have designed numerous buildings, used by many people.... We know about users. We know well their complaints: buildings that get in the way of the things they want to do.... We also know well users' joy of relaxing, working, learning, buying, manufacturing, and

worshipping in buildings which were designed with love and tender care as well as function in mind.... We're committed to the belief that buildings help people to do their jobs or impede them and that good buildings bring joy as well as efficiency."[67]

### Exercise 5.3.2: Organizational Structures for Information Management in a Hospital

Look at a real hospital that you know and at its information system.

- Which institutions are involved in information management?
- Which boards and persons are involved in information management?
- Who is responsible for strategic information management?
- Who is responsible for tactical information management?
- Who is responsible for operational information management?
- Who is the CIO, and what is his or her responsibility?

### Exercise 5.3.3: Centralization of Organizational Structures

Discuss the pros and cons for centralization and decentralization of strategic, tactical, and operational information management. Find concrete examples for your arguments.

### Exercise 5.3.4: Organizational Structures for Information Management at PMC

Look at the description of the organizational structures for information management at the Plötzberg Medical Center and Medical School (PMC) from example 5.3.1. Discuss the advantages and disadvantages of this organizational structure and discuss alternatives.

## *Summary*

Each hospital should have an adequate organization for strategic, tactical, and operational information management.

In general, a chief information officer (CIO) is responsible for strategic information management. This role may be filled by one person or by an information management board. The CIO's most important tasks should be the strategic alignment of business plans and information management plans and the strategic planning of the hospital's information systems.

There is typically one central unit or department for tactical and operational information management of the computer-supported part of the HIS. This ICT department is usually directed by the CIO. In addition, there may

---

67. Caudill WW et al. Architecture and You. New York: Whitney Library of Design; 1978. p.6.

also be decentralized information management staff, located at the individual departments of the hospital.

## 5.4 Strategic Planning of Hospital Information Systems

Strategic information management deals with the hospital's information processing as a whole. It comprises planning of HIS architecture and of the organization of information management. In this section, we look at the strategic planning of HIS.

After reading this section, you should be able to answer the following questions:

- What are the typical tasks for strategic HIS planning?
- What are the typical methods for strategic HIS planning?
- What is the goal and typical structure of a strategic information management plan?

### *Tasks*

The most important tasks of strategic HIS planning are the strategic alignment of business plans and information management plans, long-term HIS planning, and short-term HIS planning.

### Strategic Alignment of Business Plans and Information Management Plans

The basis for strategic information management in a hospital are the strategic goals as defined in the hospital's business plan. Advances in ICT may influence these strategic business goals. Therefore, it is one main task of strategic information management to align business plans and information management plans. Hospitals aim to provide efficient, high-quality health care. However, this mission may be further refined, for example,

- to increase the number of outpatients,
- to decrease the average duration of inpatients' stays,
- to perform best quality patient treatment,
- to improve collaboration with healthcare institutions in the surrounding region,
- to increase competitiveness by promoting an image of being a modern hospital with all the latest technical means,
- to offer high-quality patient care through less technical but more personal engagement, or
- to increase profit.

These very different and partly conflicting goals have to result in different information management strategies and different architectures of HIS. If goals are conflicting, strategic information management must try to solve these conflicts and establish a clear order of priorities in accordance with the enterprise's business plan.

It is clear that people or institutions responsible for strategic information management (the CIO) need knowledge about the enterprise strategy and the enterprise business plan. In addition, the hospital's management needs knowledge about the significance and possibilities of information processing with regard to formulation, realization, and evaluation of the hospital's strategy. Strategic information management must be able to offer this information to hospital management in adequate and understandable form.

Methods for strategic alignment are presented in the methods section, below.

## Long-Term HIS Planning

The strategic planning of HIS can be separated into long-term and short-term HIS planning.

The strategic information management plan contains the long-term planning of HIS. It describes the hospital's goals, the information management goals, the current HIS state, the future HIS state, and the steps to transform the current HIS into the planned HIS. Strategic information management must create and regularly update this plan. The strategic plan must take into account quality criteria for HIS structures, processes, and outcome. It must be guaranteed that the strategic information management plan is the basis for all other information management activities. HIS planning is an ongoing task, and there is no use in trying to solve all problems at the same time. On the contrary, only a stepwise approach, based on different levels of priorities, is possible and useful. The strategic information management plan, therefore, will contain a general priority list of the most important tasks and projects to be done in the coming years.

The detailed structure of strategic information management plans is described later on.

## Short-Term HIS Planning

The long-term strategic information management plan is usually valid for a longer period of time (e.g., 3 to 5 years). However, requirements (e.g., due to legal changes or new user requests) and resources (staff, money) change quicker than the strategic information management plan.

One task of strategic information management, therefore, is to establish an (annual) project list with recent projects, priorities, and upcoming planned projects. This project list, also called the *project portfolio*, has to be approved by the hospital management, which decides which projects to execute and how to organize necessary resources. This project portfolio must match the (more general) priority lists described in the strategic information management plan. However, its annual update reflects detailed prioritization and changes in the environment.

Because of the temporal limited validity of the strategic information management plan, HIS planning is a permanent task of strategic information management in hospitals.

## *Methods*

## Strategic Alignment

The role of information management varies between two extremes. At one extreme, information management may be seen as a purely supporting function; that is, the hospital strategy determines the information management planning activities. This is called organizational pull. At the other extreme, information management is seen as the strategic resource from which the hospital gains competitive advantage. The application of technological advances mainly determines the further development of the hospital and its position on the healthcare market. This is called technology push. Strategic alignment describes the process that balances and coordinates the hospital goals and the information management strategies to get the best result for the hospital.

Several models exist for strategic alignment. The component alignment model (CAM)[68] considers seven components—the external environment, emerging information technologies, organizational infrastructure, mission, ICT infrastructure, business strategy, and ICT strategy—that should be continually assessed with respect to their mutual alignment. The critical success factor (CSF)[69] approach is a top-down approach that first identities factors critical to the hospital's success or failure. Strategic information management planning is then derived with regard to these factors.

Successful strategic alignment requires that hospital top management as well as information managers have a basic knowledge of each other's competence and share the same conception of the role of information management.

---

68. Martin JB, Wilkins AS, Stawski SK. The component alignment model: a new approach to healthcare information technology strategic planning. Top Health Inf Manage 1998; 19(1): 1-10.

69. Tan JK. The critical success factor approach to strategic alignment: seeking a trail from a health organization's goals to its management information infrastructure. Health Serv Manage Res 1999; 12(4): 246-57.

## Portfolio Management

An important instrument for information management strategic planning is *portfolio management*. Originally coming from the field of finance to acquire a well-balanced securities portfolio, today the term portfolio management is used to refer to multiple strategic management problems.

Portfolio management concerning information management categorizes certain components of an information system, like application components or physical data processing components, but also projects, using certain criteria to assess the value of these components for the enterprise and to balance risks and returns. The assumption is that there are different management issues and priorities for each class.

Project portfolio management categorizes projects, looking, for example, at project objectives, costs, time lines, resources, risks, and other critical factors. McFarlan[70] proposes eight distinct project categories along the dimensions of project size, experience with the technology, and project structure. Each category carries a different degree of risk, and thus he recommends different project management tools to use. Today project portfolio management is primarily used to plan and control IT investments.

The portfolio proposed by the Gartner Group[71] distinguishes three categories according to the contribution of an application component to the hospital's performance. Utility applications are application components that are essential for the hospital's operation, but have no influence on the success of a hospital, and, therefore, are independent of the hospital's strategic goals. A good example is the patient administration. Enhancement applications are application components that improve the hospital's performance, and, therefore, contribute to the hospital's success (e.g., computer-based nursing documentation). Frontier applications are application components that influence the hospital's position in the healthcare market, for example, the enforced use of telemedicine. Information management planning should aim at a well-balanced application portfolio—on the one hand, to efficiently support essential hospital functions and, on the other hand, not to miss future technological innovations.

### *The Strategic Information Management Plan*

An important aim of strategic HIS planning is to establish the *strategic information management plan*. The previous sections made clear that without a strategic information management plan, neither tactical nor operational

70. McFarlan FW. Portfolio approach to information systems. Harvard Business Review Sept.-Oct. 1981; 142-150.

71. Rosser B. A management tool to facilitate decision making. Gartner Group. Research Note TU 03-4804; 1998.

management would work appropriately. A strategic information management plan is an important precondition for systematic directing and monitoring of the hospital information system.

The strategic information management plan should be written by the CIO and approved by the hospital management. Without proper strategic planning, it would be a matter of chance if a hospital information system fulfilled strategic information goals. But considerable efforts have to be made for creating strategic plans.

In this section, the goals and structure of strategic information management plans are presented in more detail. Figure 5.9 presents the overall view on strategic information management planning.

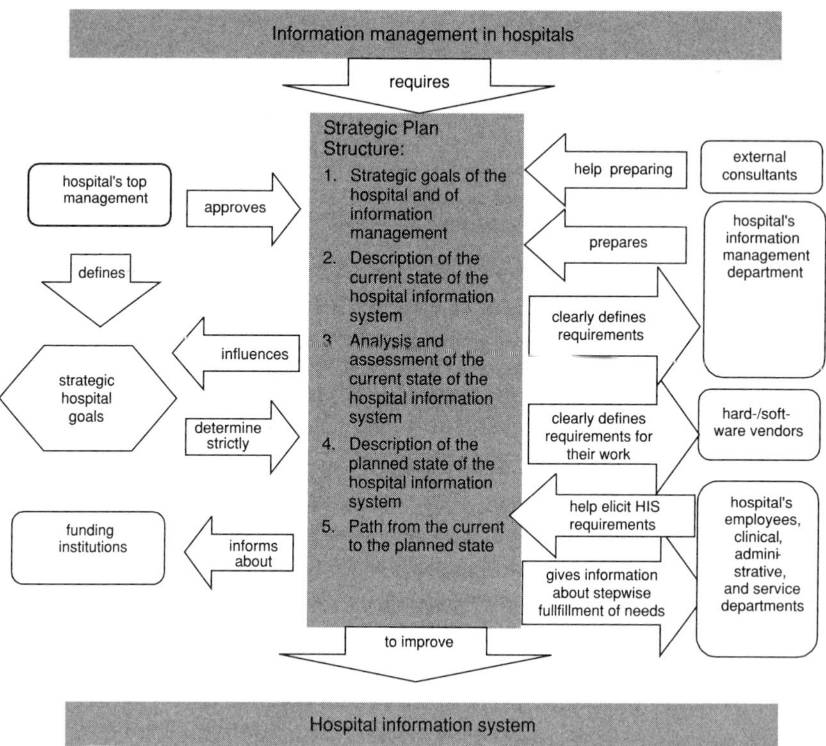


Figure 5.9: Strategic information management planning of hospitals.[72]

72. Adapted from: Winter AF, Ammenwerth E, Bott OJ, Brigl B, Buchauer A, Gräber S, et al. Strategic Information Management Plans: The Basis for Systematic Information Management in Hospitals. Int J Med Inform 2001; 64(2-3): 99-109.

## Purpose of Strategic Information Management Plans

A strategic information management plan gives directives for the construction and development of a hospital information system. It describes the recent and the intended hospital information system's architecture.

Different stakeholders[73] are involved in the creation, updating, approval, and use of strategic plans. Such stakeholders may include

- top management;
- employees, e.g., physicians, nurses, administrative staff;
- clinical, administrative, service departments;
- information management department (ICT department);
- funding institutions;
- consultants; and
- hardware and software vendors.

These stakeholders may have different expectations of a strategic plan and are involved in different life-cycle phases for strategic plans:

- *creation*, i.e., writing a first plan;
- *approval*, i.e., making some kind of contract among the stakeholders;
- *deployment*, i.e., asserting that the plan is put into practice;
- *use*, i.e., the involved stakeholders refer to the plan when needed;
- *updating* when a new version is required (because of new requirements, new available technologies, failure to achieve individual tasks, or just leaving the time frame of the plan). After the first version, the creation and update phases merge into a cyclic, evolutionary development of the plan.

The CIO and the ICT department usually create and maintain proposals for the strategic information management plan. They are interested in clearly defined requirements for their work, which is greatly concerned with tactical management issues. Top management is interested in the seamless and cost-effective operation of the hospital. Top management approves the plans (probably together with the funding institutions). Representatives of the employees should be involved in eliciting the requirements, since they will use the resulting information systems. The current strategic plans will be used by the ICT departments and the vendors of HIS components when constructing or maintaining components of hospital information systems. External consultants may help to create plans, but also be engaged in negotiations for the approval of the plans.

The most essential purpose is to improve a hospital information system so that it can better contribute to the hospital's goals. This purpose should determine the structure of strategic plans; that is, it should show a path from

---

73. The term stakeholder is used to refer to anyone who has direct or indirect influence on or interest in a component of an information system.

the current situation to an improved situation, in which the hospital's goals are achieved as far as possible and reasonable.

## Structure of Strategic Information Management Plans

A strategic information management plan should encompass the hospital's business strategy or strategic goals, the resulting information management strategies, the current state of the hospital information system, and an analysis of how well the current information system fits the strategies. The planned architecture should be derived as a conclusion of this analysis.

The strategic plan also has to deal with the resources needed to realize the planned architecture, and has to include a strategy for the operation of the resulting hospital information system and a description of appropriate organizational structures. Examples of resources are money, personnel, soft- and hardware, rooms for servers and (paper-based) archives, and rooms for training. The resources should fit the architecture and vice versa.

The general structure of strategic information management plans in hospitals can be summarized as follows:

1. strategic goals of the hospital and of information management,
2. description of the current state of the hospital information system,
3. analysis and assessment of the current state of the hospital information system,
4. description of the planned state of the hospital information system, and
5. path from the current to the planned state.

This is only a basic structure that may be adapted to the specific requirements of individual hospitals. Particularly, a short management summary and appendices describing the organizational structure, personnel resources, the building structure, etc., are likely to complement a strategic plan.

### Strategic Goals of the Hospital and of Information Management

Based on a description of the hospital's strategic goals (e.g., presented in a mission statement), the strategic information management goals should be presented using the method of strategic alignment as presented earlier in this section. Goal conflicts especially need to be taken into account and resolved.

### Description of the Current State of the Hospital Information System

Before any planning commences, the hospital information system's current state should be described. This may require some discipline, because some stakeholders may be more interested in the planned (new) state than in the current (obsolete) state.

The description of the current state is the basis for identifying those functions of the hospital that are well supported, for example, by information and communication technology, and those functions that are not (yet) well supported. Thus, application components as well as existing information and communication technology have to be described, including how they contribute to the support of the hospital's functions.

### Analysis and Assessment of the Current State of the Hospital Information System

When the current state is described, it should be analyzed with respect to the achievement of information management strategies. Note that missing computer support for a certain function may not be assessed in all cases as being poor support for that function. For example, missing computers in patient rooms and consequently paper-based documentation of clinical findings may be conforming more to the goal of being a humane hospital than the use of computers and hand-held digital devices in this area.

### Description of the Planned State of the Hospital Information System

Based on the analysis of the current state, a new state should be described that achieves the goals better than does the current state, provided that the current state does not already achieve the hospital's goals. Note that besides technical aspects, organizational aspects also have to be discussed. The description of the planned state can thus be completed by the description of the planned organizational structure of information management. In many cases, this is an opportunity to introduce a CIO or to clarify his or her role.

### Path from the Current to the Planned State

This section should describe a step-by-step path from the current to the planned state. It should include assigned resources, that is, personnel, estimated investment costs as well as future operating costs, etc., and concrete deadlines for partial results. This path could also assign priorities to individual projects as well as dependencies between projects.

## *Example*

### Example 5.4.1: Structure of a Strategic Information Management Plan

Table 5.2 presents the structure of the strategic information management plan for 2002-2007 of the Plötzberg Medical Center and Medical School (PMC).

Table 5.2: Structure of the strategic information management plan (2002-2007) of the Plötzberg Medical Center and Medical School (PMC).

| |
|---|
| **1. Goal of this strategic information management plan** |
| **2. Plötzberg Medical Center and Medical School (PMC)** |
| 2.1 Mission statement |
| 2.2 Strategic goals |
| 2.3 Environment analysis |
| 2.4 Organizational structure |
| 2.5 Hospital indicators |
| 2.6 Hospital layout |
| **3. Current state of the information system** |
| 3.1 Goals of information management |
| 3.2 Organization of information management |
| 3.3 Guidelines and standards for information processing |
| 3.4 Functionality |
| 3.5 Application components |
| 3.6 Physical data processing components |
| **4. Assessment of the current state of the information system** |
| 4.1 Goals attained |
| 4.2 Weak points and strengths of the information systems |
| 4.3 Required activities |
| **5. Future state of the information system** |
| 5.1 Visions and perspectives |
| 5.2 Planned functionality |
| 5.3 Planned application components |
| 5.4 Planned physical data processing components |
| 5.5 Planned organization of information management |
| **6. Planned activities until 2007** |
| 6.1 Overview |
| 6.2 Task planning |
| 6.3 Time planning |
| 6.4 Cost planning |
| **7. Conclusion** |

## *Exercises*

### Exercise 5.4.1: Life Cycle of a Strategic Information Management Plan

Why is a strategic information management plan usually valid for 3 to 5 years? Could there be situations where a shorter or longer period may be useful? Explain your answer.

### Exercise 5.4.2: Deviation from a Strategic Information Management Plan

A strategic information management plan should serve as a guideline for information management. Could there be situations where information management is allowed to deviate from the strategic information management plan after it has been approved? Explain your answer.

### Exercise 5.4.3: Strategic Information Management and Strategic Hospital Management

We have discussed the strategic alignment of business plans and information management plans. Could you imagine situations where this alignment is difficult? Find examples where the hospital's goals and the information management goals may conflict. Discuss reasons and possible solutions.

### Exercise 5.4.4: Establishing a Strategic Information Management Plan

Imagine that you are the CIO of a hospital in which almost no computer-based tools are used. One of the hospital's goals is to support healthcare professionals in their daily tasks by offering up-to-date patient information at their workplace.

Which main goals for information management would you define based on this information? Which hospital functions should be supported by new computer-based information processing tools?

## *Summary*

Strategic information management deals with the hospital's information processing as a whole. It comprises planning of the HIS architecture and of the organization of information management.

Tasks of strategic HIS planning comprise the strategic alignment of business plans and information management plans, long-term HIS planning, and short-term HIS planning. Strategic alignment describes a process in which the hospital goals and the information management strategies are well balanced and coordinated to get the best result for the hospital. The long-term planning of HIS is defined in the strategic information management plan. Short-term strategic HIS planning comprises the establishing of an (annual) project portfolio.

A strategic information management plan is an important precondition for systematic monitoring and directing of the hospital information system. A strategic information management plan should encompass the hospital business strategy or strategic goals, the resulting information management strategies, the current state of the hospital information system, and an analysis of how well the current information system fits the strategies. The planned architecture should be derived as a conclusion of this analysis. Finally, the path from the current to the planned state should be described.

The strategic information management plan should be written by the CIO and adopted by the hospital management.

## 5.5 Strategic Monitoring of Hospital Information Systems

### *Introduction*

AN HIS may operate well in most of its functions, with most of its information processing tools, and in many parts of its information processing organization. However, problems may also occur. Problems may have their origins in general deficiencies, for example, the HIS architecture has not been designed well. They may also occur when a formerly good HIS component is not working well anymore, for example, a component may not be cost-efficient anymore due to progress in technology. Note that, as discussed before, the lack of computer support for a certain function may not be assessed in all cases as being poor support for that function.

The monitoring criteria used are usually those described in Chapter 0. Monitoring verifies whether the hospital information system fulfills these different quality criteria.

After reading this section, you should be able to answer the following questions:

- What are the typical tasks of strategic HIS monitoring?
- What are the typical methods of strategic HIS monitoring?

### *Tasks*

The task of strategic HIS monitoring is to continually audit the quality of the hospital information system, that is, to initiate, collect, and analyze feedback on the functioning of the hospital information system. Monitoring results are compared to the strategic information management plan's directives and goals, which themselves depend on the quality criteria for hospital information systems as described in Chapter 0.

Feedback should be systematically gathered (e.g., by regularly asking staff), but it can also occur unexpectedly (e.g., report in the local press about HIS problems). It can come from tactical or operational information management, from HIS users, from hospital management, from patients and relatives, or from external institutions.

Typical questions that should be answered by strategic HIS monitoring are:

- Are the HIS users satisfied with the HIS (e.g., concerning information logistics, functionality, usability of components)?
- Does the HIS reflect the state of the art of HIS (e.g., concerning functional support, technology, standards)?
- Are external institutions satisfied with the HIS?
- Did the planned projects attain their defined goals?
- What is the quality of the HIS architecture?
- What is the quality of the organization of information management?

To answer these questions, strategic HIS monitoring must fulfill the following tasks:

- Scan the local press for comments on the hospital and its HIS.
- Regularly arrange for validation of HIS, for example, by external experts.
- Compare HIS with state-of-the-art reference models for hospital functions, HIS architectures, and organization of information management.
- Define the criteria for HIS structure, process, and outcome quality.
- Integrate the views of all main user groups (e.g., physicians, nurses, administrative staff, top management) in monitoring activities.
- Initiate projects for monitoring certain hospital functions (e.g., the cost-effectiveness of nursing documentation).
- Initiate assessment studies to evaluate cost-effectiveness of certain interventions and projects of tactical information management (e.g., Did electronic report writing improve the timeliness of discharge reports? Did the introduction of the healthcare professional workstations facilitate attaining the project goals?).
- Check the relevant legislation to see if the HIS meets its requirements as well as new legal requirements.
- Initiate formal certification and accreditation of the hospital.

Both permanent monitoring activities as well as ad hoc monitoring activities should be combined for strategic HIS monitoring.

## Permanent Monitoring Activities

A hospital information system is too complex to allow monitoring all its components. However, it is useful to define subsets of criteria that should then be monitored on a regular (daily, weekly, monthly, yearly) basis, such as

- the number of electronically transmitted findings,
- access numbers to the central knowledge server, or
- the average length of days between discharge of patient and writing of the discharge report.

Those criteria should be collected automatically, if possible, and displayed in reports. Sudden changes in those numbers can then indicate problems (for example, malfunctioning of the knowledge server), which could then initiate more detailed analysis and corrections.

These permanent monitoring activities are also supported by national and international standardized efforts for the certification, accreditation, and excellence programs of hospital information systems described later in this section.

## Ad Hoc Monitoring Activities

There will always be HIS projects, such as the introduction of healthcare professional workstations or the introduction of a case-based billing system, that are of great importance for the whole hospital. The effects of those projects should always be closely monitored. For example, during the introduction of healthcare professional workstations, the effects on information logistics and user acceptance should be monitored to see if the projects attained their goals, and if there were unexpected positive or adverse effects (e.g., significantly increased time for documentation coding). The execution of those activities entails systems evaluation or assessment studies as tactical information management projects. However, strategic HIS monitoring should collect and report the results, which will then directly give feedback to strategic HIS planning.

### *Methods*

Typical methods of strategic HIS monitoring are systems analysis projects (assessment studies), and certification, accreditation, and excellence programs of HIS.

## Systems Analysis and Assessment Projects

HIS monitoring is usually based on specific tactical information management projects, which analyze and evaluate an information system component. These *assessment studies* focus on certain questions and evaluation criteria to assess an information system component. The quality criteria used are similar to those described in Chapter 4.

Assessment studies typically comprise two main phases:

- Systems analysis: During systems analysis, the state of the information systems component is thoroughly addressed. Methods such as observation, questioning, document analysis, and simulation can be used. The results may be a description or a model of the component (see section 3.3).

- Systems evaluation: During systems evaluation, the results of systems analysis is used to assess predefined aspects of the information component (e.g., its strength and weaknesses, costs and effects, stability and user friendliness, user acceptance, etc.).

As studies can focus on multiple questions, and can use multiple methods, each study must be systematically planned and executed. Steps for assessment studies include:

1. Definition of the goals of the study.
2. Definition of the component that is to be assessed.
3. Definition of clear and answerable study questions.
4. Definition of the environment in which the component is used.
5. Selection of valid and reliable measuring methods.
6. Definition of study design.
7. Execution of the study (i.e., systems analysis and systems evaluation).
8. Answering of the study questions.
9. Discussion of validity of results.

Studies analyzing the effects of an information system component can focus, for example, on effects on data quality, the time needed for documentation or information retrieval, waiting times, or quality of patient care.

The selection of systems analysis methods and study designs depends on the questions, the component that is evaluated, and the circumstances. Quantitative methods (e.g., standardized questionnaires, time measurements) allow quantifying the effects and showing causal relationships. Qualitative methods (e.g., open interviews, participating observation) allow the detection and further investigation of unexpected effects and relationships. Often, a combination of different methods may help to better answer the study questions.

Depending on the study questions and study methods, specific types of assessment studies can be defined, such as:

- *SWOT analysis:* Analysis of the most significant *s*trengths (positive features), *w*eaknesses (negative features), opportunities (potential strengths), and *t*hreats (potential weaknesses) that characterize an information system component.
- *User acceptance study:* Analysis of the acceptance of an information system component as the main criterion for the system's success.
- *Effectiveness study*: Objective analysis of the effects of an information system component.
- *Cost-effectiveness analysis:* An economic analysis to compare the costs and consequences of an information system component. It does not require that all important effects and benefits be expressed in monetary terms.

- *Cost-benefit analysis:* An economic analysis that converts effects of an information system component into the same monetary terms as the costs and compares them.
- *Utility analysis:* An economic analysis that compares costs and consequences of an information system component, taking personal preferences into account by including weighting factors for each criterion.
- *Return-on-investment (ROI) studies*: An economic analysis that describes how much an investment on an information system component paid back in a fixed period of time.

To gain clear answers regarding the effects of a component, a controlled randomized trial can be conducted. However, in a clinical environment, the definition of an adequate control group may be difficult (e.g., there may be no or not enough participating wards or departments). On the other hand, some questions can be better answered by in-depth case studies. For example, the question "Why don't the users accept the new application component?" may best be answered by more qualitative methods. Statistical and methodological support is thus very important in selecting adequate methods and in planning and executing any assessment study in a rigorous and methodological way.

The task of performing evaluation studies in a clinical environment is demanding. A detailed explanation is not possible here due to space limitations. It is suggested that the reader consults basic references on technology assessment in health care for further information.[74]

## Certification, Accreditation, and Excellence Programs of HIS

There are several quality management approaches for hospitals, which we can classify as certification, accreditation, and excellence programs.

*Certification* in hospitals concentrates mostly on the *ISO 9000 standard*[75] and primarily assesses compliance with quality management standards. An ISO 9000 certificate states that a hospital meets the standards, but says nothing about outcome quality. There are no official healthcare guidelines for ISO 9000 certification.

The goal of *accreditation* programs is total quality management (TQM) and continuous quality improvement (CQI) of organizations, focusing on the delivery of health care as a process crossing departmental lines. Existing accreditation programs in the United States, Australia, Canada, and France

---

74. For example: Friedman CP, Wyatt J C. Evaluation Methods in Medical Informatics. New York: Springer; 1997.

75. International Organization for Standardization. ISO 9000 standards on quality management, http://www.iso.org.

are healthcare specific and based on predefined standards. The assessment of to what extent a hospital complies with these standards is performed by independent, specially trained surveyors. The accreditation is good for a certain period of time, after which it must be performed again. An internationally recognized example of accreditation is the *JCAHO* program.[76] An accreditation program currently being prepared in Germany is called *KTQ*,[77] which strives to integrate aspects of ISO 9000, EFQM, and JCAHO.

So-called *excellence programs*, such as the *EFQM*[78] model in Europe or the Malcolm Baldrige National Quality Award[79] in the United States also—like accreditation programs—strive for TQM, but use a scoring system that makes it possible to compare organizations to one another and to continually observe quality improvement. The best organizations each year get an award. Whereas no healthcare-specific standards exist for the EFQM, the Baldrige program has already defined them.

To assess the contribution of information processing to the quality of a hospital, most certification or accreditation programs also check information management criteria. The Baldrige program and the JCAHO accreditation standards offer healthcare-specific information management criteria to different extents.

## *Examples*

### Example 5.5.1: An Information Processing Monitoring Report

The CIO of the Plötzberg Medical Center and Medical School (PMC) annually reports to the hospital's management about the amount, quality, and costs of information processing of Plötzberg's hospital information system. The report is structured as shown in Table 5.3.

---

76. Joint Commission on Accreditation of Healthcare Organizations, http://www.jcaho.org. (See also example 4.6.3 in Chapter 4.)

77. Kooperation für Transparenz und Qualität im Krankenhaus (cooperation for transparence and quality in the hospital), http://www.ktq.de. (See also example 4.6.4 in Chapter 4.)

78. European Federation for Quality Management (EFQM), http://www.efqm.org/new_website.

79. National Institute of Standards and Technology, Baldrige National Quality Program, http://www.baldrige.org. (See also example 4.6.1 in Chapter 4.)

Table 5.3: A structure for an information processing monitoring report.

**Amount of information processing**

- Number of patients (inpatients, outpatients, ...)
- Number of examinations (laboratory, radiology, ...)
- Number of documents created
- Number of coded diagnoses
- Number of coded medical procedures (operations, ...)

**Tools for information processing**

- Number of application components (list and diagram)
  - Functionality
  - Number of users
  - Availability of communication interfaces, communication standards
- Number of physical data processing components (list and diagram)
  - Performance, storage capacity
  - Number, functionality, and availability of terminals (healthcare professional workstations, mobile computers, terminals, modalities such as computed tomography)
  - Network structure, data transmission standards, active components, connections

**Organization of information processing**

- Institutions for information processing with their responsibilities
- Boards and groups (steering committees, projects groups ...)

**Quality and costs of information processing**

- Relevant quality indicators (timeliness of reports; quality, timeliness, and completeness of coded diagnoses, planned and unplanned down times for important application and physical data processing components, education of staff, ...)
- ICT investment costs
- ICT operational costs (components)
- ICT staff costs (per institution)

**Tasks of strategic, tactical, and operational information management**

- Status report
- List of projects (goal, size, state of project, results, problems)
- List of ongoing tasks (description, state, problems)

## Example 5.5.2: Assessment Study of a Telemedicine System to Improve Care[80]

Objective: The goal of this study was to evaluate an Internet-based telemedicine program designed to reduce the costs of care, and to provide enhanced medical, informational, and emotional support to families of very low birth weight (VLBW) infants during and after their neonatal intensive care unit stay.

Background: Baby CareLink is a telemedicine program that incorporates videoconferencing and World Wide Web technologies to enhance interactions among families, staff, and community providers. The videoconferencing module allows virtual visits and distance learning from a family's home during an infant's hospitalization as well as virtual house calls and remote monitoring after discharge. Baby CareLink's WWW site contains information on issues that confront these families. It also allows sharing of patient-based data and communications among authorized hospital and community users.

Design and methods: A randomized trial of Baby CareLink was conducted in a cohort of VLBW infants born between November 1997 and April 1999. Eligible infants were randomized within 10 days of birth. Families of intervention group infants were given access to the Baby CareLink telemedicine application. A computer and videoconference equipment was installed in their home. The control group received care as usually practiced. Quality of care was assessed using a standardized family satisfaction survey administered after discharge. In addition, the effect of Baby CareLink on hospital length of stay as well as family visitation and interactions with infant and staff were measured.

Results: Thirty control and 25 study patients were enrolled. Families in the CareLink group reported significantly fewer problems with the overall quality of care received by their family (mean problem score: 3% vs. 13%). They also reported greater satisfaction with the unit's physical environment and visitation policies (mean problem score: 13% vs. 50%). The duration of hospitalization was similar in the two groups. All infants in the CareLink group were discharged directly to home, whereas 20% of control infants were transferred to community hospitals before ultimately being discharged to home.

Conclusion: CareLink significantly improves family satisfaction with inpatient VLBW care and definitively lowers costs associated with hospital-to-hospital transfer.

---

80. This example is based on Gray JE, Safran C, Davis RB, et al. Baby CareLink: Using the Internet and Telemedicine to Improve Care for High-Risk Infants. Pediatrics 2000; 106(6):1318-24.

## *Exercises*

### Exercise 5.5.1: An Information Processing Monitoring Report

Look at the annual information processing monitoring report in example 5.5.1. Figure out some numbers for a hospital you know. It may help to look at the strategic information management plan of this hospital.

### Exercise 5.5.2: Organizing User Feedback

You are asked to organize regular user feedback facilities for the healthcare professional workstation of your hospital. How would you proceed? How would you gather user feedback? Which user groups would you take into account? Which technical means would you use? Discuss different possibilities.

### Exercise 5.5.3: Planning of an Assessment Study

Your task is to prepare an assessment study of a newly introduced computer-based nursing documentation system. The goal of this study is to calculate the cost-benefit ratio of the documentation system. Define an adequate assessment plan. What would the questions be? What measuring methods would be used? What would an adequate study design be? Discuss the different possibilities.

## *Summary*

The task of strategic HIS monitoring is to continually audit the quality of the hospital information system, that is, to initiate, collect, and analyze feedback on the functioning of the hospital information system. Feedback should be systematically gathered, but it can also occur unexpectedly.

Permanent monitoring activities comprise the definition of a definite subset of central quality criteria that are to be monitored on a regular (daily, weekly, monthly, yearly) basis. Permanent monitoring is supported by national and international certification and accreditation activities.

Certification in hospitals concentrates mostly on the ISO 9000 norm and primarily assesses compliance with quality management standards. The goal of accreditation programs is total quality management and continuous quality improvement of organizations. An example of accreditation is the JCAHO program, which also comprises 10 information management standards. So-called excellence programs such as the EFQM model for Europe use a scoring system that makes it possible to compare organizations to one another.

Besides those permanent monitoring activities, ad hoc monitoring activities are typically assessment studies as tactical information management projects. Assessment studies can focus on multiple questions, and can use multiple methods. Each study must be systematically planned and executed.

## 5.6 Strategic Directing of Hospital Information Systems

### *Introduction*

Strategic directing of HIS is a consequence of planning and monitoring hospital information functions, HIS architectures, and information management organizations.

After reading this section, you should be able to answer the following questions:

- What are the typical tasks of strategic HIS directing?
- What are the typical methods of strategic HIS directing?

### *Tasks*

Strategic directing of information systems mainly transforms the strategic information management plan into projects. These projects are taken from the strategic project portfolio as established by strategic information planning. The decision to initiate projects is done by strategic information planning; the execution of this decision is the responsibility of strategic information directing.

Planning, running, and (successfully) finishing projects is a task of tactical information management. However, strategic directing must initiate them and prepare an adequate framework for them. In detail, the following main tasks can be identified:

- initiation of projects,
- general resource allocation,
- general time allocation,
- general controlling of the project progress, and
- adoption of the project's results.

### *Methods*

The typical method used for strategic HIS directing is general project management, including as allocation planning and project controlling. For projects of important strategic relevance (e.g., introduction of a hospital-wide electronic patient record system), a project management board will typically be established.

Such a *project management board* plans, directs, and monitors a bundle of tactical information management projects. For introducing an electronic patient record system, for example, different projects have to be executed, such as introduction of a nursing documentation system, an order entry system, and electronic patient record archiving. The project management board guarantees that these projects are coordinated and executed efficiently.

Typically, the project management board comprises representatives from the strategic information management, as well as representatives from the ICT department and from the departments involved. The project managers report to this board and should be part of it.

Important tasks of a project management board are setting priorities and long-term planning for the projects; making all relevant strategic decisions on this project, especially with respect to investments, staff, and organization; establishing and controlling the projects; and identifying and solving serious project problems. In this role, the project management board supports the CIO in directing the most important HIS projects.

## *Example*

### Example 5.6.1: Project Management Boards at PMC

Currently, two project management boards are established at Plötzberg Medical Center and Medical School (PMC):

1. Project management board for the healthcare professional workstation. Head of the board is the CIO. Members are representatives from the hospital board of managers (vice president for nursing, vice president for administration), representatives from the main user groups (senior physician from the surgery department, senior physician from the internal medicine department), as well as the project managers of the different subprojects.
2. Project management board for the introduction of a new computer-based intensive care data management system. Head is the manager of the quality assurance department. Members are the manager of the ICT department, representatives from main user groups (senior physician and head nurse from the surgery department), and the project managers.

## *Exercise*

### Exercise 5.6.1: A Project Management Board at PMC

At the Plötzberg Medical Center and Medical School (PMC), a project is going to be initiated to introduce a hospital-wide nursing documentation system. This application component comprises functionality of comprehensive nursing data management as well as supporting communication with other healthcare professionals.

Due to the high significance of nursing documentation, a project management board will be installed. Who should the members of this board be? Explain your answer.

## *Summary*

Strategic directing of information systems mainly consists of transforming the strategic information management plan into projects. It is at least as important as strategic planning and strategic monitoring, but often, from a methodological point of view, an immediate consequence of them.

For projects of important strategic relevance (e.g., introduction of a hospital-wide electronic patient record system), a project management board typically is established. This project management board plans, directs, and monitors a bundle of tactical information management projects.

# 5.7 Examples

### Example 5.7.1: Information Management Responsibilities[81]

The senior executives (chief executive officers, chief operating officers, or chief information officers) at 10 healthcare organizations conducted audits to evaluate the effectiveness of information management in their own organizations. The organizations ranged from rural hospitals to university affiliated teaching hospitals, with bed size ranging from 60 to 1232.

The audits evaluated how well the following seven information technology management responsibilities were carried out: (1) strategic information systems planning; (2) employment of a user focus in system development; (3) recruiting of competent IT personnel; (4) information systems integration; (5) protection of information security and confidentiality; (6) employment of effective project management in system development; and (7) postimplementation evaluation of information systems.

The audit results suggest that most of these responsibilities are being met to a considerable extent by a majority of the organizations studied. However, substantial variation across organizations was noted. Executives participating in the study were able to define areas in which the management of information resources in their organizations was in need of attention. The audit process encourages senior management to provide the leadership re-

---

81. This example is based on Austin KD, Hornberger JE, Shmerling JE, Managing information resources: a study of ten healthcare organizations, J Healthc Manag 45 (4) (2000) 229-38; discussion 238-9.

quired to ensure that information technology is used to maximum advantage.

## Example 5.7.2: Computer Network Failures[82]

The computer system of Plötzberg Medical Center and Medical School (PMC) crashed repeatedly over 3 1/2 days last week, periodically blocking access to patient records, prescriptions, laboratory reports, and other information, and forcing the hospital to revert to the paper-based systems of what one executive called "the hospital of the 1970s."

Hospital executives said yesterday that patient safety was never jeopardized. But scores of employees worked overtime printing records, double-checking doses, physically running messages from the labs to the wards and back—even rushing to buy copier paper on the credit card of the chief operating officer (COO), Dr. E. The crisis, which lasted from Wednesday afternoon until Sunday, took the hospital by surprise. Its electronic network was named the nation's best in health care last year by the magazine *Information Week*, and its chief information officer (CIO), Dr. H., is an authority on medical computing.

As hospitals are urged to convert their record keeping to computers as part of the battle against errors, hospital and public health officials are calling the incident a wake-up call for hospitals across the country, whose computer systems may not be able to keep up with their growing workload. At PMC, the systems handle 40 terabytes of information daily—or 40 times the information in the Library of Congress.

"Imagine if you built a house and you put in an extension cord to it, and then you hook up a lawnmower, and then you hook up a barbecue. Eventually the breaker is going to blow," the CIO, Dr. H., said. "I as CIO feel a moral obligation to share the lessons we have learned over the last few days with every other CIO in the country. Have you got systems in place to deal with a problem like this? And if you have infrastructures that are at risk, have you done due diligence to really look at your hospital and make changes?"

Although computer systems have allowed hospitals to work with more speed and flexibility, executives said, last week's events showed how frightening it can be when they fail. "Any time you're taking care of very sick patients, when everything isn't as you're used to it, you get a little nervous," said the COO, Dr. E.

The crisis began when a researcher installed software to analyze data, and a large amount of information started flowing over the network. Doctors noticed intermittent problems with e-mail and data entry. But at 4 p.m. on Wednesday, most of the systems—from e-mail to accessing patient re-

82. This example is based on a report in Boston Globe, November 19th, 2002, page B1.

cords to entering laboratory data—slowed or stopped and stayed down for 2 hours.

The hospital called in a special forces team of specialists from the manufacturer that provides and maintains its computer networks. But the crashes kept happening every 4 to 6 hours, so rather than go back and forth between paper and computer systems, the hospital decided to switch to all-paper.

The emergency room shut down for most of Friday, and the hospital decided to refuse all transfers except in life-threatening emergencies. Some lab tests that normally take 45 minutes to complete took closer to 2 hours, so doctors reverted to lower-tech methods of diagnosis. "There was a sense of old-fashioned medicine," said Dr. S., an intensive-care physician.

In response to the incident, the manufacturer plans to warn hospitals to update their systems, the CIO said. He also plans to talk about the subject with the systems managers of the state's hospitals Thursday, at a previously planned meeting of the regional Health Data Consortium.

All hospitals were required to put in disaster plans for Y2K. PMC had such a plan in place, but because systems evolve so quickly, it was already outdated. The hospital has not calculated how much the computer setbacks will cost. The COO said there may be some delay in receiving payments from insurers because billing relies on the computer network.

## Example 5.7.3: Deficiencies in Information Management

The following letter was written by the head of the Department of Internal Medicine of the Plötzberg Medical Center and Medical School (PMC) to the chief executive officer. He complains about failures in information management.

"Dear colleague,

I am sitting here again, having organized the duties for Good Friday and the whole Easter weekend in a way that patient care as far as the physicians are concerned is guaranteed. I can also be sure that nursing is well organized for these days, so I want to use the holidays to catch up with my work in the clinic. On the other hand, I have to realize that the network of our clinic is down yet again and that consequently, starting from the doorkeeper's office to every ward and every lab, there isn't any kind of data processing or EDP support. The doorkeeper sends visitors coming to see their relatives to the wards by trusting their luck. At the wards, essential information is missing and scientific work is delayed by the cutting off of all internal and external scientific networks.

With this letter I want to express my protest once again and complain about the fact that the way information processing is managed in our hospital is completely unacceptable. I do not know what still has to happen so that we can finally get an emergency service for nights and for holidays. This is why I want to ask you to immediately make sure in the board of the PMC and in the Committee for Information Processing that such a technical standby service is installed for the maintenance of the network and for breakdowns in the same way that we provide on-call services for all important clinical processes.

In summary, I want to express my deep disappointment about the whole situation. Nowadays, information processing has gained such an important standing in daily patient care that we can really put patients at risk if we do not immediately—and with this I mean at once—find a remedy for this problem.

Yours sincerely,
in a very annoyed mood

Prof. Dr. K.
Director of the Dept. of Internal Medicine

### Example 5.7.4: Cultivating Hospital Information Systems

Look at the following description of the duties of a forest's owner and discuss the similarities and differences of cultivating a forest and of information management in a hospital:

"The duties of a forest's owner are

- to cultivate the forest according to its purpose,
- lastingly ...
- carefully ...
- systematically ... and
- competently ...
- using recognized forest-managerial methods ..."[83]

## 5.8 Exercises

### Exercise 5.8.1: Management of Other Information Systems

Are there any differences between management of hospital information systems and management of other information systems? Explain your answer.

### Exercise 5.8.2: Beginning and End of Information Management

When does hospital information management start, and when does it end? Directing and monitoring are ongoing tasks of information management. Is this true for planning as well?

83. Forest law of the state of Baden-Württemberg, Germany, August 31st, 1995, §12, translated from German.

**Exercise 5.8.3: Lessons for Information Management**

Look at examples 5.7.1, 5.7.2 and 5.7.3. What have the reasons been for these failures of the computer-based part of the hospital information system? What can information management learn from those reports? Analyze the problems and suggest appropriate activities to prevent the described deficiencies.

**Exercise 5.8.4: Problems of Operational Information Management**

Look at the following problems, derived from the report of the assessment of the operational information management at Plötzberg Medical Center and Medical School (PMC). How would you proceed to solve these problems?

- The Department of Medical Informatics, which is partly responsible for operational management, is distributed over several areas that are some miles away from the hospital's building. This causes long delays, loss of information, and delayed response times in case of local problems.
- The responsibilities of the different institutions involved in information management (e.g., ICT department) are not clearly defined. For example, the responsibilities of the network backbone and the local networks are not clearly separated.
- The cost of information management and information processing are unclear. For example, the total costs of the introduction of an electronic mailing system for all staff of the hospital are not exactly known.
- In the case of emergencies (e.g., fire) in the central ICT department, there may be extensive data losses and a longer unavailability of important application components.

# 5.9 Summary

The tasks of information management in hospitals are planning, directing, and monitoring of HIS. It can be distinguished into strategic, tactical, and operational information management. Strategic information management deals with the hospital's information processing as a whole. Tactical information management deals with particular enterprise functions or application components. Operational information management is responsible for operating the components of the hospital information system.

Each hospital should have an adequate organization for strategic, tactical, and operational information management. In general, a chief information officer (CIO) should be responsible for strategic information management. There should be at least one central ICT department for tactical and operational information management of the computer-supported part of the

HIS. In addition, there may be decentralized information management staff, located at the individual departments of the hospital.

Strategic HIS planning deals with planning of HIS architecture and of the organization of information management. Tasks of strategic HIS planning are the strategic alignment of business plans and information management plans, the long-term HIS planning, and the short-term HIS planning. The main methods are the strategic alignment of hospital goals and information management goals, adequate portfolio management, and the establishment of a strategic information management plan.

Strategic HIS monitoring aims to continually audit the quality of the hospital information system, that is, to initiate, collect, and analyze feedback on the functioning of the hospital information system. It comprises permanent monitoring activities, which can be based on standardized certification, accreditation and excellence programs, as well as ad hoc monitoring activities such as assessment studies.

Strategic HIS directing mainly consists of transforming the strategic information management plan into projects.

Summarizing, some quality criteria for an efficient information management can be defined, such as:

- Clear decision structures, roles, and responsibilities for strategic, tactical, and operational information management.
- Systematic strategic information management with a strategic information management plan as the basis.
- Systematic tactical information management, with clear management of the projects.
- Systematic operational information management, with an appropriate support strategy to guarantee the continuous and faultless operation of the information processing tools.
- Sufficient and ongoing training of the users.
- Motivation and competence of IT staff, which is essential for the efficient functioning of the information systems and for a high acceptance by the users.

# 6
# Final Remarks

Hospital information systems are sometimes compared to large tankers crossing the oceans. Like tankers, hospital information systems need careful and long-term planning (planning its course), they need continual monitoring to ensure their course is still followed (staying on course), and they react only very slowly to directing (steering) activities.

Well-educated health informatics specialists (who are comparable to tanker captains and officers), with the knowledge and skills to systematically manage and operate hospital information systems, are therefore needed to appropriately and responsibly apply information and communication technology to the complex information processing environment of a hospital.

This book discussed the systematic management of hospital information systems in detail. The reader should now be able to answer the following questions:

- Why is systematic information processing in hospitals important?
- What do hospital information systems look like?
- What are good hospital information systems?
- How can we strategically manage hospital information systems?

This book should be regarded as an introduction to this complex subject. For a deeper understanding, the reader will need additional knowledge and, foremost, practice in this field.

*And now one last exercise: Four medical informatics VIPs volunteered to pose in some of the figures used in this book: Prof. Marion Ball (United States), Prof. K.C. Lun (Singapore), Prof. Jochen Moehr (Canada), and Prof. Gustav Wagner (Germany). Did you recognize them? Good luck in finding them!*

# Appendix A: Thesaurus

This chapter defines the most important concepts and terms used in this book. Cross-references between entries are indicated by ‚→'.

### 3LGM

Abbreviation for →three-layer graph-based metamodel.

### Access integration

Condition of an →information system where the →application components needed for the completion of a certain task can be used where they are needed.

Synonymous term: Zugangsintegration (German)

### Accreditation

To certify that an institution meets predefined quality standards. An example of an organization that evaluates and accredits hospitals in the United States is JCAHO (Joint Commission on Accreditation of Healthcare Organizations).

Synonymous term: Akkreditierung (German)

### Activity

Instantiation of an →enterprise function working on an individual entity.

Synonymous term: Aktivität (German)

### Administrative admission

→Patient identification and documentation of main administrative data during the admission of a patient to an institution. Includes assignment of a →patient identification number and of a visit number (case identifier).

Synonymous term: Administrative Aufnahme (German)

**Administrative documentation**

Documentation of patient-related data as basis for billing, controlling, cost center accounting, internal budgeting, or other economic analysis, sometimes done for legal reasons. Includes recording of diagnoses and procedures in a standardized way. Administrative documentation should be at least partly derivable from →clinical documentation.

Synonymous term: Administrative Dokumentation (German)

**ADT**

Admission, discharge, and transfer of a patient.

**Application component**

Responsible for the storage and for the communication of →data about entities of a specific type. Supports →enterprise functions. Computer-based application components are controlled by application programs, which are adapted →software products; paper-based application components are controlled by working plans that describe how people use paper-based →physical data processing components.

Synonymous term: Anwendungsbaustein (German)

**Application component configuration**

Within the →3LGM, the relationship between →enterprise functions and →application components. It states, that a →hospital function may be supported by several application components together, by a single application component, or by combinations of the two.

Synonymous term: Anwendungsbaustein-Konfiguration (German)

**Architectural style**

Summarizes →architectures of information systems that are equivalent with regard to certain characteristics.

Synonymous term: Architekturstil (German)

**Architecture of an information system**

Fundamental organization of an →information system, represented by its →components, their relationships to each other and to the environment, and by the principles guiding its design and evolution.

Synonymous term: Architektur eines Informationssystems (German)

### Archiving

Long-time storing (e.g., for 10 or 30 years, depending on legal regulations) of documents and records, especially of →patient records, after discharge of a patient.

Synonymous term: Archivierung (German)

### Assessment study

Specific →project of →tactical information management, which tries to analyze and evaluate a →component of an information system, thus supporting →monitoring of →HIS.

Synonymous term: Bewertungsstudie (German)

### Asynchronous communication

Form of communication where the process in the →application component that initiated communication with another application component does not have to be interrupted while awaiting or obtaining response data from the communication partner. This form of communication usually occurs through the sending of →messages. The opposite is →synchronous communication.

Synonymous term: Asynchrone Kommunikation (German)

### Basic data-set documentation

Standardized documentation of few particularly important attributes of all patients of a healthcare institution. It permits the retrieval of all patients with particular attributes and enables access to their healthcare documents. Moreover, statistics on those attributes can be produced. Thus, a healthcare institution gets a relevant current overview about its patients' characteristics. In Europe, uniform attributes for outpatient and inpatient basic data-set documentation have been suggested, and termed minimum basic data sets (MBDS).

Synonymous term: Basisdokumentation (German)

### Business process

Sequence of →activities together with the conditions under which they are invoked, in order to achieve an enterprise goal.

Synonymous term: Geschäftsprozess (German)

### Business process model

→Model focusing on the dynamic view of →information processing. Elements offered are typically →activities and their chronological and logical order. Often, other elements can be added, such as the role or unit that performs an activity, or the →information processing tools that are used. Due to the amount of different perspectives, various business process →metamodels exist, such as simple process chains, event-driven process chains, activity diagrams, and petri nets.

Synonymous term: Geschäftsprozess-Modell (German)

### CCOW (clinical context object workgroup)

Develops standards for the synchronization of independent →application components on a →healthcare professional workstation, in order to support →contextual integration.

### Certification

Assessment of the compliance with →quality management standards. Certification in hospitals concentrates mostly on the ISO 9000 standard. An ISO 9000 certificate states that a hospital meets the standards, but says nothing about →outcome quality.

Synonymous term: Zertifizierung (German)

### Chief executive officer (CEO)

Responsible for setting and carrying out the strategic plans and policies of an enterprise.

Synonymous term: Geschäftsführer, Vorstandsvorsitzender (German)

### Chief financial officer (CFO)

Responsible for financial planning and record keeping of an enterprise.

Synonymous term: Leiter der Finanzabteilung (German)

### Chief information officer (CIO)

Responsible for the →strategic, →tactical and →operational information management in an enterprise. The CIO usually has the authority for all employees concerned with →information management. The specific position of the CIO demands dedicated professional skills.

Synonymous term: Leiter des Informationsmanagements (German)

## Client-server architecture

→Architectural style at the →physical tool layer, comprising various servers and clients, interconnected by a network. The servers can be application file servers or database servers. The server offers services that can be accessed by the workstations as clients. The workstations are usually typical personal →computer systems with their own memory and data processing units. They can offer access to →application components installed on the application file server as well as to locally installed application components.

Synonymous term: Client-Server-Architektur (German)

## Clinical admission

Admission of patient to an institution from a medical and nursing point of view. It typically comprises the patient history and the introduction of the patient to the ward. Clinical admission usually follows →administrative admission. activities.

Synonymous term: Klinische Aufnahme (German)

## Clinical documentation

Recording all clinically relevant patient →data (such as vital signs, orders, results, decisions, dates) that arise during patient care as completely, correctly, and quickly as possible. This supports the coordination of patient treatment between all involved →healthcare professionals, and also the legal justification of the actions taken. Structured documentation of data is a precondition for data aggregation and statistics, computerized decision support, and retrieval of data.

Synonymous term: Klinische Dokumentation (German)

## Clinical information system

→Application component supporting →clinical documentation, →order entry and result reporting, and ward management.

Synonymous term: Klinisches Informationssystem (German)

## Communication server

→Application component supporting →asynchronous communication between application components. Stands at the center of the →logical tool layer of a →hospital information system. This architectural principle can be found in most hospital information systems with the →$DB^n$ architectural style. The communication server provides the asynchronous sending, receiving, monitoring, and buffering of →messages.

Synonymous term: Kommunikationsserver (German)

### Communication standard

Consensus on the syntax and semantics of →messages that are to be exchanged between →application components. Two important communication standards in health care are →HL7 and →DICOM.

Synonymous term: Kommunikationsstandard (German)

### Component of an information system

Typical components of →information systems are →enterprise functions, →business processes, →application components, and →physical data processing components.

Synonymous term: Komponente eines Informationssystems (German)

### Computer system

A computer-based →physical data processing tool, for example, a terminal, server or personal computer. Computer systems can be physically connected via data wires, leading to physical networks.

### Content integrity

Condition of an →information system in which the same →data that are used in different →application components in a hospital are interpreted in the same way. Content integrity can be supported by →medical data dictionaries (MDDs).

Synonymous term: Inhaltliche Integrität (German)

### Contextual integration

Condition of an →information system in which the context (e.g., patient identification) is preserved when an →application component is changed, for example, at a →healthcare professional workstation. The general aim is that a task that has already been executed once for a certain purpose does not need to be repeated again to achieve the same purpose. This type of →integration is also referred to as visual integration.

Synonymous term: Kontext-Integration (German)

### Controlled redundancy

Systematic management of redundantly stored →data. Usually, redundant data storage should be avoided. However, there are situations in which redundant data storage is unavoidable or even desirable. In any case, data redundancy must be systematically managed. In particular, it must be clear which database system is the →master database system for these data, when data copies are made, for which purpose they are made, and in which case changes of the master data are communicated to the data copies.

Synonymous term: Kontrollierte Redundanz (German)

### Controlling

Collecting and analyzing financial and other data about the hospital's operation in order to manage and optimize it. This covers, for example, staff controlling, process controlling, material controlling, and financial controlling.

### CORBA (Common object request broker architecture)

→Architectural style for distributed object systems, proposed by the object management group (OMG). The object request broker (ORB) carries an index of all services provided by the objects that are part of the architecture. The index is updated at run time, so that the ORB can support an object demanding a certain service (client) by selecting the most suitable offering object (server). The domain task force CORBAmed works on standardization of the services for the medical area.

### Cost-benefit analysis

An economic analysis to compare the costs and consequences of a →component of an information system. It converts effects of an information system component into the same monetary terms as the costs.

Synonymous term: Kosten-Nutzen-Analyse (German)

### Cost-effectiveness analysis

An economic analysis to compare the costs and consequences of a →component of an information system. It does not require that all important effects be expressed in monetary terms.

Synonymous term: Kostenwirksamkeitsanalyse (German)

### Data

Reinterpretable representation of →information or →knowledge in a formalized manner suitable for communication, interpretation, or processing by humans or machines (ISO 2382, DIN 44300[84]). Formalization may take the form of discrete characters or of continuous signals (e.g., sound signals). To be reinterpretable, there have to be agreements on how data represent information.

Synonymous term: Daten (German)

### Data integration

Condition of an →information system in which each data item needs to be recorded, changed, deleted, or otherwise edited just once, even if it is used in several →application components. Data integration is a prerequisite for the →multiple usability of data.

Synonymous term: Datenintegration (German)

### Data model

→Model focusing on the data processed and stored in an →information system.
Elements offered are typically entity types and their relationships. A typical →metamodel for data modeling is offered by the class diagrams in the Unified Modeling Language (UML) .

Synonymous term: Datenmodell (German)

### Data processing component configuration

Within the →3LGM, the relationship between the → application components and the →physical data processing components. It states, that an application component may be installed on several physical data processing components together (e.g., typical client-server installations), on a single physical data processing component (typical stand-alone application components), or through combinations of these two.

Synonymous term: Konfiguration der Datenverarbeitungsbausteine (German)

### DB[1] architectural style

→Architectural style where a →hospital information system (or a →sub-information system) comprises only one →application component containing a database system. In this case, all patient-related data are stored in exactly one database system. The precondition for this is that the different computer-based application components all only work with the database system of the central application component. This architectural style, therefore, can be

84. DIN. Deutsches Institut für Normung. http://www.din.de.

found mostly in HISs using application components that are based on homogeneous →software products.

Synonymous term: $DB^1$-Architekturstil (German)

**$DB^n$ architectural style**

→Architectural style in which a →hospital information system (or a →sub-information system) comprises several →application components containing their own database systems. As a consequence of this architectural style, patient-related data are stored redundantly in database systems of different application components. Therefore, in this architectural style, great emphasis has to be placed on the →integrity of redundant data.

Synonymous term: $DB^n$-Architekturstil (German)

**DICOM (Digital Imaging and Communication in Medicine)**

Important →communication standard in health care, used for the transfer of medical images. With DICOM, not only images (e.g., the results of radiological examinations) can be sent from their digital modalities to the resulting workstations or into the PACS, but also data describing the originating requests (e.g., from the radiology information system) can be sent to the required digital modalities. DICOM not only defines a →message format, but also couples this closely with exchange formats.

**Directing**

An important task of →information management is directing the establishment and operation of an →information system. Directing in →strategic information management means to transform a →strategic information management plan into action, that is, to systematically manipulate a hospital information system to make it conform to the strategic information management plan. Directing in →tactical information management means the execution of →projects, based on a project plan. Directing in →operational information management means the sum of all management activities that are necessary to ensure proper reactions to operating problems of →components of a hospital information system.

Synonymous term: Steuerung (German)

**Domain layer**

A set of →enterprise functions in the →3LGM that describe an enterprise independent of its implementation. Enterprise functions need →information of a certain type about physical or virtual entities of the hospital. These types of information are represented as entity types.

Synonymous term: Fachliche Ebene (German)

**Electronic patient record (EPR)**

Complete or partial →patient record stored on an electronic storage medium. Given this definition, every computer-based →application component with →clinical documentation functionality contains at least a partial electronic patient record.

Synonymous term: Elektronische Krankenakte (EKA), elektronische Patientenakte (EPA) (German)

**Enterprise function**

Describes what humans or machines have to do in a certain enterprise to contribute to its mission and goals. Enterprise functions are ongoing and continuous. They describe what is to be done, not how it is done.

Synonymous term: Unternehmensaufgabe (German)

**Enterprise modeling**

Comprises various modeling aspects such as modeling of →functional models, →technical models, →organizational models, →data models, or →business process models, and the dependencies between those models.

Synonymous term: Unternehmensmodellierung (German)

**Federated database system**

Integrated system of autonomous (component) database systems. The point of →integration is to logically bring the database schemata of the component database systems to a single database schema, the federated database schema, in order to attain →data integration even when there is redundant data in information systems with a →$DB^n$ architectural style.

Synonymous term: Föderiertes Datenbanksystem (German)

**First level of operational support**

User support unit serving as first contact for all user groups with any kinds of information processing problems. It may consist, for example, of a central 24-hour-hotline team, responsible for management of user accounts and first troubleshooting, or of a decentralized information processing staff. When the first level of operational support cannot solve the problems, they are handed over to the →second level of operational support.

Synonymous term: First level support (German)

**Formal integrity**

Comprises →object identity and →referential integrity.

Synonymous term: Formale Integrität (German)

**Functional leanness**

Condition of an →information system where an →enterprise function is supported by one and only one →application component. The opposite is →functional redundancy.

Synonymous term: Funktionale Schlankheit (German)

**Functional model**

→Model focusing on the functions of a hospital (what is to be done). Elements offered are typically →enterprise functions that are supported by the →application components of an → information system.

Synonymous term: Aufgaben-Modell (German)

**Functional redundancy**

Condition of an →information system where an →enterprise function is supported by more than one →application component. The opposite is →functional leanness.

Synonymous term: Funktionale Redundanz (German)

**Healthcare professional**

Staff member directly contributing to patient care, such as a physician or nurse.

Synonymous term: Klinisches Personal (German)

**Healthcare professional workstation (HCPW)**

Specific →information processing tool in hospitals, consisting of a (mobile or stationary) personal computer, connected to the hospital's computer network, together with the →application components installed and the →hospital functions supported. An HCPW usually provides extensive functionality for →healthcare professionals.

Synonymous term: Klinisches Arbeitsplatzsystem (German)

### Health information system

→Information system spreading over institutional boundaries to support trans-institutional patient care.

Synonymous term: Informationssystem des Gesundheitswesens (German)

### Health Level Seven (HL7)

Important →communication standard in health care supporting the transfer of patient- and case-based messages, excluding image data. HL7 describes the events and structure with which, →messages are exchanged between →application components.

### HIS

Abbreviation for →hospital information system.

### Hospital function

→Enterprise functions of a hospital.

Synonymous term: Krankenhausaufgabe (German)

### Hospital information system (HIS)

Socio-technical →subsystem of a hospital that comprises all →information processing as well as the associated human or technical actors in their respective information processing roles.

Synonymous term: Krankenhausinformationssystem (KIS) (German)

### Hospital management

The executives responsible for attaining the strategic hospital goals.

Synonymous term: Krankenhausleitung (German)

### Information

Specific →knowledge about entities such as facts, events, things, persons, processes, ideas, or concepts that, within a certain context, have a particular meaning (ISO 2382).

### Information management

Planning the →information system of an enterprise and its architecture, directing its establishment and its operation, and monitoring its development and operation with respect to the planned objectives. Encompasses the management of all →components of an information system: the management of →information, of →application components, and of →physical data processing components. The goal of information management is systematic information processing that contributes to the enterprise's strategic goals. With respect to its scope, information management can be divided into →strategic, →tactical, and →operational information management.

Synonymous term: Informationsmanagement (German)

**Information management board**

Responsible for →strategic information management in a hospital. Members should include representatives from the hospital's board of directors, representatives from the main departments and user groups, and the director of the ICT department. If no dedicated →CIO position exists, the president of this board can be regarded as the CIO of the hospital.

Synonymous term: Ausschuss für das Informationsmanagement (German)

**Information processing**

In the context of →hospital information systems, refers to the processing of →data, →information, and →knowledge.

Synonymous term: Informationsverarbeitung (German)

**Information processing tool**

An →application component or →physical data processing component. Can be either computer-based or paper-based.

Synonymous term: Werkzeug der Informationsverarbeitung (German)

**Information system**

Socio-technical →subsystem of an enterprise that comprises all →information processing as well as the associated human or technical actors in their respective information processing roles.
Synonymous term: Informationssystem (German)

**Infrastructure of an information system**

Types, number, and availability of →information processing tools used in a given enterprise.

Synonymous term: Infrastruktur eines Informationssystems (German)

### Integrated healthcare delivery system

System of healthcare institutions that join together to consolidate their roles, resources, and operations in order to deliver a coordinated range of services and to enhance effectiveness and efficiency of patient care.

Synonymous term: Integriertes Gesundheitsversorgungssystem (German)

### Integration

A union of parts making a whole, which as opposed to its parts, displays a new quality. We speak of integrated information processing if we want to express that a →hospital information system is a union that represents more than just a set of independent →components. We expect positive consequences for the quality of →information processing by integration. Different qualities of integration are →data integration, →access integration, →presentation integration, and →contextual integration.

### Integrity

The correctness of →data. Two main aspects of integrity are →formal integrity and →content integrity.

Synonymous term: Integrität (German)

### Interlayer relationship

Relationships among →components of different layers in the →3LGM. Relationships exist between classes at the →domain layer and the →logical tool layer (→application component configuration) and between classes at the logical tool layer and the →physical tool layer (→data processing component configuration).

Synonymous term: Interebenen-Beziehung (German)

### Knowledge

General →information about concepts in a certain (scientific or professional) domain (for example, about diseases or therapeutic methods). Knowledge contrasts with specific information about particular individuals of the domain (e.g., patients).

Synonymous term: Wissen (German)

### Knowledge server

→Application component supporting access to medical and nursing →knowledge for →healthcare professionals (e.g., medical and nursing guidelines and standards, reference databases, scientific papers, drug databases).

Synonymous term: Wissensserver (German)

### Laboratory information system (LIS)

→Application component supporting the management of analysis in a clinical laboratory: the receipt of the order and the sample, the distribution of the sample and the order to the different analysis tools, the collection of the results, the validation of results, the communication of the findings back to the ordering department, as well as general →quality management procedures.

Synonymous term: Labor-Informationssystem (German)

### Leanness of information processing tools

For a given task, from the point of view of the user, there should be as many different →information processing tools as necessary, but as few as possible.

Synonymous term: Schlankheit von informationsverarbeitenden Werkzeugen (German)

### Logical tool layer

A set of →application components and their communication interfaces in the →3LGM.

Synonymous term: Logische Werkzeugebene (German)

### Mainframe-based architecture

→Architectural style at the →physical tool layer, consisting of one or multiple (networked) mainframe systems to which various terminals are attached. The terminals can be used to access the →application components that are installed on the mainframe system. The terminals do not have their own data processing facilities or local memories.

Synonymous term: Großrechner-basierte Architektur (German)

### Management of information systems

Management can stand for an institution or an →enterprise function. As an institution, management comprises all organizational units of an enterprise that make decisions about planning, monitoring, and directing all activities of subordinate units. As an enterprise function, management comprises all leadership activities that determine the enterprise's goals, structures, and behaviors. Management of information systems both as an institution or as a function is a synonym to →information management.

Synonymous term: Management von Informationssystemen (German)

**Master database system**

Leading database system in which datasets of redundantly saved entity types are allowed to be inserted, changed and deleted.

Synonymous term: Führendes Datenbanksystem (German)

**Media crack**

Change of the storage media during the →transcription of data.

Synonymous term: Medienbruch (German)

**Medical data dictionary (MDD)**

Central catalog of medical concepts and terms that offers the possibility of representing the semantic relationships among all →data stored in a →hospital information system, and to link that local vocabulary to internationally standardized nomenclatures and knowledge sources. An MDD can be realized as an independent →application component or as part of an existing application component. A MDD is normally composed of a system of medical concepts and terms, an information model, and a knowledge base.

Synonymous term: Medizinischer Thesaurus (German)

**Message**

Set of →data that is put together for the purpose of transmission and that is considered to be one entity for this purpose (DIN 44300).

Synonymous term: Nachricht (German)

**Metamodel**

Language for describing →models of a certain class. It usually describes the modeling framework, which consists of the modeling syntax and semantics (the available modeling objects together with their meaning), the representation of the objects (how the objects are represented in a concrete model, e.g., often in a graphical way), and (sometimes) the modeling rules (e.g., the modeling steps). An example of a metamodel for →hospital information systems is the →3LGM.

Synonymous term: Metamodell (German)

**Middleware**

Software components of a computer-supported →information system that serve for the communication between →application components.

**Mobile personal digital assistant**

Mobile →information processing tool, supporting personal organization (e.g., task lists, scheduling), the writing of notes, and information access.

Synonymous term: Mobiler persönlicher digitaler Assistent (German)

**Model**

A simplified depiction of reality or excerpts of it. Models are usually adapted to answer certain questions or to solve certain tasks.

Synonymous term: Modell (German)

**Monitoring**

Checking on the development and operation of a →hospital information system with respect to the planned objectives. Monitoring in →strategic information management means continually auditing its quality as defined by means of its →strategic information management plan's directives and goals. Monitoring in →tactical information management means continually checking whether initiated →projects are running as planned, and whether they will produce the expected results. Monitoring in →operational information management means verifying the proper working and effectiveness of all →components of a hospital information system.

Synonymous term: Überwachung (German)

**Multiple usability of data**

Condition where →data are captured once but used for more than one task. A prerequisite is →data integration. Multiple usability of data is one important benefit computer-support can bring to →information systems.

Synonymous term: Multiple Verwendbarkeit von Daten (German)

**Nursing documentation system**

→Application component for nursing documentation, supporting all phases of the nursing process such as nursing patient history, nursing care planning, execution of nursing tasks, and evaluation of results.

Synonymous term: Pflegedokumentationssystem (German)

**Object identity**

Condition of an →information system where the representation of every entity is uniquely identifiable. In a →hospital information system, this is especially important for patients and cases since all medical data need to be assigned to a particular patient and his or her cases. →Patient identification numbers and case identification numbers are used for that purpose.

Synonymous term: Objektidentität (German)

**Operation documentation system**

→Application component that supports operation documentation. The planning data are taken from the operation planning systems to be updated and completed during and after the operation. Based on these data, an operation report can be created, which may be completed by further comments of the surgeons.

Synonymous term: Operations-Dokumentationssystem, OP-Dokumentationssystem (German)

**Operation planning system**

→Application component supporting planning of surgical interventions. It should allow assigning of date and time of surgery, and, therefore, should be available on wards as well as in offices and management units of an operating unit.

Synonymous term: Operations-Planungssystem, OP-Planungssystem (German)

**Operational information management**

Responsible for operating all →components of an information system. It cares for its smooth operation, usually in accordance with the →strategic information management plan of a hospital.

Synonymous term: Operatives Informationsmanagement (German)

### Order entry

The process of entering and transmitting a clinical order to a diagnostic or therapeutic service unit (e.g., lab, radiology, surgery) or to another →healthcare professional. The available service spectrum offered by a service unit may be presented in the form of catalogs.

Synonymous term: Leistungsanforderung (German)

### Order entry and result reporting

Comprises →order entry of diagnostic or therapeutic procedures, appointment scheduling, printing of labels, as well as the communication and presentation of findings or reports.

Synonymous term: Auftragskommunikation (German)

### Organizational model

→Model focusing on the organization of an enterprise. Elements offered are typically units or roles that have a defined organizational relationship to each other.

Synonymous term: Organisations-Modell (German)

### Outcome quality

Describes in health care the effects of patient care, that is, the changes in the health status of the patient (e.g., mortality, morbidity). In the context of →hospital information systems, outcome quality describes whether the goals of →information management have been reached, or, in a broader sense, to what extent the hospital information system contributed to the goals of the hospital and to the expectations of different →stakeholders.

Synonymous term: Ergebnisqualität (German)

### Patient administration

→Hospital function comprising patient admission, discharge, and transfer (→ADT), →basic data-set documentation, and billing. A patient-related (not only case-related) patient administration can be regarded as the center of the memory of a →hospital information system.

Synonymous term: Patientenverwaltung (German)

### Patient data management system (PDMS)

→Application component in intensive care units to automatically monitor, store, and present a vast amount of patient-related clinical →data. In this area, the requirements for the permanent availability of the application components and their data is of highest importance to guarantee patient's safety.

Synonymous term: Patientendaten-Managementsystem (PDMS) (German)

### Patient identification

To determine and record a patient's identity. As a result of patient identification, a unique →patient identification number (PIN) should be assigned.

Synonymous term: Patienten-Identifikation (German)

### Patient identification number (PIN)

Number for the unique identification of a patient. Should be used in all parts of a →hospital information system for →patient identification. Is the precondition for the →object identity of the entity type "patient," and for a patient-oriented combination of all →information arising during the patient's recent as well as future hospitalizations. Should have no internal meaning, and should thus be created sequentially.

Synonymous term: Patienten-Identifikationsnummer (PIN) (German)

### Patient management system (PMS)

→Application component supporting →patient administration.

Synonymous term: Patientenmanagementsystem (PMS) (German)

### Patient record

Comprises all →data and documents generated or received during patient care at a healthcare institution. Document carriers may be paper-based or electronic media. Nowadays, many documents in the paper-based patient record are computer printouts, and the portion of documents created on a computer will further increase, leading to the →electronic patient record.

Synonymous term: Krankenakte, Patientenakte (German)

### Physical data processing component

→Information processing tools used to realize computer-based and paper-based →application components. They can be human actors (such as the person delivering mail), paper-based physical tools (such as printed forms, telephones, books, paper-based patient records, administrative stickers), or →computer systems.

Synonymous term: Physischer Datenverarbeitungsbaustein (German)

**Physical tool layer**

A set of →physical data processing components in the →3LGM that are physically connected via so-called data transmission connections (e.g., data wires).

Synonymous term: Physische Werkzeugebene (German)

**Picture archiving and communication system (PACS)**

→Application component that supports the storage, management, and presentation of digital images and their communication from the storage media to the attached workstations for the diagnosing specialists or for the ordering departments.

Synonymous term: Bildarchivierungs- und Kommunikationssystem (German)

**Planning**

One task of →information management is planning the →hospital information system and its →architecture. Planning in →strategic information management results in a specific →strategic information management plan, describing the HIS with the supported →hospital functions, its architecture, and its organization. Planning in →tactical management means planning →projects and of all resources needed for them. Planning in →operational information management means planning organizational structures, procedures, and all resources such as finances, staff, rooms, or buildings that are necessary to ensure the faultless operation of all components of the hospital information system.

Synonymous term: Planung (German)

**Plötzberg Medical Center and Medical School (PMC)**

Plötzberg ([pløts'berg]) is a hypothetical medical school associated with a tertiary care hospital. Most of the examples in this book are located at the PMC. The PMC is fictitious, but similarities with real hospitals are certainly not Synonymous term: Zugangsintegration (German)

Synonymous term: Medizinische Hochschule Plötzberg (MHP) (German)

### Portfolio management

Important instrument for strategic →planning of a →hospital information system. Originally coming from the field of finance to acquire a well-balanced securities portfolio, today the term is used to refer to multiple strategic management problems. We can distinguish application portfolio management and →project portfolio management.

Synonymous term: Portfolio-Management (German)

### Presentation integration

Condition of an →information system where different →application components represent →data as well as user interfaces in a unified way.

Synonymous term: Präsentations-Integrität (German)

### Project

A unique undertaking that is characterized by management by objectives, by restrictions with regard to available time and resources, and by a specific project organization (DIN 69901).

Synonymous term: Projekt (German)

### Project portfolio

Describes recent →projects, priorities, and upcoming planned projects of →information management. Its establishment is one important task of →strategic information management.

Synonymous term: Projektmappe, Projektbestand, Projektportfolio (German)

### Quality

Degree to which a set of inherent characteristics fulfills requirements (ISO 9000). We can typically distinguish three major approaches to quality assessment: →quality of structures, →quality of processes, and →outcome quality.

Synonymous term: Qualität, Güte (German)

### Quality management

All activities of a healthcare institution's management that ensure and continually improve the quality of patient care. This includes setting the goals, defining the responsibilities, and establishing and monitoring the processes to realize these goals. For hospitals, there are several quality management approaches such as →certification, →accreditation, and excellence programs.

Synonymous term: Qualitätsmanagement (German)

**Quality of data**

The correctness, integrity, reliability, completeness, accuracy, relevancy, authenticity, availability, confidentiality, and safety of →data.

Synonymous term: Datenqualität (German)

**Quality of processes**

In health care, quality of activities carried out by care providers (e.g., adherence to professional standards, appropriateness of care). In the context of →hospital information systems, quality of processes deals with the quality of the information processes that are necessary to meet the user's needs.

Synonymous term: Prozessqualität (German)

**Quality of structures**

In health care, the human, physical, and financial resources that are needed to provide medical care (e.g., educational level of staff, availability of medical equipment). In the context of →hospital information systems, quality of structures refers to the availability of technical or human resources needed for →information processing. It comprises quality characteristics for →data, for →information processing tools, and for →integration of →components.

Synonymous term: Strukturqualität (German)

**Radiological information system (RIS)**

→Application component supporting the management of a radiological department, comprising appointment scheduling, organization of examinations and staff (work flow management, working lists), provision of patient data and examination parameters, and creation of reports.

Synonymous term: Radiologie-Informationssystem (RIS) (German)

**Reference model**

→Model pattern for a certain class of aspects. On the one hand, these model patterns can help to derive more specific models through modifications, limitations, or add-ons (generic reference models). On the other hand, these model patterns can be used to directly compare models e.g. concerning their completeness (nongeneric reference models).

Synonymous term: Referenzmodell (German)

### Referential integrity

Correct assignment of entities, for example, the assignment of cases to a certain patient, or of results to a case.

Synonymous term: Referenzielle Integrität (German)

### Return-on-investment (ROI) study

An economic analysis to describe how much an investment in a →component of an information system pays back in a fixed period of time.

Synonymous term: Rendite-Studie (German)

### Second level of operational support

User support unit addressing information processing problems that cannot be solved by →first level of operational support. It may consist, for example, of specially trained informatics staff in the central information management department, responsible for the operation of a specific →application component. When the second level of operational support cannot solve the problems, they are handed over to the →third level of operational support.

Synonymous term: Second level support (German)

### Socio-technical system

A (man-made) →system that consists of both human and technical components.

Synonymous term: Sozio-technisches System (German)

### Software ergonomics

Comprises suitability for a task, suitability for learning, suitability for individualization, conformity with user expectations, self-descriptiveness, controllability , and error tolerance of a →software product (ISO 9241).

Synonymous term: Software-Ergonomie (German)

### Software product

An acquired or self-developed piece of software that is complete in itself and that can be installed on a →computer system.

Synonymous term: Software-Produkt (German)

### Software quality

Comprises quality of functionality, reliability, usability, efficiency, maintainability, and portability of a →software product (ISO 9126).

Synonymous term: Software-Qualität (German)

### Stakeholder

Anyone who has direct or indirect influence on or interest in a →component of an information system.

Synonymous term: Interessensgruppe (German)

### Strategic alignment

The process that balances and coordinates the hospital goals and the →information management strategies to get the best result for the hospital. Important task of →strategic information management.

Synonymous term: Strategische Anpassung, Angleichung (German)

### Strategic information management

Deals with the enterprise's →information processing as a whole and establishes strategies and principles for the evolution of the →information system. An important result of strategic information management activities is a →strategic information management plan that includes the direction and strategy of →information management and the →architecture of an enterprise information system.

Synonymous term: Strategisches Informationsmanagement (German)

### Strategic information management plan

Contains the long-term planning of a →hospital information system, describing the hospital's goals, the →information management goals, the current HIS state, the future HIS state, and the steps to transform the current HIS into the planned HIS. Its establishment is an important task of →strategic HIS planning. The strategic information management plan should be written by the →CIO and approved by the →hospital management.

Synonymous term: IT-Strategieplan, IT-Rahmenkonzept (German)

**Sub-information system**

A subset of the components of an →information system and the relationships between them. A sub-information system is a →subsystem of the overall information system and thus itself again an information system.

Synonymous term: Sub-Informationssystem (German)

**Subsystem**

A subset of all components of a →system, together with the relationships between them.

**SWOT analysis**

Analysis of the most significant *s*trengths (positive features), *w*eaknesses (negative features), *o*pportunities (potential strengths), and *t*hreats (potential weaknesses) that characterize a →component of an information system.

**Synchronous communication**

Form of communication in which the process in the →application component that initiated communication with another application component is interrupted as long as the system is awaiting or obtaining response data from the communication partner. The opposite is →asynchronous communication.

Synonymous term: Synchrone Kommunikation (German)

**System**

Set of persons, things, and/or events that forms an entity, together with their relationships. We distinguish between natural systems and artificial (man-made) systems. A system can be divided into →subsystems.

**Tactical information management**

Deals with particular →enterprise functions or →application components that are introduced, removed, or changed. Usually these activities are done in the form of →projects.
Synonymous term: Taktisches Informationsmanagement (German)

**Technical model**

→Model focusing on →information processing tools used in an enterprise. Elements offered are typically →physical data processing components (e.g.,

→computer systems, telephones, forms, pagers, records) and →application components (application programs, working plans).

Synonymous term: Technisches Modell (German)

### Third level of operational support

User support unit addresses the more severe information processing problems that cannot be solved by →second level of operational support. It may consist, for example, of specialists from the software vendor.

Synonymous term: Third level support (German)

### Three-layer graph-based metamodel (3LGM)

→Metamodel that can be used to model →hospital information systems. It distinguishes three layers of information systems: →domain layer, →logical tool layer, and →physical tool layer. It aims to support the systematic →information management, especially of heterogeneous hospital information systems, as well as the quality assessment of →information processing.

Synonymous term: Grafisches Drei-Ebenen-Metamodell (3LGM) (German)

### Transcription of data

Transfer of →data from one storage device to another storage device, for example, transfer of patient diagnoses from the →patient record to an order entry form, or copy of data from a printout into a computer-based →application component. Transcription usually leads to the duplication of data.

Synonymous term: Transkription von Daten (German)

### Utility analysis

Economic analysis that compares costs and consequences of a →component of an information system, taking the staff's personal preferences into account by including weighting factors for each criterion.

Synonymous term: Nutzwertanalyse (German)

# Appendix B: Bibliography

The following books, proceedings, journals, associations, and Internet resources address hospital information systems.

## *Books*


Ball MJ, Douglas JV, Garets DE, editors. Strategies and Technologies for Healthcare Information—Theory into Practice. Health Informatics. New York: Springer; 1999.

Cassidy A. A Practical Guide to Information Systems Strategic Planning. Boca Raton, Boston, London: St. Lucies Press; 1998.

CSTB. For the Record: Protecting Electronic Health Information. Washington: National Academy Press—Committee on Maintaining Privacy and Security in Healthcare Applications of the National Information Infrastructure; 1997. http://www.nap.edu/books/0309056977/html/index.html.

Degoulet P, Fieschi M. Introduction to Clinical Informatics. New York: Springer; 1997.

Dick RS, Steen EB, Detmer DE, editors. The Computer-Based Patient Record: An Essential Technology for Healthcare (revised edition). Washington: National Academy Press—Institute of Medicine; 1997. http://www.nap.edu/books/0309055326/html.

Dudeck J, Blobel B, Lordieck W, Bürkle T. New Technologies in Hospital Information Systems. Amsterdam: IOS Press; 1997.

Federal Statistical Office. Statistical Yearbook for the F.R.G. Wiesbaden: Metzler Poeschel; annual edition.

Friedman CP, Wyatt JC. Evaluation Methods in Medical Informatics. New York: Springer; 1997.

Haux R, Kulikowski C, editors. Yearbook of Medical Informatics. Stuttgart: Schattauer; annual edition.

Hsu LD, Glaser JP. The Strategic Application of Information Technology in Healthcare Organizations. New York: McGraw-Hill; 1999.

Lorenzi NM, Riley RT, editors. Organizational Aspects of Health Informatics—Managing Technological Change. New York: Springer; 1995.

Lorenzi NM, Riley RT, Ball MJ, Douglas JV, editors. Transforming Healthcare Through Information—Case Studies. New York: Springer; 1995.

Mantas J, Hasman A, editors. Textbook in Health Informatics—A Nursing Perspective. Amsterdam: IOS Press; 2002.

Martin J. Information Engineering. Book II: Planning and Analysis. Englewood Cliffs: Prentice Hall; 1989.

Prokosch HU, Dudeck J. Hospital Information Systems: Design and Development, Characteristics; Impact and Future Architecture. Amsterdam: Elsevier; 1995.

Shortliffe E, Perrault L, Wiederhold G, Fagan L. Medical Informatics: Computer Applications in Healthcare and Biomedicine. 2nd edition. New York: Springer; 2001.

van Bemmel JH, Musen MA, editors. Handbook of Medical Informatics. Houten/Diegem: Springer; 1997.

Ward J, Griffiths P. Strategic Planning for Information Systems. 2nd edition. Chichester: John Wiley & Sons; 1996.

## *Proceedings*

Proceedings of the Annual American Medical Informatics Association (AMIA) Symposium (formerly known as SCAMC) (published as supplement to the Journal of the American Medical Informatics Association). http://www.amia.org.

Proceedings of the Annual Symposium of the German Association for Medical Informatics, Biometry and Epidemiology (GMDS) (last issues published by Urban & Vogel, München). http://www.gmds.de.

Proceedings of Medical Informatics Europe (MIE) (in the years where no Medinfo takes place) (last issues published by IOS Press, Amsterdam). http://www.efmi.org.

Proceedings of the Triennial World Congress on Medical Informatics (Medinfo) (last issues published by Elsevier North Holland, Amsterdam). http://www.imia.org.

## *Journals*

Health Informatics Online: http://www.healthcare-informatics.com.

The Informatics Review: http://www.informatics-review.com.

International Journal of Medical Informatics: http://www.elsevier.com/locate/ijmedinf.

Journal of the American Medical Informatics Association: http://www.jamia.org.Journal of Healthcare Information Management: http://www.himss.org/templates/journals_issue.asp.

Journal of Healthcare Information Management: http://www.himss.org/templates/journals_issue.asp.

Methods of Information in Medicine: http://www.methods-online.com.

## *Associations*

American Health Information Management Association (AHIMA): http://www.ahima.org.

American Medical Informatics Association (AMIA): http://www.amia.org.

Association for Computing Machinery (ACM): http://www.acm.org.

Center for Health Information Management (CHIM): http://www.chim.org.

College of Healthcare Chief Information Executives: http://www.cio-chime.org.
European Federation for Medical Informatics (EFMI): http://www.efmi.org.
European Federation for Quality Management (EFQM), http://www.efqm.org.
European Information Technology Observatory (EITO): http://www.fvit-eurobit.de/def-eito.htm.
German Association for Medical Informatics, Biometry and Epidemiology (Deutsche Gesellschaft für Medizinische Informatik, Biometrie und Epidemiologie, GMDS) with its working groups: http://www.gmds.de.
German Computer Society (Gesellschaft für Informatik, GI) with its working groups: http://www.gi-ev.de.
German Institute for Standardization (Deutsches Institut für Normung, DIN), http://www2.din.de.
German Professional Association for Medical Informatics (Berufsverband Medizinische Informatik, BVMI): http://www.bvmi.de.
German Research Association (Deutsche Forschungsgemeinschaft, DFG): http://www.dfg.de.
Healthcare Information and Management Systems Society (HIMSS): http://www.himss.org.
Institute for Electrical and Electronic Engineering (IEEE): http://www.ieee.org.
International Federation for Information Processing (IFIP): http://www.ifip.org.
International Medical Informatics Association (IMIA) with its special interest groups and working groups: http://www.imia.org. In particular working group on Health Information systems.
International Organization for Standardization (ISO). http://www.iso.org.
Joint Commission on Accreditation of Healthcare Organizations, http://www.jcaho.org.
Joint Healthcare Information Technology Alliance (JHITA): http://www.jhita.org.
National Committee on Vital and Health Statistics (NCVHS). http://ncvhs.hhs.gov.
National Institute of Standards and Technology (NIST), http://www.nist.gov.
Object Management Group (OMG). http://www.omg.org.
Organization for Economic Cooperation and Development (OECD): http://www.oecd.org.
World Health Organization (WHO): http://www.who.int.

## *Internet Resources*

CEN/TC 251. European Standardization of Health Informatics. http://www.centc251.org.
DICOM. Digital Imaging and Communications in Medicine. http://medical.nema.org.
HIPAA. Health Insurance Portability and Accountability Act. http://www.hipaa-iq.com.
HL7. Health Level Seven. http://www.hl7.org.
HON. Health on the Net Foundation. http://www.hon.ch.
IMIA Yearbook of Medical Informatics. http://www.yearbook.uni-hd.de.
KTQ. Kooperation für Transparenz und Qualität im Krankenhaus. http://www.ktq.de.
Nicholas E. Davies CPR Recognition Award of Excellence Program. http://www.cpri-host.org/davies/index.html.

NIST. Baldrige National Quality Program. http://www.baldrige.org.

NLM. National Library of Medicine. PubMed. http://www.ncbi.nlm.nih.gov/entrez/query.fcgi.

OECD. OECD Health Data 2001. A comparative analysis of countries. http://www1.oecd.org/els/health/software/index.htm.

PITAC. National Coordination Office for Information Technology Research and Development. President's Information Technology Advisory Committee. Reports to the President. http://www.ccic.gov/pubs/pitac/index.html.

Requirements Index for Information Processing in Hospitals. http://www.umit.at/reqhis.

UML. Unified Modeling Language. http://www.uml.org.

WHO. World Health Report 2000. http://www.who.int/whr/2000/en/statistics.htm.

# Appendix C: List of Examples and Exercises

## *Examples*

## *Exercises*

# About the Authors

**Prof. Dr. Reinhold Haux**

Reinhold Haux is a professor of medical informatics at the University for Health Informatics and Technology Tyrol (UMIT), Austria. He is the rector of UMIT and director of the Institute for Health Information Systems. From 1989 to 2001 he was a professor and director of the Department of Medical Informatics at the University of Heidelberg, Germany. From 1987 to 1989, he was associate professor of medical informatics at the University of Tübingen, Germany.

He studied medical informatics at the University of Heidelberg/University of Applied Sciences, Heilbronn, Germany. He received a Ph.D. from the Faculty for Theoretical Medicine, University of Ulm in 1983, and a license for lecturing (German "Habilitation") for medical informatics and statistics from the medical faculty of the Technical University of Aachen in 1987.

At the University of Heidelberg and at UMIT, he has chaired the strategic IT management boards of the respective university medical centers. At the Universities of Tübingen and Erlangen-Nuremberg he was also a member of such boards. At all these university medical centers, he participated in the elaboration of their strategic IT plans.

His current research field is health information systems (strategic IT management, patient-centered, shared care, clinical documentation, electronic patient record, knowledge-based decision support for diagnosis and therapy) as well as the design of curricula in health and medical informatics. He is lecturing on hospital information systems at UMIT and at the Universities of Amsterdam, Heidelberg, Heilbronn, and, formerly, in Athens and Prague. Reinhold Haux is vice president of the International Medical Informatics Association (IMIA). He is editor-in-chief of *Methods of Information in Medicine*, and editor of the IMIA *Yearbook of Medical Informatics*.

## Prof. Dr. Alfred Winter

Alfred Winter is a professor for medical informatics at the Institute of Medical Informatics, Statistics, and Epidemiology of the University of Leipzig, Germany.

He studied informatics at the Technical University in Aachen, Germany, and received his Ph.D. and a license for lecturing (German "Habilitation") for medical informatics from the Faculty of Theoretical Medicine at the University of Heidelberg.

His research focuses on methods and modeling tools for the management of hospital information systems. He teaches information management in hospitals in a medical informatics course at Leipzig University. He is responsible for co-ordinated strategic information management at Leipzig University Hospital and Leipzig University Medical Faculty. He works as a consultant concerning telemedicine and evaluation projects for the German state of Saxony. He has been head of the joint medical informatics division of the German Association of Medical Informatics, Biometry and Epidemiology (GMDS) and the German Association of Informatics (GI).

## Prof. Dr. Elske Ammenwerth

Elske Ammenwerth is assistant professor and head of the Research Group Assessment of Health Information Systems at the University for Health Informatics and Technology Tyrol (UMIT) in Innsbruck, Austria.

She studied medical informatics at the University of Heidelberg/University of Applied Sciences Heilbronn, Germany. Between 1997 and 2001, she worked as a research assistant at the Institute for Medical Biometry and Informatics at the University of Heidelberg, Germany. In Heidelberg, her work comprised the evaluation of hospital information systems (e.g., evaluation of mobile technology), the introduction and evaluation of nursing documentation systems, and requirements analysis for hospital information systems. In 2000, she received her Ph.D. from the Medical Faculty of the University of Heidelberg for her work on requirements modelling.

Since her time at UMIT, she has worked on evaluation methods for hospital information systems. Here, she also participates in the elaboration of the strategic IT plan of the University Medical Center of Innsbruck. She lectures on hospital information systems, evaluation of information systems, and project management at UMIT, and formerly lectured at the University of Heidelberg and the University of Applied Sciences, Heilbroun.

She is head of the working group Assessment of Health Information Systems of the European Federation for Medical Informatics (EFMI).

## Dr. Birgit Brigl

Birgit Brigl is a research scientist at the Institute of Medical Informatics, Statistics, and Epidemiology of the University of Leipzig, Germany. Her current research interests cover the management of hospital information systems, with a special focus on hospital information systems modeling.

She studied medical informatics at the University of Heidelberg/University of Applied Sciences, Heilbronn, Germany. Between 1992 and 1998 she worked as a research assistant at the Institute for Medical Biometry and Informatics at the University of Heidelberg, focusing on the integration of decision support systems in hospital information systems. In 1997, she received her Ph.D. from the Faculty of Theoretical Medicine at the University of Heidelberg for her work on knowledge acquisition.

The authors of this book. From left: Reinhold Haux, Alfred Winter, Birgit Brigl, and Elske Ammenwerth.

# Index

D



F

## Health Informatics Series

*(formerly Computers in Health Care)*

*(continued from page ii)*

Introduction to Clinical Informatics
P. Degoulet and M. Fieschi

Behavioral Healthcare Informatics
N.A. Dewan, N.M. Lorenzi, R.T. Riley, and S.R. Bhattacharya

Patient Care Information Systems
*Successful Design and Implementation*
E.L. Drazen, J.B. Metzger, J.L. Ritter, and M.K. Schneider

Introduction to Nursing Informatics, Second Edition
K.J. Hannah, M.J. Ball, and M.J.A. Edwards

Strategic Information Management in Hospitals
*An Introduction to Hospital Information Systems*
R. Haux, A. Winters, E. Ammenwerth, and B. Brigl

Information Retrieval
*A Health and Biomedical Perspective*, Second Edition
W.R. Hersh

The Nursing Informatics Implementation Guide
E.C. Hunt, S.B. Sprout, and R.R. Kitzmiller

Information Technology for the Practicing Physician
J.M. Kiel

Computerizing Large Integrated Health Networks
*The VA Success*
R.M. Kolodner

Medical Data Management
*A Practical Guide*
F. Leiner, W. Gaus, R. Haux, and P. Knaup-Gregori

Organizational Aspects of Health Informatics
*Managing Technological Change*
N.M. Lorenzi and R.T. Riley

Transforming Health Care Through Information
*Case Studies*
N.M. Lorenzi, R.T. Riley, M.J. Ball, and J.V. Douglas

Trauma Informatics
K.I. Maull and J.S. Augenstein

Consumer Informatics
*Applications and Strategies in Cyber Health Care*
R. Nelson and M.J. Ball

Public Health Informatics and Information Systems
P.W. O'Carroll, W.A. Yasnoff, M.E. Ward, L.H. Ripp,
and E.L. Martin

Advancing Federal Sector Health Care
*A Model for Technology Transfer*
P. Ramsaroop, M.J. Ball, D. Beaulieu, and J.V. Douglas

Medical Informatics
*Computer Applications in Health Care and Biomedicine,* Second Edition
E.H. Shortliffe and L.E. Perreault

Filmless Radiology
E.L. Siegel and R.M. Kolodner

Cancer Informatics
*Essential Technologies for Clinical Trials*
J.S. Silva, M.J. Ball, C.G. Chute, J.V. Douglas, C.P. Langlotz, J.C. Niland,
and W.L. Scherlis

Clinical Information Systems
*A Component-Based Approach*
R. Van de Velde and P. Degoulet

Knowledge Coupling
*New Premises and New Tools for Medical Care and Education*
L.L. Weed